Media
Madness

Media Madness
Public Images
of Mental Illness

Otto F. Wahl

Rutgers University Press
New Brunswick, New Jersey

Published by Rutgers University Press, New Brunswick, New Jersey
Manufactured in the United States of America

Library of Congress Cataloging-in-Publication Data

Wahl, Otto F.
    Media madness : public images of mental illness / Otto F. Wahl.
      p.   cm.
    Includes bibliographical references and index.
    ISBN 0 8135 2212 9 (acid-free paper)
    1. Mental illness in mass media—United States.   I. Title.
P96.M452U68 1995
362.2—dc20   95-6402
                                                        CIP

British Cataloging-in-Publication information available

To the memory
of my mother, Hazel L. Wahl,
and my father, Otto F. Wahl, Sr.
I wish they were here to read this.

Contents

Illustrations

Preface

I confess. I am a cardinal member of the television generation. As a child, I hurried home from school to beat my siblings to the living-room chair closest to the television in order to watch black-and-white cartoon animals move awkwardly across the small screen. The most eagerly anticipated event of each week was a trip to my grandmother's house, because she was the first person we knew to have a large-screen television set (and, eventually, a large color TV). We would go on Sundays so my siblings and I could watch *Walt Disney Presents* while the adults played pinochle in the kitchen. I grew up with *The Lone Ranger*, *Sky King*, and *Captain Midnight*. Even in college, group viewing of *Star Trek* and *Mission Impossible* was an important part of my social and recreational life.

When I began to study clinical psychology in graduate school and to learn about psychiatric disorders, however, my television viewing took on added dimensions. I began to notice how frequently mentally ill characters appeared in the shows I was watching, and how commonly those depictions deviated from what I was learning about mental illnesses. I could not help but notice, in addition, how generally unfavorable television depictions of mentally ill persons seemed to be, with most of these characters appearing as killers and villains.

As a student of psychology, I also learned how people's ideas and images of persons and events could influence attitudes and behavior. I learned that beliefs about mental illness did indeed seem to influence people's attitudes toward psychiatric patients and that others often responded to those with mental illnesses solely on the basis of their psychiatric labels, regardless of the specific symptoms or behaviors observed. People responded to "mental illness" by recalling the mental images and stereotypes conjured up by the term. I began to wonder about the extent to which those internal images that formed the basis of public responses to mental illness corresponded to those images of mental illness I was encountering on television.

Direct clinical work with people with mental illnesses taught me also of the embarassment, shame, and discouragement experienced by psychiatric patients in reaction to the real and perceived negative attitudes of the public toward them. Most felt stigmatized by their illnesses and expressed reluctance to disclose to others that they were or had been receiving psychiatric treatment. Many reported that unfavorable public attitudes were as difficult to deal with as the illnesses themselves. It became clear to me, as it was to the psychiatric patients with whom I worked, that inaccurate and demeaning public images of mental illness and mentally ill people had significant practical—and often undesirable—consequences.

Such observations led me to a more professional consideration of the public images of mental illness. The images of mental illness in the mass media became more than just objects of bemusement for me; I began to see them as phenomena for serious study and clinical concern. In the more than fifteen years I have focused on this topic as a clinician and researcher, I have learned a great deal about mass media images of mental illness, about their impact on society, and about efforts to modify and improve such images. This book is a synthesis and articulation of that learning.

It is the intention of this book to examine the extent, nature, accuracy, and potential impact of public images of mental illness. It addresses not what scientists and mental health professionals communicate to one another, but what is being communicated to the person on the street—or, more accurately, to the person in his or her living room enjoying a new book, the day's newspaper, or the evening's television fare. This book, in other words, is about what everyday people are learning, from everyday sources, concerning mental illnesses. Its goal is to increase readers' and viewers' awareness and understanding of the media inputs that may shape public conceptions of mental illness, to inform them of some of the facts of mental illness that may be obscured or even contradicted by mass media portrayals, and, in addition, to enable them to be more enlightened consumers of the vast amount of mental health information conveyed in everyday, nonprofessional sources.

In order to understand the media's potential for influencing public attitudes and behavior regarding mental illness, it is necessary to appreciate the extraordinary frequency with which mental illnesses are depicted. This book begins with an examination of how often mental illnesses appear in mass media and calls upon both examples and research to demonstrate the variety of media sources in which information about mental illness is presented to the public. The problematic nature of those numerous depictions is considered in the next several chapters. I first describe the tendency of mass media to treat mental illness as an object of ridicule, to use psychiatric terminology inaccurately, and to overuse slang and disrespectful terms for mental illness, while in subsequent chapters I focus on media presentations of mentally ill people as fundamentally different from others and on the image of individuals with mental illnesses as violent, criminal, and dangerous. I next explore the impact and potential impact of such images, presenting evidence that underscores the fears of mental health advocates that current media images of mental illness have many harmful consequences.

That harmful images of mental illness are so pervasive and persistent in mass media calls strongly for change. The final chapters of the book, then, explore issues related to the need for change. I begin by considering the forces that may shape and support current media images; I attempt to explain why and how inaccurate images have come to dominate mass media presentations of mental illness. Following this, I describe specific efforts to modify the problematic patterns of the depiction of mental illness as well as the growing number of organizations involved in such efforts.

Finally, several appendices can be found at the end of this book that provide more extensive examples of the number, variety, and nature of depictions of mental illness in movies, television shows, and popular novels. Appendix A presents descriptions of over 150 movies released since 1985 that have acknowledged mental illness themes; Appendix B presents a similar list of television programs with mentally ill characters. Brief summaries of fifteen "psycho-killer" novels from the past decade are provided in Appendix C to highlight the characteristic depiction of mental illness in this increasingly popular genre.

As may already be apparent, I am not a totally unbiased observer. I have a point of view, based both on personal experience and on collected research, and what I present here conveys that point of view. I believe that mass media images of mental illness are altogether too frequently inaccurate, unfavorable, and, as such, harmful to mentally ill people and to mental health goals. Let me be clear, however, that my criticisms of the mass media in no way constitute a blanket indictment. My goal is to elucidate what I believe to be a problem situation, not to assign blame. I am a member of the mass media generation, and I will continue to be entertained by the television programs, movies, and novels that I eagerly consume. Yet overall satisfaction with mass media productions does not preclude looking carefully, and critically, at some aspects of those media; it does not prevent identifying, and trying to rectify, problems in media depiction if and when they do occur. It is my intention in this book to take a critical look at mass media depictions of mental illness and to identify problems in that depiction without rejecting or villifying the media themselves.

I am indebted to many people for their assistance in completing this project. Jean Arnold and the National Stigma Clearinghouse provided me with inspiration, encouragement, and much of the illustrative material used here. Leslie Mitchner, Editor in Chief at Rutgers University Press, offered excellent suggestions and guidance. Her enthusiasm for the topic and willingness to blend her critical feedback with needed support are greatly appreciated. Kimberly Baker gave much-needed help with some of the typing and Karen Alarie and Chris Boes bailed me out when computer hardware wouldn't do what I wanted it to. Most of all, I thank my family—my wife, Anne, and my daughters, Johanna and Sasha—who not only put up with my distraction as I attempted to complete this book but also let me get away with recounting every detail of the process to them.

Media
Madness

Chapter One

Madness, Madness Everywhere

Not long ago I attended a zoning board meeting in suburban Northern Virginia, where I live. The issue being considered was the proposed establishment of a group home for six adult females with mental illness. I was there to testify on behalf of the group home as an affordable housing alternative that would enable these women to leave the hospital and return to their communities. Others from the community were there, as is often the case with group home hearings, to oppose the residence, and their arguments against establishment of the home were sometimes quite remarkable. One longtime resident observed that the neighborhood had many elderly citizens and many children and that, therefore, it would be inappropriate to place psychiatric patients there. Her implication was that both young and old residents of the community would be vulnerable to the dangers mentally disabled neighbors would pose. A similar sentiment was expressed by a man who said simply that the home should not come to his neighborhood "because I'm small" (referring, I assume, to his short stature); being a small person, he suggested, meant that he would not be able to defend himself well. Still another spokesperson argued that the neighborhood was unsuitable for psychiatric patients because it was near a very busy intersection and that the former patients would have difficulty crossing the streets safely.

It was clear that the community members' acceptance of or resistance to the proposed group home was based on their (often inaccurate) ideas about mental illness. They appeared to see people with mental illnesses as dangerous and potentially assaultive as well as childlike and incompetent. I could not help but wonder where these images were coming from.

A similar question could be posed for a variety of other situations in which laypersons must make decisions related to mental illness. Consider the jurors chosen to decide the fate of Ricardo Caputo, who in March 1994 turned himself in to the New York State Police and confessed to killing several women. Almost immediately after Mr. Caputo's arrest, his lawyer began tossing out a variety of psychiatric and pseudopsychiatric labels, including schizophrenia, multiple personality disorder, "repressed psychotic character," and "psychotic personality," to account for his client's actions and, apparently, to set up some sort of psychiatric defense.[1] How would the average citizens serving on Ricardo Caputo's jury sort out this jumble of psychiatric claims? On what information about mental illness might they base their judgments? From where would their ideas and impressions about mental illness have come?

In the heated debate over new schemes for health-care coverage for all Americans, one issue has been the extent of coverage of mental health problems. Most agree that mental illnesses typically have not had the same degree of insurance coverage as physical disorders. There has been substantial disagreement, however, as to whether or not this inequality is appropriate. What ideas about mental illness lead some to argue that "the mentally ill deserve equality so that they can find the therapy and medication they need without overwhelming concerns about the costs" (as one individual suggested in a March 29, 1994, letter to the *Washington Post*)? From what sources did another person, on the same page of the *Post*, get the information that led him to argue against equal coverage for "fake disease, or mental illness" and to assert that "the diagnosis and treatment of mental illness have no place in health care reform because neither have anything to do with the legitimate practice of medicine"?[2]

I am quite certain that public knowledge of mental illness does not come from the professional journals through which mental health professionals share their research and ideas with one another. The layperson who is willing to subscribe to and wade through such journals is rare indeed. Nor do the newsletters or educational campaigns of mental health organizations reach more than a small audience, usually those already invested in learning about mental health issues. Academic experience, through psychology courses in high school and college, may contribute knowledge to substantially more people, but there are still many who never take such courses.

It is far more likely that the public's knowledge of mental illness comes from sources closer to home, sources to which we all are exposed on a daily basis—namely, the mass media. Representatives of the public, in fact, report exactly that. In 1991 the Robert Wood Johnson Foundation, in conjunction with the Daniel Yankelovich polling organization, conducted a telephone survey of approximately thirteen hundred adults representative of the population of the United States. Among the questions about mental illness in this survey was one asking about the sources of respondents' information concerning mental illness. Far and away the most-cited sources were mass media ones—for example, television and news reporting.[3] Americans themselves identify mass media as the source from which they get most of their knowledge of mental illness. That they do so is certainly no surprise, for not only are these media ubiquitous in our lives, but mental illness is a very common theme in their presentations.

The movies we watch, for example, have a long history of treatment of psychiatric topics. According to Michael Fleming and Roger Manvell's 1985 book, *Images of Madness*, the introduction of the "subjective use" of the camera—a now-familiar device in which camera images are used to express the inner emotions of the movie's characters—occurred in a film focusing on the actions of a mad protagonist.[4] In that 1919 film, *The Cabinet of Dr. Caligari*, Robert Wiene used unusual camera angles to suggest (among other things) the world as seen by a mentally ill man. The technique, of course, has been imitated many times since to create an impression of the "skewed" inner world of mental illness.

Early films commonly presented "madmen, demented doctors, and psychopath scientists," as one chapter in Alan G. Frank's 1974 history of horror films is titled, to create horror and suspense.[5] Mad doctors, played by such prominent actors as Boris Karloff, Peter Lorre, Bela Lugosi, and George Zucco, were staples of the early film industry. Such unstable villains were sometimes more famous than the heroes of those early movies, and many a patron eagerly attended the matinees that promised some doctor or scientist who had dared to tinker with nature and had lost his sanity in the process. Frank observes, "A general distrust and fear of doctors and scientists sustains the steady flow of mad-doctor, screwball-scientist, and maniac-next-door films."[6]

B-movie matinees have hardly been the only places where audiences could see mentally ill characters on screen, however. Over the years, films about mental illness, mentally ill people, and psychiatry have included many well-crafted and critically acclaimed, as well as financially successful, film ventures. Ingrid Bergman's performance in *Gaslight* as a woman struggling to maintain her recovery from a nervous breakdown earned her a 1944 Academy Award. Edmund Gwenn, as a man whose sanity is questioned when he insists that he is the real Kris Kringle, won a Best Supporting Actor Award in 1947 for his work in the timeless classic *Miracle on 34th Street*. Joanne Woodward received a Best Actress Oscar for her portrayal of a multiple personality patient in *The Three Faces of Eve* (1957), and *One Flew Over the Cuckoo's Nest*, Ken Kesey's allegory of authority and rebellion set in a psychiatric hospital, was the runaway Oscar winner in 1975, with Best Picture, Best Actor, and Best Actress awards. More recently, *Rain Man*'s 1988 portrayal of an autistic man won awards for Best Picture, Actor, Director, and Screenplay, while *The Silence of the Lambs*, featuring a search for a mentally ill killer, garnered most of the major Oscars in 1992. These movies, of course, live on in video stores and on television and thus provide additional audiences with their portrayals of mental illness.

The examples given so far barely scratch the surface, moreover. There remain a large number of other less memorable and/or less successful films that have also presented mental illness to the public. I have been monitoring the movie descriptions published in the weekly television guide in my local newspaper, the *Washington Post*, for a number of years now, and I have identified films that, according to their printed descriptions, involve mental illness or mental illness themes. Even excluding films dealing only with mental retardation, alcohol or substance abuse, or mental health therapists rather then patients, I have found well over four hundred films, from all decades of moviemaking, that were *advertised* to potential viewers as involving mental illness.[7] According to other research on the representation of disability in movies, mental disorder has been the most commonly depicted disability in feature films.[8]

Of course, what I have been talking about so far is largely film history. Historically, mental illness has been a common topic in movies.

This does not necessarily say anything about the current selection of movies available to influence those deciding about issues related to mental illness. To take a careful look at the prevalence of mental illness depictions in more current films, I called upon *Entertainment Weekly* magazine, a publication that, each week, provides reviews of new films, books, and television shows. In its first year of publication (February 1990–February 1991), *Entertainment Weekly*'s reviewers described 177 new movies. Of those, according to the descriptions provided in the reviews, 18 involved portrayals of mental illness. These films included: *Loose Cannons*, with Dan Akroyd playing a police officer with multiple personalities; *Blue Steel*, which featured "a gnomish stockbroker with pleading eyes who turns out to be a lunatic";[9] *Crazy People*, in which Dudley Moore is committed to a mental institution; *Sleeping with the Enemy* ("What happens," wrote the reviewer, "when a beautiful young woman finds and marries her Prince Charming—and he turns out to be a psychotic monster?"[10]); and *The Silence of the Lambs*. Eighteen films may seem, at first, like a relatively small number of movies, but those 18 represent more than 10 percent of the films reviewed that year. If this was a typical year—and there is no reason to believe it was not—current moviegoers can expect to find depictions of mentally ill characters in one out of every ten new films they see. Mentally ill characters in feature films are hardly a relic of the past; they are in strong supply in films from all time periods, including the present.

As common as mental illness themes may be in feature films, however, they are even more available through television. Television is certainly the medium about which I am asked the most concerning media depictions of mental illness. As a parent, for example, I have more than once participated in "Career Week" at my children's schools, attending their classes to talk about my profession. When I explain that, as a clinical psychologist, I help people with mental illnesses, I usually get questions about specific disorders class members have heard of. Many of the questions are phrased in terms such as: "I saw a program on TV the other night, and they said this guy was borderline psychotic. What does that mean?" On a recent visit, one teenager explained that he had seen a villain on a Batman cartoon who had developed two brains and was said to be schizophrenic; he wondered if it were true that people with schizophrenia have mutated brains.

Just how much information about mental illness is available on television is a question a colleague, Rachel Roth, and I attempted to address a number of years ago. To get an idea of how common television portrayals of mental illness were, we enlisted the cooperation of the National Citizens' Committee on Broadcasting and several local organizations to monitor and rate the content of prime-time television in the Washington, D.C., metropolitan area.[11] Volunteers in this Media Watch study rated prime-time television on five local stations (ABC, NBC, CBS, and two major independents) for an entire month (February 1981). Viewers were instructed to identify any program in which a character was labeled as mentally ill. We were insistent that viewers not make their own psychiatric judgments; they were not to judge whether they thought the character had psychiatric problems but to restrict themselves to only those characters designated *in the program* as "mentally ill," "insane," "schizophrenic," "psychotic," and so on.[12] Out of 385 programs watched during that month, 35 (approximately 9 percent) were identified as depicting mental illness. In the Washington, D.C., area, viewers were able to see 35 mentally ill characters in a single month. If one accepts this as a typical month, it would appear that, on the average, television viewers—even those without access to 100 cable stations—can find at least one mentally ill person on their home screens each and every night of the year. Moreover, other research, using similar ratings of prime-time television, indicate that, if anything, the prevalence of mentally ill characters on television is steadily increasing.[13]

Because examples can sometimes be more enlightening than statistics, let me provide a few. To begin with, consider a single series, the popular and long-running comedy, *M*A*S*H*: within its 251 episodes over eleven seasons (during which the show was nominated for nearly one hundred Emmy awards), there were frequent psychiatric themes. Corporal Klinger (played by Jaime Farr) was a continuing character who constantly tried to earn a Section 8 psychiatric discharge by convincing superiors that he was "crazy." He wore women's clothing, tried to eat a jeep piece by piece, and acted as if he believed he were back home in Toledo rather than in the army, among other ploys. In addition, in several episodes, Klinger faced competition from other soldiers similarly seeking psychiatric discharges. According to Suzy Kalter's *The Complete Book of M*A*S*H*,[14] psychiatrists visited the MASH unit in at least eleven different episodes to examine the staff. Ultimately, Col. Frank Burns (Larry Linville), the show's original villain/buffoon, ended up committed to a psychiatric hospital.

Psychiatric disorders, such as hysterical paralysis, battle fatigue, and amnesia were treated by the series hero Dr. Benjamin Franklin (Hawkeye) Pierce (Alan Alda) and a frequent MASH visitor, the psychiatrist Sidney Freedman (Alan Arbus). Hawkeye himself was frequently shown suffering from psychological symptoms—nightmares and sleepwalking in one episode, psychosomatic sneezing, swelling, and hives in another. The final episode, one of the most watched programs in television history (by an estimated 125 million Americans), featured Hawkeye's recovery from a nervous breakdown as well as the return home of the major characters at the end of the Korean War. That final show, in fact, began with Hawkeye in a psychiatric hospital observing, in a letter to his father: "For the first time, I understand what a nervous disorder is because it seems I've got one. I guess I'll be seeing you soon since I doubt they'll let a surgeon operate whose cheese has slipped off his cracker. Sorry I haven't written you for a while, but I've been on R & R at this wonderful resort—The Seoul Old Soldiers Never Die They Just Giggle Academy. We're planning on having a bridge tournament here as soon as we can find someone with a full deck."

Might some of the participants in the zoning board meeting have been among the 125 million people viewing *M*A*S*H*'s final episode, and, if so, what might they have learned from it? Perhaps some good things, such as the ideas that mental illnesses are treatable and that even competent, heroic figures can have psychiatric problems. Perhaps some not so desirable things, such as disparaging metaphors that can be used to refer to mental illness. It is hard to say. What is clear, in any case, is that, even in this one series, there was (and is, thanks to syndication and cable options) ample opportunity for communities to learn about mental illness.

Furthermore, as the statistics mentioned previously suggest, there is similar opportunity across all types of television programming. Whatever the viewing tastes of individuals, they will find images of mental illness to engage them. If they are devotees of daytime television, they will surely find mental health topics—schizophrenia, bulimia, autism, psychiatric hospitalization—mixed in with the mothers and daughters pregnant by the same men, the believers in past lives, and other exotic topics on the expanding number of talk shows competing for audiences. Viewers will also witness frequent psychiatric disorder on their favorite soap operas. Indeed, a 1979 study of daytime soaps by Mary Cassata and her colleagues led them to conclude that "psychiatric illness is the number one health-related problem in the soap opera world,"[15] with numerous instances of "mental problems" such as schizophrenia, manic-depression, amnesia, and hysterical blindness. A 1985 study by Laurel Fruth and Allan Padderud of 14 daytime serials, including *Guiding Light*, *The Young and the Restless*, and *As the World Turns*, indicated that fully half of them featured a mentally ill character and that 11.4 percent of the available programming time for the fourteen programs was devoted to the portrayal or discussion of mental illness.[16]

If community residents and potential jurors and voters wished to transfer their affections to prime-time soaps, they would find similarly high levels of psychopathology. They would have been able to see *Dallas*'s J. R. Ewing and *Falcon Crest*'s Angela be admitted to psychiatric hospitals. So common were mentally disordered characters in *Knot's Landing* that *Entertainment Weekly*'s April 19, 1991, cover story on the series was captioned "Nutty, Naughty, 'Knots': After 300 episodes full of sex, scandal, and psychos, what will 'Knots Landing' do for an encore? Plenty!"

Should viewers' tastes run more toward police and detective dramas, they would have encountered still more mentally ill characters. Among the episodes on the popular *Hill Street Blues* were ones in which (according to the newspaper descriptions of the shows): "Bates goes undercover to find a psychopath who's killing prostitutes"; "Henry tries to deal with a murder suspect's multiple personalities"; and "Coffey deals with a disturbed man who has taken 8 hostages." From *The Untouchables* ("The syndicate engages a psychotic war veteran to dispose of Ness") to *Hunter* ("A popular female radio talk-show host, whose past includes a series of lovers who have been killed, fears a psychopath may be responsible for the deaths"), *Kojak* ("A psychotic killer terrorizes Manhattan with a series of seemingly indiscriminate murders"), and even *Charlie's Angels* ("A revenge-seeking psychopath booby traps the cabs of a small company he's out to destroy"), television detectives have confronted mentally ill characters on their shows.[17]

Almost all drama series on television have found occasion to portray mental illness. MacGyver, in the show by the same name, has used his ingenuity to frustrate "an escaped madman [who] plots to kill the policewoman who arrested him." On L.A. Law, "Rollins defends a deranged ventriloquist who speaks through his dummy." After a Quantum Leap through time to a mental institution, "Sam undergoes electroshock therapy which results in his having multiple personalities." In outer space, Captain Kirk of the original Star Trek "finds his brother dead and the entire population of the planet Deneva insane," while later the officers of Star Trek: The Next Generation are "trapped in a Tyken's Rift with the crew slowly going insane."

Lest one think that mental illness is confined to television drama, however, let me add a few comedy examples: "A mad bomber threatens to turn the late shift into the last shift" in one Barney Miller episode. On Cheers, "Diane fears she's being followed by a deranged actor." Night Court's Harry Anderson has dealt with "a psychiatric patient posing as Santa" and with "four mental patients charged with defrauding a cab driver." A mentally ill character even appeared on The Simpsons, suffering from the delusion that he was Michael Jackson, with the voice provided by no less a celebrity than Michael Jackson himself.

These examples and statistics, furthermore, because they deal only with mental illness as a prominent theme, still merely scratch the surface of film and television communications about mental illness. There are many more instances in which mental illness is included as a smaller part of a film or program and thus probably would not be featured in a film review or program description. Nevertheless, these less central portrayals provide images and information about mental illness from which the lay public may be learning.

Take, for example, the highly successful movie Terminator 2, viewed, it is estimated, by more than 160 million people.[18] Much attention was paid to its impressive special effects and its breath-taking action sequences; most would recall its "Arnold saves the world" plot, but probably few would think of it as involving portrayals of mental illness. Yet much of the opening half hour of the movie takes place in a psychiatric hospital where the heroine (Linda Hamilton) is being confined. Audiences received inaccurate diagnostic information about schizoaffective disorder ("The usual indicators," says the doctor in charge, "depression, anxiety, violent acting out, delusions of persecu-tion") and glimpses of hospital life that included gray-clothed patients being herded by burly attendants with billyclubs.

Two of Disney's highly successful animated films, *Beauty and the Beast* and *Aladdin*, have included segments related to mental illness. Beauty's eccentric father, referred to by the townspeople as "crazy old Maurice," is threatened with commitment to an asylum, and Aladdin rescues Princess Jasmine from palace guards in the marketplace by telling them that "she's a little crazy" and that she thinks his monkey is the Sultan, indicating also that her plight deserves their pity and sympathy. "Come along, Sis," Aladdin says as if to a child, "time to go see the doctor."

Even in films such as these, with their incidental references to psychiatric problems, people may be learning about mental illness. They may be learning, for example, that people with mental illnesses need forceful control, that communities seek to punish those with mental illnesses, and that people with mental illnesses are best treated like children.

No accounting of media images of mental illness can be complete without also considering the written word. Here, too, mental illness is a common theme. Lay readers have many opportunities to read about mental illness in the magazines they buy, for example. According to the *Readers' Guide to Periodical Literature*, a yearly comprehensive index of magazine articles published in the United States, there were almost four hundred articles with mental health themes published in 1988 in such high-circulation publications as *Time*, *Newsweek*, and *Glamour*.[19] Reviews of current books from *Entertainment Weekly* show that mental illness depictions from such sources include biographical or autobio-graphical accounts of people with mental illnesses (for example, *Dark-ness Visible: A Memoir of Madness* by William Styron) and detective thrillers with mentally ill villains (such as L. R. Wright's *A Chill Rain in January*, Robert Ferrigno's *The Horse Latitudes*, and Whitley Streiber's *Billy*) as well as general fiction (such as Sue Miller's novel, *Family Pictures*, about a family's experience with an autistic child and Mary McGarry Morris's account of how a mentally different person can be-come *A Dangerous Woman*).[20]

And, of course, there are newspapers. Although precise counts of the number of newspaper stories about mental illness that appear in any given year are not available, one can easily imagine a front-page story of a dramatic crime involving a person with mental illness— someone like Jeffrey Dahmer, for example, whose crimes and subsequent trial filled newspaper columns across the country and generated editorials, analyses, and even cartoons for many weeks. Insanity pleas of lesser-known defendants likewise often make the papers, as do periodic exposés of psychiatric care facilities. Recently, mental health care providers have been in the news along with their patients—the psychiatrist Margaret Bean-Bayog, whose unusual relationship with her patient may have led to his suicide, and the therapist to whom the Menendez brothers spoke of their hatred for their parents. Concerns about the increasing number of homeless people living on our streets have led to frequent newspaper stories and, with them, to frequent consideration of the proportion of those with mental illnesses within the homeless population. These and other news stories bring a steady flow of information about mental illness to the lay public.

Moreover, these major media sources—television, print, and film— are not the only mass media to bring images of mental illness to the general population. Depictions of mental illness can be found in almost any public media one might select. Should individuals reject the large and small screens in favor of live theater, for example, they still would find mental illness portrayals in abundance. From *Hamlet* and *King Lear* to *Suddenly Last Summer* to *Equus* to *Nuts*, theatrical offerings have portrayed mental illness. In the 1992 Tony award winner, *Blood Brothers*, theatergoers see a man destroyed by depression who seeks revenge on his blood brother while the musical background intones, "He's a madman." They would find that even in Agatha Christie's venerable *The Mousetrap*—a play performed continuously in London since its opening in November 1952, translated into twenty-four different languages, performed in forty-four other countries throughout the world, and viewed by more than eight million people in London alone—there is a young man labeled as schizophrenic ("A bit queer in the head, that's to say," according to the police officer on hand to solve the mystery).

If people were to pay close attention to the lyrics of the music they and their offspring listen to, they likewise would notice much about mental illness. From sing-along children's tunes ("Boom, boom, ain't it great to be crazy")[21] to Helen Reddy's *Delta Dawn* ("All the folks 'round Brownsville say she's crazy"),[22] from David Bowie ("I'd rather stay here with all the madmen than perish with the sad men roaming free")[23] to Stephen Sondheim ("He's crazy. He's a troubled person. He's a truly crazy person himself")[24], and from Dr. Demento ("They're coming to take me away, ha ha")[25] to Metal Church ("Twisting under schizophrenia, falling deep into dementia, old habits reappear, fighting the fear of fear")[26] to Billy Joel ("It just might be a lunatic you're looking for"),[27] musicians sing to us about troubled minds.[28]

It is clear that madness is indeed everywhere in the mass media. Even if members of a community have never read a professional journal or taken a psychology course, they will have been exposed to a great deal of information about mental illness. And whether they are deciding about a group home, making hiring decisions about someone with a psychiatric history, consoling a friend whose sibling has been diagnosed with mental illness, or sitting on a jury asked to rule on an insanity plea, their reactions and decisions may well be based on the images they have encountered and the information they have received through the mass media.

The fact that mental health themes and information are so prevalent in mass media, it should be noted, could be a very positive circumstance. Mental health advocates have long been concerned that mental illness has been "kept in the closet," much as cancer used to be. It was something people did not talk about, and even mass media sometimes considered the topic too frightening or too depressing to present.[29] Advocates still argue that public knowledge about mental illness needs to be increased and that discussions and depictions in the mass media are important means to that end. That information about mental illness is available in so many different and easily accessible sources seems in line with mental health goals.

Sheer numbers and availability, however, tell only part of the story. One must also pay close attention to the nature of the mental illness references and depictions with which the mass media inundate us. It is the specific information and impressions that are conveyed, the stereotypes presented and reinforced, that will determine whether the high visibility of mental illness in mass media will be helpful or harmful.

Unfortunately, media images of mental illness do not measure up well. Overall, the mass media do a poor job of depicting mental illness, with misinformation frequently communicated, unfavorable stereotypes of people with mental illnesses predominating, and psychiatric terms used in inaccurate and offensive ways. Members of the public, if they are to make fair decisions about issues related to mental illness, need to understand the nature of the media images of mental illness that may shape their ideas and the relationship of those images to the facts of mental disorder.

Chapter Two

Words and Laughter

Words have power. They have the power to hurt or soothe, to honor or insult, to inform or misinform. Words reflect and shape prevailing attitudes, attitudes that in turn shape social behavior. Words both mirror and influence the ways we treat people and the ways they view themselves. And words—disparaging and disrespectful labels in particular—inflict emotional pain on those to whom they are applied. The words used by mass media to refer to mental illnesses and to the people who suffer from mental illnesses have such power, making it important to consider those words and the ways they are typically used—and misused.

A common complaint of mental health advocates about mass media is that psychiatric labels are often used incorrectly and serve to misinform and confuse viewers and readers. One of the most widely misused and misunderstood psychiatric terms is "schizophrenia." Schizophrenia is a severe mental disorder suffered by over two million people in the United States. It is characterized by dramatic disturbances in thought, perception, and emotion. Symptoms include delusions (false but seemingly unshakable beliefs), hallucinations (for example, hearing voices), and disorganized thinking and speech. The symptoms are typically overwhelming to the person with schizophrenia and produce significant impairment in social, occupational, and recreational functioning to a point where hospital care is often needed. Schizophrenia is the most common diagnosis among those hospitalized in psychiatric facilities and is the condition closest to what might be called "classical madness," the disorder most lay people are probably thinking about when they speak of madness, insanity, or asylums.

What schizophrenia is *not* is split personality. Split, or multiple, personality is a disorder in which a person has one or more alternate personalities. Each personality functions relatively well (except that it may not be aware of the existence of other personalities), is reality-oriented, and lacks the hallucinations, delusions, and thought disorganization characteristic of schizophrenia.

Although the word "schizophrenia" means literally "split psyche" or "split personality," it reflects the conceptualization of Eugen Bleuler, who coined the term in the early 1900s, that the disorder involves the splitting, or fragmentation, of the personality into many *disorganized* parts—not splitting into two or more relatively well organized alternate personalities (as in multiple personality disorder).

The mass media, however, strongly and repeatedly communicate that schizophrenia and split personality are one and the same. To begin with, the use of the term "schizophrenia" (or "schizophrenic") by writers and reporters as a shorthand to describe a state of affairs in which there are dramatic contrasts has become widespread. The *New York Times*, for example, in a February 1990 article, labeled Berlin "this schizophrenic city" not only because of its divided history but also implicitly because it is "yanked at every quarter by contradicting tugs."[1] *Time* magazine, in its August 6, 1990, issue, described the perceived contradiction in the behavior of some members of congress concerning cuts in the defense budget in this way: "Congress keeps insisting on cuts in the defense budget, but one of the biggest obstacles is the schizophrenia on Capitol Hill: members who fight a rear-guard defense to prevent the Pentagon from cutting weapons made in their districts."[2] The variety of contexts in which the term "schizophrenia" is used in this way, furthermore, continues to grow. I have seen the term used to indicate inconsistent political actions ("Schizophrenic Environmental Policy," cried one editorial headline),[3] to characterize incongruent food choices ("Cereal schizophrenia strikes at grocery store"),[4] to suggest paradoxical attitudes ("Poll finds Americans have schizophrenic views of the rich"),[5] to describe rivalries within the U.S. Navy ("Reformers now seek an antidote for the Navy's schizophrenia"),[6] and even to highlight the up-

and-down performance of sports teams (such as the "Schizophreknicks," as one sportscaster dubbed the New York Knicks because of their erratic NBA play).[7]

The concept of schizophrenia as equivalent to multiple personality, moreover, is not confined to newspaper shorthand. It often finds its way into humor as well. In one of Art Sansom's *Born Loser* cartoons, for example, one man asks the other, "Something wrong?" "I feel a little schizophrenic today for some reason," is the reply, whereupon the questioner notes, "That makes four of us." The *M*A*S*H* psychiatrist Sidney Freedman insults the Army intelligence villain Col. Flagg by stating, "I'd like to go on talking to you, Flagg, but, with your schizophrenia, I'd have to charge you double." Another cartoon shows a banner above a crowded room identifying a meeting of the "United Schizophrenics of America," and each person in the cartoon has two or more name tags, implying, of course, that each has many identities. To spread the misconception further, bumper stickers, t-shirts, and coffee mugs can be purchased that declare, "I am schizophrenic . . . and so am I." It is small wonder that the public continues to confuse schizophrenia and multiple personality disorder when the terms are so often equated in such a multitude of media sources.[8]

Other psychiatric labels frequently misused and misunderstood include "psychotic" and "psychopathic." It is common to find these terms used almost interchangeably. A February 10, 1991, *New York Times* review of *The Silence of the Lambs*, for instance, referred to the character played by Anthony Hopkins—Dr. Hannibal Lecter—as "the most current example of the psychopath in popular narrative art."[9] At another point, however, the reviewer asked, with respect to Hopkins, "What is it like for an actor to inhabit the character of a depraved psychotic killer?" The killer in Robert B. Parker's 1988 novel, *Crimson Joy*, is authoritatively labeled in the text by the psychologist Susan Silverman (girlfriend of the novel's detective hero, Spenser) as a psychopath, while the first page of the book reproduces praise from the *Buffalo Times* to the effect that the killer "may be the best fictional representation of a psychotic murderer we've had in some time." The terms "psychotic" and "psychopathic," however, are not interchangeable. They have specific psychiatric meanings and refer to very different types of disorders.

Although the term "psychotic" lacks a precise definition, it is generally used in psychiatry to refer to conditions that involve severe impair-

1. *Media images equate schizophrenia with multiple personality.* *Reprinted by permission from Bill Lee.*

ments of thought, speech, and behavior, particularly hallucinations and delusions.[10] These impairments result in grossly distorted perceptions or understandings of external reality. Psychotic disorders are also often professionally referred to as serious, severe, or chronic mental disorders. Their symptoms markedly impair a person's ability to continue to function socially, academically, or occupationally. Disorders considered psychotic include schizophrenia; severe mood disorders such as mania, major depression, and manic-depression; and some brain disorders.

"Psychopathic," by contrast, is a descriptor taken from a no longer officially used diagnostic label—"psychopathy." One central feature of this disorder (now called Antisocial Personality Disorder) is "a pervasive pattern of disregard for, and violation of, the rights of others that begins in childhood or early adolescence and continues into adulthood."[11] Often this antisocial pattern includes unlawful behavior and numerous arrests, but it may also include things like repeated failure to fulfill work or financial obligations, lying, and substance abuse. Like other personality disorders (and unlike psychosis), psychopathy does not involve symptoms with clear onset that are disruptive and intrusive; rather, they seem to involve gradually developed, lifelong patterns of behavior with which the individual himself or herself is relatively comfortable. Unlike those with psychoses, individuals labeled psychopathic usually have an adequate sense of reality and may even lack other pathology beyond their antisocial actions. (It is noteworthy that laws in many states explicitly exclude this type of disorder from definitions of legal insanity. Psychopathy does not diminish one's capacity to understand the wrongness of one's actions, as psychosis may do, and therefore is not accepted as a condition that diminishes criminal responsibility.) Psychopathic individuals are also said to be characterized by a lack of remorse for their harmful actions toward others. They seem to develop few personal loyalties and have little compassion for their victims—they seem, as early clinicians noted, to lack a conscience. Rather than acting out of passion, compulsion, or confusion, the psychopathic person tends to commit antisocial acts mainly for emotional and physical gain.

Although psychopathic individuals do not necessarily become murderers, psychopathic (*not* psychotic) is probably an appropriate appellation for real-life serial killers like Ted Bundy or Kenneth Bianchi. Such criminals (who are far rarer than their appearance in books, television, and films would suggest) typically have long histories of illegal and antisocial behavior, despite otherwise intact psychological functioning. They may hold jobs and develop successful (though usually shallow) social relationships. They are organized, deliberate, and even clever and creative in the crimes they perpetrate. Their murders are committed because of lack of inhibitions to such actions—because they do not value the lives of their victims and see their victims as little more than vehicles for the satisfaction of their sexual or other needs. Rarely are psychotic symptoms, such as hallucinations and delusional thinking, found to be involved in their actions.[12]

The majority of books, films, and television programs showcasing serial killers, however, mix psychotic and psychopathic in their portrayals as well as in their advertising. Typically, fictional serial killers are portrayed as intelligent and resourceful, often with jobs, social position, and financial comfort. At the same time, however, they are shown to have obsessions, delusions, and even hallucinations, with these psychotic symptoms unrealistically encapsulated such that no one else is aware of them. Furthermore, when these serial killers are finally captured or confronted at the end of the movie, book, or show, they suddenly beginning shouting, voice their delusions, appear wide-eyed and distracted, or display other overtly disorganized behavior not seen before.

Take, for example, Thomas Harris's prototypical serial killer novel, Red Dragon. In this novel, the serial killer has achieved an occupational position of considerable responsibility through his effective work and is thoughtful and efficient in his savage murders of entire families. At other points in the book, however, he is shown to have clearly psychotic symptoms, including delusional ideas about "becoming" and command hallucinations (voices giving him forceful instructions on how to act) from a painting with which he is obsessed. To further the confusion, the killer is variously labeled as a "psychopath," a "madman," and "crazy" by authorities in the novel.[13] Robert Ressler, an FBI expert on serial killers (and the person credited with coining the term "serial killer"), has written of Harris's depiction: "As fiction, both the Harris novels are superb, though they are not truly realistic in their portrayals either of killers or of the heroes and heroines inside the FBI. For instance, in the serial killer of [Red Dragon], Harris combines attributes of several different sorts of killers, personality dynamics that would be highly unlikely to coexist in one person in the real world."[14]

Mental health and criminal justice professionals are in agreement that the blending of the manipulative, antisocial, but clear-thinking aspects of psychopathic individuals with the disabling pathology of the person with psychosis represents a decidedly unlikely combination. Despite its apparent popularity, the psychotic psychopath is a very unrealistic and misleading media characterization.

Another confusion of terms is also worth noting—namely, the confusion of "mental retardation" and "mental illness." Mental retardation refers to lifelong limitations of intellect that in turn translate into limitations on learning. People who have mental retardation typically are "slow" in the classroom; they have difficulty learning the material as rapidly or as fully as others. They may also have difficulty learning life skills and thus have problems in coping and social adaptation. Mental illness, by contrast, typically refers to a spectrum of psychiatric conditions that interfere with the individual's usual or prior level of functioning.[15] People with mental illnesses do not necessarily suffer from fundamental limitations of intellect. They may be just as bright, just as academically able as anyone else, but are plagued by specific symptoms that disrupt their lives. In addition, while mental retardation, as a condition, does not change or diminish, mental illnesses wax and wane and often may be relieved altogether. It is possible, of course, for a person to suffer from both mental retardation and mental illness—just as one can have both pneumonia and cataracts. The majority of the millions of people with mental illnesses are not mentally retarded, however, just as the majority of those with mental retardation are not also mentally ill.

Mass media presentations, however, sometimes mix, or fail to differentiate between, the two conditions. Program or film descriptions of mentally retarded characters as "mentally handicapped," "mentally impaired," or "mentally disabled" make them easy to confuse with mentally ill characters. People hearing of my interest in media depictions of mental illness have frequently said to me, "Oh, you mean like Benny on *L.A. Law*?" or, "Like that kid on *Life Goes On*"? Both characters are mentally retarded and not mentally ill. Movies, like *Benny & Joon*, in their otherwise praiseworthy attempts to make mentally ill characters more sympathetic, may present them as basically slow, backward, and inarticulate, traits that most people associate more with intellectual limitations and that, therefore, depict mental retardation more than mental illness. Occasionally there is even more blatant mislabeling, as in one newspaper article I came across about the generally good work habits of mentally retarded employees that was incorrectly headlined

"Loyalty, Pride, Hiring Pluses for Mentally Ill." Mental illness and mental retardation are two distinctly different conditions, despite what one reads in the papers.

Finally, there is still another, somewhat more subtle problem in the use of psychiatric labels. The problem is that forms of these labels are frequently used to characterize people rather than to name their disorders. People with schizophrenia are frequently referred to as "schizophrenics," persons with psychosis as "psychotics," and so forth. Use of such terms in this way subtly dehumanizes the afflicted person, implying that the disorders *define* the individual rather than describe a fluctuating or temporary psychiatric condition. An article in the June 1994 *APA Monitor* (the monthly newsletter of the American Psychological Association),[16] for instance, identified a defendant in a recent court case as "a diagnosed paranoid schizophrenic"—and did so before giving the man's name, implying that his disorder was a more important aspect of his identity than his given name.[17]

Even references to "a schizophrenic person," while preferable to "a schizophrenic," places the emphasis on the disorder rather than the person. More appropriate designations would be "a person experiencing psychotic symptoms" or "an individual with schizophrenia." Although admittedly more awkward, these suggested references are consistent with our designations of other health conditions: people suffering from cancer are unlikely to be referred to as "cancerous people" or "the cancerous." Nevertheless, use of psychiatric labels to refer to sufferers rather than disorders remains common in media and public utterances.

Another troubling aspect of media presentations is the media's tendency to use slang in referring to mental illnesses and to people with those illnesses. One study of television drama, for example, found that technical terms for psychiatric disorders—that is, accepted diagnostic labels—were rarely used when identifying characters as mentally ill. Rather, the most frequently used terms for designating psychiatric problems were "crazy," "sick," and "nut" and also included "wacko," "weirdo," "screwy" and, with lesser frequency, "fruitcakes," "kooks," and "cuckoo-birds."[18] A scan of any guide to television programming will reveal a similar preference for slang descriptors. Television guide descriptions of upcoming programs and films routinely use terms such as "deranged" (on *L.A. Law*, "Rollins defends a deranged ventriloquist who speaks through his dummy") and "demented" (on *The New Avengers*, "a demented genius plots to take over the world using an army of birds") to indicate the psychiatric status of featured characters.[19]

The problem with these terms, as with slang terms for other groups, is that they are fundamentally disrespectful and, therefore, offensive. Just as psychiatrists prefer not to be called "shrinks," because the term conveys less respect for their profession, people with mental illnesses would like not to be called "loons," because such language conveys less respect—and less sympathetic understanding. Virtually all slang terms for mental illness have undertones of disapproval or negative judgment of some sort. In addition, many of the slang terms are residuals of past unflattering conceptions of mental illness (for example, "lunatic"), leftovers of a time when people with mental illnesses were seen as little more than insensate beasts, when they were chained in dungeons and treated as objects of amusement for nobles who paid to view them as if in a human zoo. Terms with such a history cannot help but convey a lack of sympathy and respect for people with mental illnesses.

What is particularly objectionable is the deliberate and exploitative use of slang references to mental illness to show wit and garner attention. It is easy to understand how a person struggling with a mental illness and/or their loving relatives might be hurt to read their cable TV guide and find a showing of *The Dream Team* announced as "Nutty Psychiatric Patients are THE DREAM TEAM," along with a subheading describing the plot as centering on "a motley group of lunatics." Yet movie reviewers often respond to films about mental illness by utilizing as many slang and disparaging references to mental illness as they can fit into their columns. *Newsday*'s review of *The Dream Team*, for example, was head-lined "Four Crazoids Hit the Streets" and included, in its text, further reference not only to "crazoids," but also to "wackos" and "loonies."[20] The *New York Post*'s review was not much better, titled "Psycho-slapstick to Sleep By" and containing references to the psychiatric patient characters in the film as "yo-yos," "loonies," and "loveably dotty."[21]

Advertisers also make frequent playful use of slang terms—and offensive images—of mental illness to grab the eye or ear of viewers and readers. New York-based Crazy Eddie's Records and Tapes was widely known for its (often imitated) advertisements involving wordplay with psychiatric terms ("Crazy Eddie's prices are innnn-sane!"). A promotion for a record album by Buster Poindexter, *Buster Goes Berserk*, involved a proclaimed "Mental Health Day." The ad, appearing, among

A motley group of lunatics scour New York.

Nutty Psychiatric Patients Are
THE DREAM
TEAM

2. *Offensive slang is often used to refer to mental illness.*

other places, in the June 6, 1989, *Village Voice* called for the attention of "Neurotics, Psychotics, Schizoids, Manics, and Music Lovers at All Levels of Mental Dysfunction" and promised that, if readers came to one of the scheduled locations for Buster Poindexter Mental Health Day, they could get their pictures taken, in a straitjacket, with Buster Poindexter himself. An Alexandria, Virginia, restaurant promoted its bargains by using the image of a grinning lobster in a straitjacket to announce its "Lobster Lunacy" prices.

There is an even stronger pull, no doubt, for makers of peanuts to be drawn to wordplay involving psychiatric terminology, and more than one sales campaign has capitalized on the double meaning of "nuts." Planters Peanuts has had a long-running ad campaign featuring people doing odd things and the tag line "Everybody Loves a Nut,"

3. *Ads can be insensitive in their use of mental health images.*

with the double entendre underscored by the finger-twirling gesture pointed at the head generally recognized as indicating that someone is "crazy." Another peanut product was a gift bag of peanuts packaged in a straitjacket and labeled "Certifiably Nuts." The package came with a "patient history" stating that the owner's family had been "nuts for generations." If one pulled a small ring on the package, hysterical laughter could be heard. The product even won a prestigious CLIO award from the advertising industry for innovative retail packaging, a circumstance that mental health advocates felt only highlighted the lack of sensitivity of the advertising industry to the plight of those with real mental illnesses.

There is differing opinion, nevertheless, about the extent to which we should be concerned about such slang and its use. Many slang terms (such as "crazy") have become very widely used in casual conversation, with no real insult intended to those with mental illnesses: "Things have been absolutely crazy today at work"; "it would be crazy not to take advantage of these opportunities." Some mental health advocates find these types of usage innocuous and generally acceptable as a part of public speech. In addition, objections to "mere words" and to playful use of those words when they involve no intention to offend or disparage those with mental illnesses are often seen as out of proportion to the offense, as carrying political correctness to an extreme, and as marking the protester as overly sensitive and lacking a sense of humor.

An editorial in the *Staten Island Advance* typifies this position. When

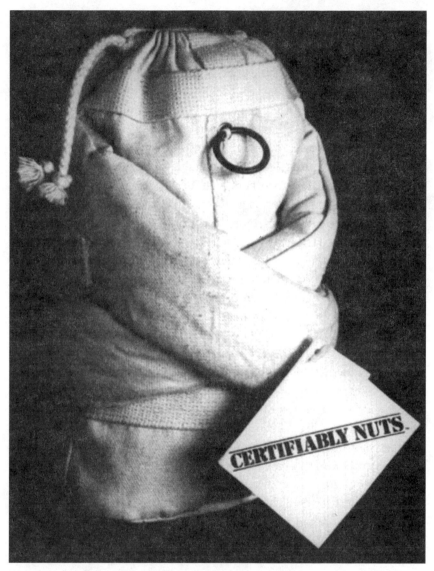

4. *This product won a marketing award but offended people with mental disorders.*

a New York assemblywoman, Elizabeth A. Connelly, expressed offense at a local lottery ad that urged people to be "crazy, nuts, out of control . . . cuckoo, wacko . . ." by playing the new instant scratch-off game called "Crazy Eights," the Staten Island newspaper headlined its piece, "Outrage at Harmless Ad Is, Well, Crazy."[22] The editorial went on to observe that "we do think the Assemblywoman is afflicted with some of the same hypersensitivity that makes every public pronouncement these days a trip through a minefield of political correctness" and that "even bright and thoughtful public officials seem to lose their sense of humor in that touchy climate."

On the other side of the issue, others—particularly those who have experienced a mental illness in themselves or loved ones—argue that even mild references (to "crazy" situations, "insane" choices, and so forth) contribute to the continued devaluation of people with mental illnesses, emphasizing to others that being "crazy" is unacceptable. Those opposed to such terms also remind us that such references are unnecessary because other, more appropriate terms are available (for instance, "wild" or "chaotic" or "foolish" as replacements for "crazy"), and that, therefore, derogatory language, however mild, should not be accepted.[23] One woman wrote in response to the *Staten Island Advance* editorial: "All stigmatized minorities know that mild slurs considered socially acceptable go hand-in-hand with the 'truly objectionable slights' you speak of."[24]

Those with mental illnesses and the families and friends who have seen the pain that such illnesses produce, furthermore, find careless and exploitative use of psychiatric terms and concepts objectionable because it conveys a lack of recognition of the seriousness of the plight of those suffering from mental disorders. Such usage trivializes what is a very painful and often prolonged struggle for millions of people. "Going psycho," to those who have experienced psychosis, means something much more than wearing wild sunglasses or cavorting with Elvira (as ads for Psycho Sunglasses and Pepsi-Cola have suggested). Being "insane" involves something far more devastating than swimming in goo (as the 1990 Fox TV program *Pure Insanity* implied). Being in a straitjacket for real is hardly a lark, and those who have had to be in one are angered when Buster Poindexter treats it as a fun experience.

In addition, advocates have pointed out that people with mental illnesses constitute one of the few remaining groups, in this era of political correctness, to be subject to such consistently thoughtless labeling. The use of slang for most other groups of people, at least in mass media, has largely been curtailed. Public media have learned to avoid slang references because of their offensiveness to those of specific ethnic background, sexual preference, and gender and because they demean those groups of people. The University of Missouri School of Journalism has even published a *Dictionary of Cautionary Words and Phrases*,[25] listing terms that journalists are advised to avoid because they are seen as objectionable. It is noteworthy that in the University of Missouri's compendium, terms for mental illness are not included, although terms for other types of disabilities are. The omission of terms for mental illness is another indication that the media do not yet recognize the need to limit slang references to mental illness.

The result is that psychiatric slang continues to appear, even in well-respected media sources, at a frequency that would be considered totally unacceptable for almost any other group. Consider, for example, *Time* magazine's coverage of a tragic event that took place at an elementary school in Winnetka, Illinois. In May 1988, thirty-year-old Lori Dann entered the school armed with several guns and shot a number of children. *Time*'s May 30, 1988, headline introducing the story of this incident was "One Lunatic, Three Guns." The event was truly tragic, and it is likely that mental illness was a contributing factor in the woman's actions. Referring to the mentally ill person involved as a "lunatic," however, was both unnecessary (*Newsweek*'s article on the same incident was titled simply " 'I Have Hurt Some Children': Nightmare in Winnetka") and inconsistent with standards applied to other groups. If the Winnetka school killings had been committed by someone in a wheelchair, it is unlikely that *Time*'s headline would have read "One Cripple, Three Guns." If the incident had involved a black woman, the headline would not have proclaimed "One Nigger, Three Guns." There seems not to be the same hesitancy about using similarly disrespectful terms in referring to people with mental illnesses.

Then, too, there is the deliberate use of psychiatric terminology to disparage others. Writers and editors (and many others) frequently, and inappropriately, apply psychiatric labels to those whose actions they do not approve of. According to various newspaper reports,[26] Saddam Hussein, following Iraq's invasion of Kuwait, was promptly labeled a "madman" by Senator Christopher Dodd and Congressman Don Riley. Senator Alphonse D'Amato of New York reportedly noted that Hussein was "as crazy and ruthless as Hitler." News agencies were quick to pass on these assertions—and to add a few of their own. *Newsweek* was led to suggest, in its January 7, 1991, cover story, that the Iraqi leader was "More than Just a Madman" (although the accompanying article, similarly titled, gave no real consideration to the question of Saddam's psychiatric status). Similarly, a brief piece in the April 14, 1991, *Parade* magazine included a picture of Muammar Qaddafi, captioned "Nutty as a Fruitcake," and then, in its March 24, 1994, issue, *Parade* expressed concern about Russia under "an unhinged leader like 'Mad Vlad' Zhirinovsky." Yet individuals such as Qaddafi, Saddam, and Zhirinovsky are not suffering from mental disorders. They are organized, functioning effectively, and—perhaps unfortunately for the rest of the world—very much in control of their faculties. That their actions are hostile, cruel, or even fanatical does not make them "madmen" in the sense of having a significant mental illness. And, if pressed, the writers who apply the madman label to our international enemies in this way would probably acknowledge that they don't really believe that these men are mentally ill. What they are communicating through the use of such labels is that these leaders are unlikable and destructive, even evil, people. These writers are, in short, using mental illness labels as discrediting insults and, by doing so, are also discrediting those with true mental illnesses.

A related issue involves the use of mental illness as a source of humor. Jokes about mental illness are common in the repertoires of comedians. One chapter of Gerald Lieberman's book of recommended jokes for speakers is titled "Psycho . . . psychiatry, psychiatrists, neurotics . . . and just plain nuts."[27] It includes numerous "a man went to a psychiatrist . . ." and inmates-in-the-asylum jokes, with disdain for the mentally ill subjects of those jokes clearly apparent in the terminology used:

> It was visiting day at the asylum. "Is there anything I can get you?" asked his brother.
> "Yes," the nut replied. "I'd like a watch that tells time."
> "Doesn't your watch tell time?"
> "No," he said dejectedly. "I have to look at it."

Even youthful comedians-to-be can easily learn that mental illness is a fruitful topic of humor, with jokes such as the following offered to them in books of children's jokes:

> PATIENT: Doctor, can you help me? I think I'm a dog. All the time I think I'm a dog.

DOCTOR: How long have you felt like this?
PATIENT: Ever since I was a puppy.[28]

Such jokes—and many others—convey that mental illness is a comical condition and involves small and laughable idiosyncrasies, such as believing that one is a dog. This notion of mental illness as a humorous oddity is commonly conveyed in many comedy contexts.

Numerous film comedies, for instance, have been based on the premise that the symptoms of mental illness are laughable. Ads for a 1990 Dudley Moore movie asked, "You wanna laugh tonight?" and urged people to go see *Crazy People* to get those laughs. *Newsday*'s film reviewer described the plot of *The Dream Team* as "four acknowledged crazy people on their own in New York City" and declared that to be "an innately funny premise"[29]—a characterization probably not shared by the growing numbers of homeless mentally ill people struggling to survive on the streets.

Comedy portrayals also tend to depict mental illness as primarily involving little more than specific comical oddities that the individuals manifest repetitively. In *Crazy People*, for example, Dudley Moore plays an advertising executive whose "truthful" ads lead him to be sent to a psychiatric hospital. There he meets a succession of patients, each of whom has a particular emphasized peculiarity. In fact, it is the peculiarity rather than the person to whom the viewer is really introduced. The first patient seen merely plays the piano endlessly. The next is seen reciting to himself statistics about Saab automobiles ("In 1975, Saab switched over from electronic fuel injection to continuous fuel injection . . ."); his symptom is that he thinks and talks almost exclusively about Saabs. Another patient, Bruce, has less clear pathology except that he comments in a somewhat hostile manner on the other patients. For example, when Dudley Moore seems perplexed by the recitation about Saab, Bruce interjects, "He's a lunatic." Daryl Hannah, whose presence in the hospital is said to be a result of the many fears she has, introduces another patient: "There's Mort. All he wants in life is to be a comedy writer and move to Hollywood." A young Asian man is seen wandering about the ward swatting flies with a fly swatter. A large black man walks up and introduces himself: "I'm Manuel Robles. I'm Latino and I enjoy it. Incidentally, I'm macho." ("Incidentally," adds

Bruce, "you're crazy.") Later Manuel is seen working on embroidery, to make his statement about being macho even more comic. Moore then sits next to a small man with mussed hair who is staring into space. The man looks at him and says "hello" repeatedly. Daryl Hannah explains that "hello" is the only word he says; he carries around a box full of signs that say hello as well. Finally, there is Judge, who introduces himself and asks for ballet tickets, explaining, "I love the ballet. I love the little toe shoes. I can't help myself."

This sort of parade-of-patients-with-funny-habits can be found in almost every comedy—film, television, or theater—with a scene in a psychiatric hospital. In television series about mental health practitioners (*The Bob Newhart Show*, *Growing Pains*, *The Robert Guillaume Show*, *Frasier*, and *Good Advice*), the parade may be week to week rather than all in the same scene, but the same pattern is apparent; one by one, new patients are introduced who each have a special amusing quirk. In *Bob Newhart*, there was Mr. Carlin, who was hostile and morose, Mr. Henderson, who was nervous and nonassertive, and so forth.

As noted previously, jokes about mental illness often convey this same idea of mental illness as a humorous habit. Cartoons may likewise communicate this when attempting to use mental illness to create humor. A widely circulated newspaper cartoon by Leigh Rubin, for instance, purports to show "where Crazy Glue comes from" and depicts horses in a field, with one dressed as Napoleon, another standing on its head, and others making funny faces and doing odd things ("crazy" horses).

Once again, there are mixed reactions to these depictions. There are many, including people with psychiatric disorders, who perceive and enjoy the wit in comic portrayals of mental illness. Others point out that such comic depictions are clearly preferable to some of the alternatives—such as the presentation of individuals with mental illness as savage and inhuman. Indeed, many comedies present their mentally ill characters as heroes of sorts. The patients from *The Dream Team* rescue their therapist from kidnappers, and those in *Crazy People* are more supportive and likable than the greedy advertising executives who commit Dudley Moore to the hospital. In addition, those who respond negatively to comedy are vulnerable to criticisms that they have no sense of humor, that they take things too seriously, and that

Rubes®   By Leigh Rubin

Where Crazy Glue comes from.

5. *Those who are "crazy" are expected to do odd and humorous things.*
Rubes by Leigh Rubin. Reprinted by permission of Leigh Rubin and Creators Syndicate.

they are unable to lighten up and to laugh at themselves in a healthy
way.

The concerns that mental health advocates express, on the other side, focus on what they see as misinformation and trivialization of mental disorders. Comedy portrayals, they note, are not depictions of real patients. They are one-dimensional caricatures that poorly represent the complexity, severity, and seriousness of mental illness. Rarely in real life are psychiatric problems as clear and circumscribed as those described above. Patients with singular obsessions about a specific kind of automobile or the word "hello" are not seen in actual practice. Mental health advocates and educators who feel it is important for the public to have a clearer and more accurate understanding of mental illnesses express concern that these one-dimensional comedy characterizations lead farther away from such understanding.

Moreover, the lack of distress and suffering shown by patients in fictional comedy, their implied comfort with their hallmark symptoms, is also quite unreal. Those with mental illnesses and their families would like the public to better appreciate how consuming and how painful mental illnesses can be, and portrayals that suggest just the opposite may understandably be experienced as hurtful and infuriating. Afflicted persons and their loved ones would like the media to understand that, as the woman who wrote to the *Staten Island Advance* commented, "poking 'gentle fun' at people with mental illness is no more acceptable than poking 'gentle fun' at people with muscular dystrophy."[30] For those personally affected by psychiatric disorders, mental illness is no laughing matter.

And as other disability groups have pointed out, it is one thing to tolerate joking about and comic depiction of your group if that group nevertheless has high standing and acceptance in the community, but quite another when your group is not respected or valued. The comments of James Gashel, an official of the National Federation of the Blind, about media depiction of people with visual disabilities apply equally well to those with mental disability: "If we were at a point where blindness was not regarded as a negative and if we had achieved equal opportunity, then we could laugh and say this is not a realistic portrayal of a blind person. But for people with visual handicaps who face discrimination in everyday life . . . such depictions are dangerous."[31] Jokes and presentation of people and problems as laughable do not aid in the restoration of status and self-esteem needed by people with mental disabilities; more likely they undermine those and encourage the continued devaluation of the group of people they portray. Under

6. *This cartoon conveys the message that praise from psychiatric patients is worth little.* KUDZU *by Doug Marlette. Reprinted by permission of Doug Marlette and Creators Syndicate.*

such circumstances, humor at one's expense, however otherwise entertaining, remains objectionable.

Furthermore, the use of humor about mental illness, as with the use of slang, can sometimes involve more clear and direct put-downs, as in the following scene from a *Barney Miller* episode:

> Barney instructs dim-witted officer Levit to take a prisoner to Bellevue Hospital. The prisoner, who has been screaming in his cell, expresses relief, saying to Captain Miller, "Bellevue. I *am* more sick than I am criminal." Barney answers, "Absolutely." As Levit is about to take the prisoner, Barney's wife enters through the squadroom door. "Hi," says the prisoner. "I'm the man who was screaming. . . . You're very lovely." "Don't mind him," Levit counters, "he's crazy."

The humor here suggests that the prisoner's opinion, even about the attractiveness of Barney Miller's wife, is not to be valued because he is mentally ill. "He's crazy" is used to mean "He's just a mentally unstable person; don't put any credence in what he thinks." A person who is "crazy" is one whose opinions or actions should be discounted.

The *Barney Miller* scene is not an isolated example of this type of

THE FAR SIDE

By GARY LARSON

7. This cartoon suggests that even therapists look down on people with psychiatric problems. *THE FAR SIDE copyright 1990 & 1992 FARWORKS, INC.* Dist. by *UNIVERSAL PRESS SYNDICATE. Reprinted by permission. All rights reserved.*

humorous devaluing of people with mental illnesses. Reverend Will B. Dunn, in one *Kudzu* comic strip, is pleased with fan mail praising his advice column until, in the final frame, he learns that the letter comes from a psychiatric institution. The implication is that praise from people with mental illnesses is worthless and nothing one can really feel good about. A Gary Larson cartoon shows a therapist writing "just plain nuts" in his notepad, conveying to the audience that even therapists have little respect for their disturbed patients. The simple respect that people with mental illness need and desire is neither presented nor encouraged in such comedic portrayals.

Words—and the images that accompany them—have power. Misused psychiatric terminology and unreal images may mislead the public and create misunderstanding rather than increase understanding about mental illness. Slang and unflattering references to mental illness, exploitative use of psychiatric concepts, and comic depictions of mental disorder fail to recognize the painful seriousness of psychiatric disorders and to respect the sensitivities of those with mental illnesses who may be in their audience. Such references put forward a view of mental illness as a trivial matter, worthy of laughter rather than empathy. They communicate that mental illness makes one less worthy of respect. And they display and encourage insensitivity in their failure to see people with mental illnesses as individuals who could be hurt or offended by being so often the butt of jokes.

Chapter Three

A
Breed
Apart

People who are perceived as "different" are often the target of disrespectful humor. So it should be no surprise that people with mental illnesses, who are frequently the subject of such humor, also tend to be viewed and portrayed as fundamentally different from others. I am not talking here simply about portrayals of the symptoms that distinguish those with mental illnesses. Such individuals do, of course, differ from others in many of the behaviors they display: they exhibit the distinct, often dramatic symptoms of their disorders. I am referring here to depictions of mental illness that suggest much more fundamental differences from others—differences in physical appearance, in background and character, even in basic humanity.

In the late 1950s, Jum Nunnally conducted an extensive rating of mass media presentations of mental illness. Trained raters sampled newspapers, magazines, television, and films and made judgments about the way mental illness was depicted. Nunnally also asked mental health professionals what they felt should be conveyed about mental illness and compared their recommendations with ratings of actual media depiction. In general, media portrayals deviated greatly from what mental health professionals felt should be communicated about psychiatric disorders. In particular, Nunnally noted a large discrepancy on a factor that he labeled "look and act different." Psychiatric experts felt fairly strongly that mental illness is only part of an individual's total functioning and that it is difficult to single out a person with mental illness from others. The mass media, however, seemed to suggest that those with mental illnesses are recognizably different from others in both manner and appearance, that they stand out as deviant and bizarre. Nunnally described the media approach: "In general, the causes, symptoms, methods of treatment and social effects portrayed by the media are far removed from what the experts advocate. In particular, the media in their overall presentations emphasize the bizarre symptoms of the mentally ill. . . . In television drama, for example, the afflicted person often enters the scene staring glassy-eyed, with his mouth widely open, mumbling incoherent phrases or laughing uncontrollably."[1]

I have heard people declare that they can tell that someone is mentally ill just by looking at them. "It's in the eyes," some have said, forgetting the times when they have been surprised to learn that someone they know has a mental illness. Others decide it is the voice, the speech, the movement that gives away one's mental disorder. Perhaps these observers' views have been shaped by the fact that actors with such distinct appearances and manners have been frequently chosen for Hollywood madman roles. Peter Lorre, with his large eyes and unusual voice, for example, was featured in many films in which he played a person with a mental disorder. One of the earliest sound films, M, was about the police search for a psychotic murderer of children. Lorre played the killer. Subsequently Lorre became identified with the role of "the insidious and deranged menace who concealed his nastiness under a cloak of gentility," as Ted Sennet notes in his book, *Masters of Menace*.[2] Lorre played the insane Dr. Gogol in *Mad Love* (1935), a deranged killer in *Stranger on the Third Floor* (1940), and sadistic prison authorities in *Island of the Doomed Men* (1940) and *The Cross of Lorraine* (1944). *The Beast with Five Fingers* (1957), Sennet writes, gave Lorre the chance "to depict again the sort of deranged and obsessed man he had played so brilliantly in M, *Mad Love*, and *The Face Behind the Mask*."[3]

That it was his unusual physical appearance and manner which contributed greatly to his being tied to these madman roles is supported by the remarks of Lorre's biographers. Peter John Dryer, for example, writes of Lorre: "He was too intractably unique in accent, form and expression for producers to reorient their attitude to him. He was too obviously nearly mad."[4] Similarly, Philip Kemp notes, in the *International Dictionary of Films and Filmmakers*: "Squat, stocky, round-faced, at once pitiable and terrifying, he seemed a textbook illustration of schizophrenia. . . . Small wonder if he found himself cast as madmen and murderers."[5] One might question, however, whether having a unique accent or being squat, stocky, and round-faced are truly signs of madness.

Drawings of people with mental illnesses for advertisements and cartoons even more consistently emphasize distinctive physical features—wild eyes and unkempt hair in particular—as characteristic of their subjects. An advertisement for *Pipe Dream*, a computer game, features a man in a straitjacket with hair going in all directions, wide eyes, and open mouth. To convey that he is crazy, Crazy Eddie's logo and ads have featured an odd cartoon face with a large nose, wild eyes, and the requisite wiry, sticking-out hair. A Volkswagen advertisement claiming that their offers warrant commitment contains a similar image, as do ads for Maniac Plus clothing stores. The consistency of these images is striking.

Gary Larson, in his caroon depiction of "Things from Ipanema," includes a "homicidal maniac" who is easy to pick out, even from the other odd-looking characters. One can obtain a Garfield bumper sticker that proclaims "Welcome to the Funny Farm" and shows the popular cat slobbering in a straitjacket, with his eyes crossed and his tongue out. Steven Spielberg's contributions to children's television programming includes *The Animaniacs*, three creatures named Yakko, Wakko, and Dot. Which character is Wakko is easily determined just by looking at drawings of the trio; Wakko is the odd-looking one with his tongue hanging out and hat askew. The idea that those with mental illnesses look different from other people is alive and well in our mass media.

Writers, editors, and directors may insist on representing people with mental illnesses as physically different even if doing so does not match their own actual experiences. The 1975 Academy Award–winning film *One Flew Over the Cuckoo's Nest* is a case in point. Its producers saw distinct physical appearance as such a necessary attribute for portrayals of mental patients in their film that one of their reported start-up problems was finding a sufficient number of competent actors who looked unusual enough to portray mental patients. Using actual patients from Oregon State Hospital, where the movie was filmed, for walk-on roles was considered, but such use was rejected because the real patients did not look distinct enough to depict mental patients on the screen.

The situation is similar to that reported more recently by *Time* magazine with respect to a film involving homeless people. According

8

9

10

11

8–11. *Odd appearance is consistently used to suggest mental illness.*

THE FAR SIDE   By GARY LARSON

8-25

the girl

the dog

the cow

the chicken

the insurance salesman

the microbe

the homicidal maniac

the cat

the nerd

Things from Ipanema

12. *Again, "maniacs" are presented as odd even in physical appearance.*

to the January 21, 1991, *Time* article entitled "Actors with Dirty Faces," Warner Brothers was filming *Curly Sue*, a story of friendship between

13. *Which Animaniac is Wakko is clear from his physical appearance.*

an eight-year-old girl and a homeless man, and decided to hire real
street people as extras. Most of the applicants from a local shelter were
reportedly rejected, however, because they were too clean. In order to
be hired to represent homeless people on the screen, the real homeless
people had to find and wear filthy clothes and a layer of dirt. *Time*
quoted a casting staff member as explaining: "When the director asks
for street people, he wants a certain look."[6] Homeless and mentally ill
people are expected to look a certain way—discernibly different from
others—and visual representations of them underscore that expectation
in their selection of images, even when that representation is contrary
to the reality encountered by those responsible for the depiction.

The mass media, however, do not stop at suggesting that those
with mental illnesses look different from others. Their images also
communicate that people with mental illnesses *are* different in many
fundamental ways. In our Media Watch study, we not only had observers identify instances of prime-time television portrayal of mental illness
but also had them record the personal and social attributes of all
characters indentified in the program as mentally ill. These characters,
we found, tended to be identified mainly by their mental illnesses.
Almost three-fourths of them had no family connections; they were
either unmarried or of unspecified marital status. Almost half had no
clear occupation.[7] Moreover, these results are hardly unique to either
the time period of our study or the time slot viewed. Nancy Signorelli,
sampling twelve years of prime-time programming as part of George
Gerbner's well-known Cultural Indicators Project, also found that mentally ill characters on television were less likely than other characters
to have identifiable occupations (and those that did were more likely
to be failures in those occupations).[8] Likewise, of the eight characters
shown as mentally ill in the fourteen daytime soap operas studied by
Laurel Fruth and Allan Padderud, six had no identifiable marital status
and five had no specified occupation.[9]

In other words, these studies showed a tendency for mentally ill
characters to be portrayed as unlike most real people (or even other
people in the television world) who have family and jobs that establish
their identities as participating members of society. Even on soap operas,
where plots move slowly and there is ample time for character development, mentally ill individuals are provided with little social identity.
They are not spouses or parents who have become mentally ill. They

are not workers whose ability to handle their jobs has been impaired by mental illness. They are not someone's friend who has developed a psychiatric disorder. They are not a part of the usual fabric of society, of home and work. And they are not, then, people with whom the average viewer can identify or empathize. Those with mental illnesses are, if the television image is to be believed, truly a breed apart, a special, distinct class of people characterized primarily, if not exclusively, by the illnesses they suffer.

The image of people with mental illnesses as fundamentally different from others is conveyed in other subtle ways as well. That image is reinforced, for example, in the generic terms used to refer to sufferers of mental disorders. News media in particular, seeking abbreviated references for their limited space and headlines, easily fall into the habit of talking about those with psychiatric disorders or psychiatric histories as "the mentally ill."[10] A December 12, 1992, story in the *New York Times*, for instance, featured "Alice, Matchmaker for *the Mentally Ill*"; a January 12, 1992, headline from the same paper declared "Big Shelters Hold Terrors for *the Mentally Ill*" (emphasis added). Just as terms like "a schizophrenic" or "a diabetic" identify individuals in terms of their illnesses as if that were their only and most important characteristic, these broad references to "the mentally ill" convey a similar lack of appreciation of the basic human character of *individuals* with psychiatric disorders. Such terminology also communicates that "the mentally ill" are a special and distinct group who are, implicitly, unlike the rest of "us." Designation of those with mental illnesses as "the mentally ill" (or to people with other disabilities as "the disabled," to people without homes as "the homeless," and so forth), advocates argue, encourages others to view them in terms of their differentness.[11]

A probably unintentional, but telling, extension of this kind of representation is found in an article in the November 2, 1982, issue of *Time* magazine. "When former Mental Patient Robert E. Pates became rowdy . . ." began the article, which then went on to describe a tragic incident in which a prisoner's carelessness with a cigarette started a jail fire and resulted in the death of many other prisoners.[12] Not only did *Time* feel it was important to note that the prisoner was a former psychiatric patient, but it apparently felt that mental illness was such a central part of that individual's identity that it capitalized "Mental Patient" as if it were a formal title—like Doctor, Senator, or Reverend.

The media also provide suggestions that people with mental illnesses are different from others in their lack of basic abilities. Those with mental illnesses, it is often suggested, can't be as smart, as talented, as dedicated as the rest of us. A book review from *Entertainment Weekly*, for example, puts forward the misconception that those with psychiatric disorders cannot possibly have the writing skills that others possess. Reviewing *Spider*, by Patrick McGrath, the reviewer observed: "McGrath isn't crazy, of course. Yet he has written a book that only a wacko could write, if only a wacko could write as well as McGrath, which a wacko probably can't."[13] When we consider that the ranks of "wackos" have included widely acclaimed authors such as William Styron, Sylvia Plath, Virginia Woolf, and Ernest Hemingway, it is clear that the expectation that "wackos" can't write well is false. Such a misconception clearly exists, however, and is part of the image of individuals with mental illnesses as different from others.

People with mental illnesses, media convey, also can't be expected to possess other traits or skills that "normal" people have. When a resident of a psychiatric hospital managed to write and have published an article in the *Military Review* about hand-held nuclear weapons, his achievement was seen as so remarkable that a Washington State newspaper reported it with the headline "Schizophrenic Writes Nuclear Weapons Article." The newspaper report highlighted the embarrassment and amazement of the officer in charge of the *Military Review*. "I just found it incredible that he could be doing this from a hospital," that officer is quoted as saying.[14] Although there are desirable aspects to this story—such as having mental illness associated with positive accomplishments rather than nefarious deeds—the newspaper report was nevertheless troubling in its implicit assumption that such an accomplishment is a newsworthy novelty. "What I find incredible," wrote one mental health advocate in response to the newspaper story, "is that someone found that to be news. . . . Why should it come as a surprise that someone with schizophrenia should be bright and talented?"[15]

Similar surprise that a person with a mental illness could possess normal human traits is implicit in a Utica (N.Y.) *Observer-Dispatch* account of an altruistic act. That newspaper story described how a man found $7,000 in cash in a bank money bag and quickly returned it to its owner. The obvious news in this story was that this person showed a higher degree of honesty and integrity than we expect from many people in today's world; he returned a substantial sum of money when he could easily have kept it without consequence. The story, however, also contained gratuitous reference to the fact that the man had been a resident of a psychiatric hospital. It is possible that the author of the story intended to suggest that the man's psychiatric status explained his honesty and to communicate that psychiatric patients are simpler, purer, more innocent, and less capable of deception than others. What seemed more clearly suggested, however, was that honesty and integrity were especially surprising from someone with a psychiatric history, as if such an individual would not be expected to have those basic human values. Both interpretations involve the inaccurate stereotype that those with mental illnesses are morally different from others.

In the extreme, there may even be explicit assertions in the media that those with mental illnesses are so different as to be virtually inhuman. In the film *Halloween II*, Donald Pleasance, the psychiatric authority tracking murderous Michael Myers, makes clear that he does not consider his former patient human:

> "I can't stop [searching for Michael Myers] until I'm certain it's dead," says the psychiatrist.
> "You're talking about him like he's some kind of animal," remarks the police officer accompanying the doctor.
> "He was my patient for fifteen years," explains Pleasance. "It became an, obsession with me until I realized there was nothing within him, neither conscience nor reason, that was even remotely human."

Similar suggestions are a common element of many thriller and detective novels with serial or multiple murderers. In Thomas Harris's *Red Dragon*, the hero offers this characterization of Dr. Hannibal Lecter: "He's a monster. I think of him as one of those pitiful things that are born in hospitals from time to time. They feed it, and keep it warm, but they don't put it on machines and it dies."[16] The mentally ill killer in Rex Miller's *Slice* is many times referred to as less than human, as more like an animal than a human being: "His natural laugh was a weird kind of barking noise . . . so he had learned to fake a passable human laugh."[17] "The thing had been honing its skills."[18] "The monster loomed over him. He could feel the thing's hot breath on him."[19] This mentally ill character is also referred to directly as a "rare subspecies of humanity."[20] Likewise, the villain in Shane Stevens's *By Reason of Insanity* is depicted as an inhuman monster of predominantly animal cunning: "He was a human robot who reacted to the feelings of others but could never act on his own feelings. . . . a shrewd cunning animal. . . . an authentic monster."[21]

Even news media often find occasion to imply that those with mental illnesses are less than human. "Village Beast May Go Free," blared the January 13, 1992, front page of the *New York Post* to introduce an article about the possible release of a psychiatric patient. "Monster Masked as a Human Being," was the headline for another *Post* article, this one on the trial of Joel Rifkin. After noting that Rifkin had been diagnosed with paranoid schizophrenia, the article went on to marvel that "he clasped his hands and coughed like a normal person. He shifted in his seat and slouched down and even dozed off, just like a human being."[22]

Such assertions of bestiality are not confined to stories of murderous villains. I was shocked to find one, for instance, in an innocuous and otherwise delightful children's book, *How to Eat Fried Worms*, by Thomas Rockwell. The book is about a wager between two children; one child boastfully bets another that he can eat fifteen worms in as many days. In a brief section totally irrelevant to the main plot, one child character sees someone behaving strangely, suggests to his friend that the person is mentally ill, and then warns him: "Don't let him see we're afraid. Crazy people are like dogs. If they see you're afraid, they attack."[23] The clear message to the children for whom this book is written is that people with mental illnesses are like animals.

Once again, the examples in this chapter represent only a small sample of what is available. Alert readers will find many more in their own experience. Even these limited selections, however, should make it clear how people with psychiatric disorders are presented in a variety of media as fundamentally different from others—in nature, in physical appearance, even in basic humanity. The reality, of course, is quite different.

The truth is that those who suffer from mental illnesses are not fundamentally different from others. Again, this is not to deny that people with such illnesses have specific symptoms that may be unusual, different, or even bizarre. When those symptoms are being displayed, individuals may indeed act and seem "different" from others without those symptoms. When the illness is severe or prolonged, it may even be difficult to recognize the sufferer as the same person we knew before the illness. Some also may be taking medications that produce tremors, facial contortions, or other odd movements. But all of this is true with almost any illness.

Even a relatively mild and short-lived illness like influenza can produce outward differentness. Those with the flu may appear "different" from those without the illness: they sneeze and sniffle; they sweat and vomit; they look pale and tired, in ways that people without the illness do not. What we think of as their personality may change, and the pleasant, humorous, outgoing friends we know can become irritable, uncommunicative, and demanding as a by-product of the discomfort they are experiencing from their flu or from the medications they are taking to treat the illness. More severe and prolonged illnesses may produce even more profound changes. Such changes, however, usually do not lead us to think of such physically ill people as fundamentally different from others. With respect to basic elements of human nature and experience—background, learning, feelings, motivations, needs, values, and so forth—the person with the illness is far more similar to than different from the person without such an illness. The same is true for those with mental illnesses.

The remarkable frequency of mental illnesses in our society tells us that those who experience those illnesses must include people who are like ourselves. In 1984, the National Institute of Mental Health undertook what it called the Epidemiological Catchment Area Study to determine the prevalence of psychiatric disorder in the United States. Researchers sent trained interviewers to three major cities (Baltimore, Maryland; New Haven, Connecticut; and St. Louis, Missouri) to conduct standardized, structured interviews with over nine thousand adults. Experienced mental health professionals then examined interview data to see whether the patterns of behavior and emotions described by interviewees corresponded to explicit criteria for selected psychiatric diagnoses and thus whether interviewees appeared to be suffering from (or to have suffered from) an identifiable psychiatric disorder. Results of this study led to the conclusion that thirty to forty million Americans, in any given six-month period, will be suffering from a diagnosable mental disorder and that, over the course of a lifetime, one out of every five citizens in this country will experience a significant mental illness.

This includes approximately two million people with schizophrenia, eight to ten million people with depressive or manic-depressive illnesses, and ten million people with anxiety disorders such as phobias and panic attacks.[24]

With numbers this high, mental illnesses cannot be thought of as confined to a small and unique group of individuals. Rather, as the study confirmed, mental illnesses afflict people from all age groups, education levels, and socioeconomic circumstances. Those millions of people with mental illnesses come from all walks of life; they are doctors, lawyers, teachers, grocers, mechanics, pilots, construction workers, and psychiatrists. With one out of five people afflicted, there is a high likelihood that someone we know well—someone from our own school, someone from our own place of business, someone from our own neighborhood, someone from our own household, someone very like ourselves—will be among the ranks of "the mentally ill."

Moreover, no amount of economic privilege, brains, talent, or courage can make one immune to mental illness. Those afflicted, for example, have included a winner of both the Pulitzer Prize and the Nobel Prize for Literature, the second person to set foot on the moon, the Oscar-winning star of *Gone With the Wind*, a Super Bowl winner, a famous painter, a senator and vice presidential candidate, the psychology director of a large psychiatric hospital, and a recent winner of the Nobel Prize for Economics.

Ernest Hemingway, is, of course, well known for his success as an author. In 1953 he was awarded a Pulitzer Prize for *The Old Man and the Sea*, and he received the Nobel Prize for Literature in 1954. It was around this same time that his mental and physical health began to deteriorate. He became depressed, socially withdrawn, and unable to write. He worried excessively about his financial status and began having delusions that he was being investigated and followed by the FBI and the IRS. Multiple hospitalizations and electroshock therapy were unable to relieve his distress, and, on July 2, 1961, Ernest Hemingway shot and killed himself in his home.[25]

Edwin (Buzz) Aldrin, a man who has done what few people have ever done—walked in space and stepped on the moon—has also struggled with depression. According to his own account,[26] he began to experience symptoms of depression not long after his walk on the moon. He reported that he would feel "an overwhelming sense of fatigue mixed with vague sadness," do little besides stay in bed or watch television, and often wept from helplessness. With medication and psychotherapy, Aldrin recovered and has sought to share his experiences with the public through an autobiographical book and through service as a spokesperson for the National Mental Health Association.

Vivien Leigh was only twenty-seven when she was voted Best Actress for her performance as Scarlett O'Hara in *Gone With the Wind*. Throughout her life, however, she suffered from what was eventually diagnosed as manic-depressive illness. She resisted psychiatric treatment for fear of public exposure and embarrassment, but, in February 1953, her condition deteriorated to a point where she was admitted to an English hospital specializing in the treatment of mental disorders. Despite treatment, which included medication, being packed in icebags, and electroshock, Leigh continued to have manic-depressive episodes, resulting in her replacement in several plays and films. On July 7, 1967, Leigh died of tuberculosis when her painful memories of past psychiatric treatments led her to refuse to enter a hospital for proper care.[27]

Lionel Aldridge played defensive end for nine seasons in the National Football League, seven of them with the Green Bay Packers, with whom he earned a Super Bowl ring. According to a 1987 story in *Parade* magazine,[28] Aldridge began to hallucinate shortly after his retirement from football in December 1973. Despite initial attempts at psychiatric treatment and success as a radio and television sportscaster, his mental condition deteriorated. He was committed to Milwaukee County Mental Health Complex but refused medication and soon drifted onto the streets, lost to even his former teammates until 1984. Eventually he sought and accepted treatment, which enabled him to recover. According to the *Parade* report, he is now working as an account supervisor for the post office and has resumed work as a radio sports broadcaster.

Vincent Van Gogh, born March 30, 1853, was seen as withdrawn, seclusive, and brooding for most of his life, and his mental condition steadily deteriorated over the years until, beginning in 1889, he underwent a series of hospitalizations. Despite being tormented by hallucinations and delusions, Van Gogh continued to paint, producing as many as two paintings a week during his one-year hospitalization in Arles,

France. On Sunday, July 27, 1890, at the age of thirty-seven, Van Gogh ended his psychological torment by shooting himself in the abdomen. He died thirty-six hours later.[29]

Thomas Eagleton graduated cum laude from Harvard University Law School in 1953 and almost immediately plunged into politics. He became the youngest circuit court attorney in St. Louis history at the age of twenty-seven. He was elected state attorney general in 1960 and then went on to become Missouri's youngest lieutenant governor. In 1968 Eagleton was elected to the United States Senate. He became nationally known, however, when he was chosen, in 1972, as vice presidential running mate for George McGovern. When Eagleton acknowledged that he had received psychiatric treatment for depression that had included electroshock, public concerns about his qualifications to be vice president led to his withdrawal from the ticket. Eagleton returned to his position as senator from Missouri and served in that role for almost twenty years.

Frederick Frese was diagnosed with schizophrenia when he was twenty-five years old. He experienced numerous episodes in which he thought he was an animal, believed he was God's messenger, and became lost in perceived complex relationships among numbers and colors, and he was hospitalized numerous times. Despite this, Frese was able to complete a doctoral program in psychology at Ohio University. He then worked at Western Reserve Hospital in Ohio, taught at local universities, and earned a reputation as a bright and hard-working professional. In 1980 he was appointed psychology director of Western Reserve, where he supervises both patient care and other psychiatric professionals. Although he has not been hospitalized since 1974, Frese continues to have occasional episodes of his illness, during which times he takes accumulated sick leave and stays home with his wife and family until he recovers. Until 1986 only his family and immediate superiors knew of his disorder. Described as a warm, polite man, Frese continues to work, to write, and to point out to others the error of assuming that someone with a serious mental illness will be unsuited for leadership roles.[30]

At the age of twenty-one, John Nash was singled out by *Fortune* magazine as a brilliant mathematician. He earned a doctorate from Princeton in 1950, at the age of twenty-two, and went on to teach at the Massachusetts Institute of Technology. His Ph.D. thesis on game theory has served as a foundation for economists since that time. In October 1994, Nash was awarded the Nobel Prize for Economics for that influential early work. In between his graduate school days and his Nobel award, however, Nash struggled with schizophrenia. For more than twenty years, Nash was in and out of psychiatric hospitals, and his ability to continue his productive work was impaired. Fortunately, friends and colleagues continued to maintain contact with him, to support him, and to see to it that he had access to Princeton's computers. His friends and colleagues were also instrumental in persuading the Nobel Prize committee not to disqualify Nash as a candidate because of his mental illness. Nash now appears to have experienced a remission of his symptoms and has begun doing mathematics again.[31]

What should be apparent from this short list of prominent people who have experienced severe psychiatric disorders is that even privileged, talented, and accomplished people are vulnerable to mental illness, just as are those of us who are more ordinary in our status and accomplishments. This shared vulnerability, of course, is one of the things that makes mental illness so frightening and that motivates us to exaggerate the differences between ourselves and those who have mental illnesses. I will be discussing this tendency to distance ourselves from that which we fear in later chapters.

Those with psychiatric disorders are like others, also, in their individual uniqueness. What I mean by this seemingly paradoxical statement is that "the mentally ill," like any other group of people who share a single label, are very diverse. Each person within this group has his or her own strengths, weaknesses, and personality, and those differences are not negated by their disorders. Susanna Kaysen's bestselling recollections of her adolescent psychiatric hospitalization, *Girl, Interrupted*, for example, movingly describes the diverse characters of the young women who share her hospital ward and mental illness label.[32] There is not even homogeneity of symptoms among those with mental illnesses. We must remember that, while the media tend to focus on severe and psychotic disorders in their presentations of mental illness, there are many different mental illnesses—literally hundreds of different disorders of varying symptoms and degrees of severity. "The mentally ill" are like us in that they cannot be characterized by any one set of specific traits, backgrounds, or behaviors. Their commonality is in the motives, feelings, aspirations, and so forth that they share with the rest of humanity.

The histories of these individuals—and of millions more like them of greater and lesser status—also challenge the notion that people, when they suffer mental illnesses, invariably lose all those attributes that characterized them before their illnesses—as media portrayals of psychiatric patients as little more than bundles of symptoms might suggest. Although well-established skills are sometimes interfered with by symptoms, they do not simply disappear. The painter may still be able to paint, the chess player to play chess, the pianist to make music, the ping pong player to compete at table tennis. Education, intelligence, and past training remain to characterize the person with mental illness despite his or her illness. Individual interests likely remain also. People within psychiatric hospitals may continue to enjoy reading, jogging, knitting, or other hobbies if those activities were routine parts of their lives outside the hospital.

Likewise, the motives, goals, and emotions of people with mental illnesses are similar to those of all of us. Contrary to media characterizations of those with mental illnesses as emotionally hollow—such as the suggestion on a March 24, 1992, *Roseanne* episode that "psychos" and "schizos" can fool lie detector tests because they have no feelings to measure—the emotions of people with mental illnesses remain the same as those of all human beings. They appreciate comforts and kindnesses. They feel guilt and fear rejection. They desire acceptance and affection from family and friends. And, when struggling with a mental illness that can be both overwhelming and uncontrollable, they feel pain—pain so deep and raw that sometimes death can be a desired release.

"In the winter of 1985–86," wrote William Styron, the acclaimed author of *Sophie's Choice*, "I committed myself to a mental hospital because the pain of the depression from which I had suffered for more than five months had become intolerable. I never attempted suicide, but the possibility had become more real and the desire more greedy as each wintry day passed and the illness became more smotheringly intense. What had begun that summer as an off-and-on again malaise and a vague, spooky restlessness had gained gradual momentum until my nights were without sleep and my days were pervaded by a gray drizzle of unrelenting horror.[33] Styron's sentiments are echoed by Buzz Aldrin, in his description of the depression he suffered: "I could see no hope, no possibility of controlling anything. I began staying up nearly all night every night with some vague fear of sleeping in the darkness. . . . The rule of my emotions was absolute and ruthless. In no way could I stop feeling anything at all. I yearned for a brightly lit oblivion and wept for it."[34]

Even the dramatic disorganization of thinking that characterizes schizophrenia does not change these basic human feelings; it does not render individuals insensate or unaware. One articulate woman, for example, described her schizophrenic experience as follows: "I have never learned to describe sensations so far removed from what is called normal. General misery, physical discomfort, degradation, not born of intellectual concept, but a deep, bodily and inner mental state; a feeling of being lost, utterly lost with no sense of place or time, no idea to whom voices belonged, no clear realization of my own identity, lost in mind and body and soul, lost to light and form and color."[35]

Those with mental illnesses are also eager to be well and, like others with serious physical illnesses, they struggle for recovery. Lara Jefferson, a woman diagnosed with schizophrenia in an era before effective medications were available to help her manage her illness, wrote often about her experiences on any scrap of paper she could find in the midwestern hospital where she spent much of her time. "Life, for anyone," she wrote, "is an individual thing. For one who is insane—it is a naked—and a lonely thing. I learned that in my days of raving. I am aware of it more than ever this morning, as I think of what is before me. Insanity—Nakedness—Loneliness—Hopeless insanity—on 'Three Building' unless I can learn to think differently. How—how—HOW? In the name of God—How does a person learn to think differently? I am crazy wild this minute—how can I learn to think straight?"[36]

Even today, despite the treatment advances in psychiatry and pharmacology, the struggle remains. Lori Schiller, whose story has been told in the *Wall Street Journal*, also wrote during her many hospitalizations with schizophrenia and described her efforts in a way remarkably similar to that of Jefferson forty years previously: "Do you know I have to fight to keep from going crazy every day? What should I do, listen to every voice? Act out every impulse? What about my fantasies? Should I make those sick thoughts a reality? I'm working hard, damn hard."[37]

As to shared human goals and motivations, one need only read Susan Sheehan's account of the life of Sylvia Frumpkin—*Is There No Place on Earth for Me?*—to appreciate how individuals with mental illnesses cling to the same basic desires all of us have—for love and affection, for family and job success, for a place in the world—even in the midst of the wildest insanity. Sylvia Frumpkin, according to Sheehan's account, was born in May 1948. She had a tested IQ of 133, earned certificates of excellence in several subjects while in junior high school, and went to a special music and art high school. Starting in 1963, however, Sylvia developed a mental illness that led to more than a dozen psychiatric hospitalizations in numerous different institutions; underwent treatments that included drugs, insulin coma, electroshock, megavitamins, religious conversion, and sheltered workshops; and received several different diagnoses including schizophrenia, manic-depressive disorder, and schizoaffective disorder. She proved to be one of the relatively uncommon patients who do not respond to the medications typically used for such disorders, and she rarely had sustained periods of successful functioning. There were many times when she was dramatically delusional, ranting incoherently about her relationships to music and movie stars, and times when even huge dosages of medication could not calm her. Yet, through all her difficulties, Sylvia held to her hope of a "real" life someday and was painfully aware of the possibility that she might not achieve it: "I once thought, when I was about to finish medical-secretarial school, before I had a breakdown on the last day of school, that I'd graduate and get a job. I was looking forward to earning my own money, to having a credit card, to being a grown woman in my own right. If you can work and earn money, you can spend money. . . . You can buy new clothes instead of wearing State clothes. And you can have fun. But if you can't have any of those things. . . . When you know all those things exist for other people but not for you, sometimes it's very hard to endure the not having."[38]

Individuals with mental illnesses—individuals like William Styron, like Lori Schiller, like Sylvia Frumpkin—are not fundamentally different from others. They share the same backgrounds, feelings, and goals as all of us and react to their illnesses as most of us would react. They are, in fact, "us"—our relatives, our friends, our co-workers, our neighbors. Media depictions, however, give the opposite impression. Television and film portrayals feature actors with unusual appearances. Advertisements and other visual depictions likewise highlight physical distinctiveness. Entertainment media present mentally ill characters as having little identity beyond their mental illnesses, and news media subtly reinforce this notion by generic references to "the mentally ill" and by stories which convey wonder that someone with a mental illness is able to do what ordinary people can. In some cases, people with mental illnesses are even characterized as inhuman. The overall inaccurate message of mass media references to mental illness is that those with mental illnesses are unlike others, that they are indeed a breed apart.

Chapter Four

Murder and Mayhem

Even more common and more pernicious than any of the media images of mental illness discussed so far is the depiction of people with mental illnesses as violent and criminal. The "mad murderer" is as persistent, pervasive, and powerful a media stereotype as one can find anywhere. It occurs repeatedly within our most popular media and consistently across virtually all forms of mass media.

Mad killers and menacing mad doctors, for example, were prominent even in early film fare. One of the very earliest films, *The Cabinet of Dr. Caligari* (1919–20), introduced the mad and evil doctor who uses his special knowledge toward nefarious ends. Later Dr. Mabuse, in *Dr. Mabuse, the Gambler* (1922), was shown attempting to use hypnosis to establish a criminal empire and ending up confined as a raving madman. Still other early mad doctors include Charles Laughton, who tries to turn animals into men in *The Island of Dr. Moreau* (1932); Boris Karloff, who, as Hjalmar Poelzig, attempts human sacrifice as part of his devil worship in *The Black Cat* (1935); and Peter Lorre, as Dr. Gogol, who grafts the hands of a murderer onto a concert pianist in *Mad Love* (1935). Vincent Price carries on the mad doctor tradition in such films as *The Abominable Dr. Phibes* (1971) and *Dr. Phibes Rises Again* (1972).

With Alfred Hitchcock's classic suspense tale *Psycho* (1960), however, the floodgates opened for the portrayal of psychotic killers who are not merely scientists gone mad, who kill repeatedly, and whose murders are accounted for almost solely by their insanity. Hitchcock's film featured Anthony Perkins as the motel manager Norman Bates, who, dressed as his dead mother, kills a motel guest, Janet Leigh, in one of the most frightening scenes in movie history. *Psycho* was followed closely by several other films with similarly gruesome mad murderers— and similar one-word titles: *Homicidal* (1961), *Maniac* (1963), *Paranoiac* (1963), and *Nightmare* (1963). Since *Psycho*, there has been a fairly steady stream of psycho-killer films. *Peeping Tom*, released the same year as *Psycho*, featured a sadistic murderer who films women as he kills them in order to capture the look of fear on their faces. In *Night Must Fall* (1964), Albert Finney played an axe murderer who collects the severed heads of his victims. *Twisted Nerve* (1968) presented a homicidal maniac who assumes the identity of a six-year-old boy as part of his pathology. In 1972 Hitchcock again featured a mad murderer and frighteningly graphic murder scenes in *Frenzy*, while Brian DePalma began his bloody contributions with *Sisters* (1973), in which a scalpel-wielding young woman takes on the homicidal impulses of her dead sister.

In the late 1970s and early 1980s the low-budget, psycho-killer "slasher" movies found their stride, leading to series that have spanned more than a decade with their sequels. The murderous Michael Meyers escaped his asylum in *Halloween* (1978) and has continued to pile up an enormous body count through *Halloween II, III*, and so on. Jason, who was merely the motivation for murder in the first *Friday the 13th* in 1980, also emerged as a lasting menace, killing his way through multiple "final" sequels. Next to emerge as a public favorite (some newspaper ads described him as "the most popular cinematic maniac since Darth Vader") was *Nightmare on Elm Street*'s Freddy Kruger. Freddy was even presented as the result of insane villainy. According to the film story, Freddy is the "offspring of 1,000 maniacs," patients on a psychiatric ward who gang-raped one of the nurses (incidentally suggesting the genetic impossibility that Freddy's insanity was "inevitable" because so many patients "contributed" their genes). Even Norman Bates was returned to the Bates Motel, after twenty years' absence, for three *Psycho* sequels between 1983 and 1990, albeit as a somewhat more sympathetic figure than in the original.

Film portrayal of mentally ill villains has not diminished in the 1990s. Many of the films noted in Chapter 1 have focused on disturbed criminals. These include, for example, *Blue Steel*, *Miami Blues*, and

14. *Mentally ill villains are common in films.*

Henry: Portrait of a Serial Killer. Innocent victims have been menaced by disturbed babysitters (*The Hand That Rocks the Cradle*), sinister tenants (*Pacific Heights*), unstable fans (*Misery*), psychopathic secretaries (*The Temp*), troubled children (*The Good Son*), traumatized football players (*Ace Ventura, Pet Detective*), and even obsessed police officers (*Unlawful Entry*). One nineties' madman who strongly captured the public's imagination is Hannibal (the Cannibal) Lecter, played by Anthony Hopkins, in *The Silence of the Lambs*. The great critical and box office success of this film—about a serial killer who abducts and skins women and the brilliant but disturbed prisoner (Lecter) who is consulted to help capture the elusive killer—led to rereleases of both the book on which the movie was based and the preceding Thomas Harris novel, *Red Dragon*, in which Hannibal Lecter first appeared. In addition, the less-successful earlier film *Manhunter*, based on that first novel, was resurrected for television audiences and retitled *Red Dragon: The Curse of Hannibal Lecter* to further capitalize on the insane villain's popularity.

The popularity of mentally ill villains—they attract large audiences and sometimes even critical industry acclaim—helps to ensure their continued appearance. It seems clear that the menace presented by such characters is exciting for those who watch them. Films about mentally ill villains provide the fear, suspense, and sometimes dramatic special effects necessary to engage paying audiences. In addition, some villains, like Hannibal Lecter, may even be admired for their cunning, while others, like Norman Bates, strike an emotional chord with their pathos. Psychotic killers are, have been, and likely will continue to be big business for Hollywood filmmakers.[1]

Mentally ill villains are no less frequent on the small screen, and readers will probably have little difficulty recalling examples. Mentally ill villains, for example, show up repeatedly in detective and police programs. Thirty-eight percent of the detective shows in our Media Watch study had mentally ill characters, and those characters were usually criminals from whom the heroes had to protect the public. There is probably no detective hero on prime-time television who has not been faced with a mentally ill villain to apprehend. As television guide descriptions tells us, Kojak has been called when "a Bellevue Hospital outpatient's demented friend believes he is protecting her by killing an aggressive suitor." Cagney and Lacey have posed "as prostitutes to trap a psychotic." Hunter has battled "a psychotic masked killer," while the detectives of Miami Vice have rolled into action when "a stripper with a dual personality goes on a killing spree." Even detectives in the tropical paradise of Hawaii have had the tranquillity of their idyllic setting disrupted by mentally ill criminals, with Steve McGarett of Hawaii, 5-O engaging in a "desperate quest for a maniac known as the Skyline Killer" and Magnum, P.I., trying to stop "a Vietnam veteran suffering from psychological problems [who] murders a beautiful surfer."[2]

Mentally ill villains, furthermore, are not confined to detective shows; mentally ill characters show up as villains in virtually every type of television show. On Civil Wars, "Sydney is taken hostage by a disturbed defendant," and, on Matlock, "a psychopath . . . holds the lawyer's associates hostage." MacGyver has been forced to use his creative wiles to prevent "a disturbed student from contaminating the campus [of his alma mater] with a plutonium bomb." The popular science fiction series Star Trek has included an episode in which inmates of a galactic asylum take over the asylum planet and, being mental patients, plot to take over the rest of the galaxy. Both Beverly Hills 90210 and Melrose Place have had their lead characters stalked by rejected and obsessed lovers. Even in many comedy programs, mentally ill characters are menacing and dangerous, as conveyed by the television guide descriptions of these programs. On Sledge Hammer, "a madwoman becomes enamored of Hammer and threatens to kill Doreau unless

Sledge gives in to her advances." On *Night Court*, "a strange defendant, claiming to be an alien from Saturn, holds Dan hostage." The multiple personalities popular on soap operas (*Santa Barbara*'s Eden/Lisa, *One Life to Live*'s Viki/Niki) invariably have one personality who is malevolent and/or violent. The already convoluted relationships of soap characters are often made even more complex by the criminal machinations of other characters who undergo or escape from psychiatric treatment (such as *General Hospital*'s Ryan, who escapes from his hospital, tries to disrupt Mack's wedding to Felicia, with whom he has been obsessed, and ends up killed in a struggle with his psychiatrist twin brother, Kevin).

Furthermore, dialogue within these programs, particularly proclamations by characters of authority, underscores the connection between mental illness and violence. In one *Simon and Simon* episode, for instance, the brothers are hired to help stop someone from causing accidents at amusement parks. A. J. Simon, the more cerebral of the Simon brothers, observes that "if this guy's a psycho, he could go off like a Roman candle all over the park." When a female police officer is taken hostage by "an escaped madman" on *T. J. Hooker*, a psychiatrist in the program explains: "Miland is a paranoid schizophrenic with a troubled past. He was on his way to being a brilliant medical student. Then he was booted out of medical school after a series of violent emotional conflicts." "And the violence is still there?" asks one of the police officers, the reply to which is: "He's deranged, a walking time bomb. Anyone who comes in contact with him is in extreme danger." When a character on *Night Court* who identifies with films she has seen (the specific idiosyncrasy image of mental illness discussed in Chapter 2) wanders off to rendezvous with Dan, the lecherous prosecutor, her psychiatrist exclaims, "My God! Don't you know that woman is dangerous?" The normally sympathetic Judge Stone also warns, "We better find her before she finds herself another innocent victim." There is strong, unmistakable, and repeated warning in television programs that people with mental illnesses are particularly dangerous, are compelled to violence, are "walking time bombs."

Individuals inclined more to reading than to viewing will also gain ample exposure to the image of people with mental illnesses as killers and villains. Mentally ill villains appear very frequently in the modern paperback thrillers that accompany readers on vacations and business travel. In these novels, mentally ill killers—often serial killers—are extraordinarily common.

John Sandford's popular *Prey* series, for example (*Rules of Prey*, *Shadow Prey*, *Eyes of Prey*, *Silent Prey*, and *Winter Prey*),[3] has featured the same detective pitted against a variety of different disturbed killers. Thomas Harris's best known works, of course (*Black Sunday*, *Red Dragon*, and *The Silence of the Lambs*—all made into films),[4] likewise involve disturbed killers, as do several of the very successful crime novels of Mary Higgins Clark (*Loves Music, Loves to Dance*),[5] Patricia Cornwell (*Body of Evidence*, *Post-Mortem*),[6] and Ira Levin (*Sliver*[7]).[8]

The connection of murder and madness is made clear even to those who never get past the covers or front pages of such novels, since the theme of the mad killer is usually what is dramatically highlighted to attract the reader's eye. The cover of James Ellroy's *Blood on the Moon*, for example, quotes the *New York Times Book Review*'s description of the novel: "A brilliant detective and a mysterious psychopath . . . come together in a final dance of death."[9] The front cover of Gary Paulsen's *Night Rituals* promises "a mind-blowing novel of murder, madness, and twisted love,"[10] while the cover of Rosamond Smith's *Soul Mate* lets would-be readers know that the book is about "a psychopathic killer with a lover's face."[11]

The more detailed descriptions of these stories which appear on the back or just inside the front cover, which even those who do not purchase the book may peruse as part of their search for exciting prose, are usually even more explicit about the books' portrayals of menacing maniacs. William Heffernan's *Ritual* is typical: "The woman's body was found behind New York's Metropolitan Museum, strangely and savagely mutilated, the first in a series of bizarre murders that share an eerie similarity to the Toltec Indian ritual of human sacrifice. . . . This chilling, edge-of-the-seat thriller follows the bloody trail of a madman as he creeps in the street shadows, waiting to stalk his next female victim for a sacrifice to a bloodthirsty god."[12] Gene Lazuta's *Bleeder* warns: "Nasty Andrew is coming. He is pure psychopath, a deranged killer who guts his victims for pleasure alone."[13] One paperback version of Thomas Harris's *The Silence of the Lambs* lures readers by announcing on its back cover: "On the loose is a psychotic killer. Locked away is a psychopathic madman. To catch one, the FBI needs the other."[14]

The connection of mental illness with violence and criminality is no less a part of children's media. Future generations are receiving repeated messages about the dangerousness of people with mental illnesses through their own special media. Characters with mental illnesses appear in comic books and cartoons—as villains to be battled by their cartoon heroes. The Teenage Mutant Ninja Turtles (TMNT), for instance, have encountered several disturbed criminals. In their Saturday morning cartoon show, the Turtles have challenged Dr. Lloyd Cycloid, referring to him as a "mad scientist who's trying to build some crazy invention," "that nutty Dr. Cycloid," "that nut case," and just plain "psycho." And in one of the TMNT's graphic novels, the Turtles encounter a scientist who has developed an army of automated "mousers" and threatens to release them at one of the World Trade Center towers unless he is paid twenty million dollars. The Ninja Turtles observe, "This man is mad! He must be stopped!" and their mentor, Splinter, commands them to "use your every skill to quench this madness."[15] The scientist's depiction includes not only pronouncements that he is "looney" but also frequent "maniacal" laughter to make clear to the youthful audience that he is an insane criminal.

The super hero Green Lantern has battled Sinestro, a villain driven insane by his expulsion from the Green Lantern Corps. Batman's chief enemy, the Joker, according to the description on his action-figure toy package, "is completely insane. . . . Is almost compelled to commit crimes" (a characterization carried over into the blockbuster *Batman* film with Jack Nicholson as the Joker; in at least six different points in the film, the Joker is explicitly labeled as insane, psychotic, and so forth). In one installment from the *Amazing Spiderman* comic strip, a man peeks around the corner, declaring, "I've escaped the asylum at last!" and his scowling face and gleaming knife tell readers what to expect from a "Madman At Large," as the frame is captioned.

Steven Spielberg's phenomenally successful efforts to entertain children have included *Tiny Toons*. One *Tiny Toons* video, *How I Spent My Summer Vacation*, includes the following segment. The pig family picks up a hitchhiker, a tall man with darkened eyes, bad teeth, and simian arms. As they drive, a news bulletin comes over the car radio, informing them that "a psychotic killer has escaped from the state maximum security prison! . . . Doctors report that the slavering lunatic has a psychotic aversion to pork." The hitchhiker is, of course, the escaped lunatic, and, as additional warnings about the "homicidal fiend" and "raving maniac" are broadcast, he dons a hockey mask, pulls out a chain saw, and tries to carve up the children in the car.

Live-action children's programs may also convey expectations about the dangerousness inherent in mental illness. *Saved by the Bell*, a Saturday morning show about high school students that has gone on to prime time as its characters have aged, provides a good example. In one of its episodes, two boys spy on a girl's sleepover party to try to find out the girl's preference for a date for an upcoming dance. The girls discover the spying and try to get even by making one of the boys believe that the girl he likes has a disturbance that causes her to physically injure boys to whom she is attracted. When the boy sneaks a look at her (falsified) school records and finds that she was once in the "Riverside Home for the Criminally Insane," he is even more convinced that she is dangerous. The boy additionally consults the school counselor, who assures him that the girl's currently threatening behavior is probably just the result of adolescent hormones—"unless she's that rare wacko who's been in an institution or something." Insanity, criminality, and a tendency toward violence are all neatly related in this episode, with the authority of the school counselor adding greater legitimacy to the connection.

As if these sources were not enough to persuade our children to be fearful and suspicious of those with mental illnesses, they are reinforced by still other presentations targeted to youth. *Uncle Shelby's ABZ Book*, a tongue-in-cheek ABC book by the cartoonist Shel Silverstein, in which Uncle Shelby gives bad advice to children whom he only purports to like, includes a picture of an ugly, ill-shaven man holding a notched knife with blood dripping from it. Readers are told: "S is for Stanley. Stanley is a crazy murderer who likes to murder little boys and girls early Sunday morning."[16] G.I. Joe action-figure toys include villains to fight against. One such villain was Zartan, described on his toy package as an "extreme paranoid schizophrenic." His special characteristic, according to the package information, was that he "grows into various multiple personalities to such an extent that the original personality becomes buried and forgotten"—thus communicating not only a connection between mental illness and villainy but also the incorrect equation of schizophrenia with multiple personality.

Even in the song lyrics of contemporary music powerful images

15. *People with mental illnesses are commonly presented as frightening in appearance and violent in behavior.* Reprinted by permission of Sterling Lord Literistic, Inc. Copyright © Sheldon Silverstein.

connect mental illnesses with violence. In addition to the sexual, misogynistic, and racist references on which recent congressional hearings have focused, contemporary music is replete with references to dangerous madmen. In *Madman*, Ugly Kid Joe sings of an axe murderer terrorizing an amusement park: "Madman is loose in Disneyland. He'll take no shit but he'll take your head."[17] The lyrics of *Psycho*, by Metal Church, warn, "He's out there waiting for you. The psycho is ready to kill"—and vividly describe the consequences of contact with a mentally ill person: "The psycho jumps out from behind, sticks a knife in your throat, and you die."[18] Even more shockingly, the GeTo Boys suggest that both murder and necrophilia are in *The Mind of a Lunatic*: "She begged me not to kill her; I gave her a rose, then slit her throat, watched her shake till her eyes closed, had sex with the corpse before I left her and drew my name on the wall like Helter Skelter."[19] Such lyrics—and sometimes the music videos that accompany them—provide a consistent and potent communication to youthful listeners that people with mental illnesses are much to be feared.

Bolstering the presentations of the entertainment media, news sources also connect mental illness and violence. Crime, along with other tragic events, is the core of "news," and when that crime involves someone with a psychiatric history to fascinate the public, it often finds its way into news copy. When one reads or hears about "escaped mental patients" commiting crimes or about apprehended lawbreakers attempting an "insanity defense," it is not difficult to infer that mental disorder and criminality, often lethal criminality, are related. It is, moreover, an inference the public is probably relieved to make. However frightening the idea of mentally ill violence may be, it is likely even more disconcerting to recognize that violent actions—actions that threaten us—could come from people without mental disorders. This issue will be discussed further in Chapter 6, exploring the factors that shape media portrayal.

It is not simply that the image of people with mental illnesses as violent and criminal appears so often and in so many different sources that troubles mental health advocates, however. It is that this image is characteristic of media portrayals. The role of violent, dangerous villain is the one most commonly assigned to mentally ill characters in the mass media. When one sees or reads about a person with a mental illness in the media, it is more likely that that person will be shown as criminal and dangerous than in any other way.

Research by George Gerbner, for example, has found that, when mentally ill characters appear on prime-time television, they are more likely to be presented as villains than as heroes. As part of his ongoing monitoring of prime-time television, Gerbner and his associates classified major characters as portrayed either favorably (heroes) or unfavorably (villains) and calculated the ratio of villains to heroes for each of a number of different groups of characters—women, Hispanics, African Americans, older adults, people with physical disabilities, and characters with mental illnesses. Mentally ill characters were far and away the most likely group to be shown as villains, and the only group of all those examined to have a villain-to-hero ratio of greater than one. All other groups, even those that had what might be considered high frequencies of unfavorable portrayal, were nevertheless more frequently depicted in favorable ways. Mentally ill characters, however, were unique in being in unfavorable roles for the majority of their appearances.[20] When prime-time television viewers encounter characters with mental illnesses, they will more likely than not be seeing villains.

Not only are mentally ill characters on television more likely to be villains, but they are also more likely to be violent. As part of our Media Watch of television portrayals of mental illness, we looked at how the mentally ill characters were depicted. In particular, raters were asked to choose, from a list of ten favorable and ten unfavorable adjectives, which descriptors best fit the mentally ill characters as portrayed in the show. The traits most often applicable to those characters were "active," "confused," "aggressive," "dangerous," and "unpredictable." While mentally ill characters were not totally without positive traits such as loyalty, friendliness, and poise, they were far more often depicted as threatening and dangerous.[21]

Our study was not the only one to find such a pattern of portrayal. The 1989 summary of Gerbner's laboratory's seventeen years of sampling of television content indicated that 72.1 percent of all mentally ill characters in prime-time drama were portrayed as violent. Over one-fifth (21.6 percent) of the mentally ill characters killed someone.[22] Gerbner also monitored daytime television and reported that two-thirds of the mentally ill characters on daytime soap operas are also criminal and violent.[23] Similarly, Laurel Fruth and Allan Padderud, in their 1986 study of daytime serials, reported that six of the eight mentally ill characters identified (among fourteen popular soaps) "were shown engaging in some sort of criminal behavior. . . . These characters were presented as tense, cold, dangerous individuals who were capable of inflicting harm on other characters."[24]

Even females, much less likely overall to be violent than male characters in prime time (only 27.2 percent were portrayed as violent), were found to show high levels of violence when characterized as mentally ill (60 percent were violent and 16.7 percent were killers).[25] As Gerbner has noted, mental illness is the only label in the world of television that renders women as violent as men.[26]

Finally, there is research indicating that the people with mental illnesses one reads about in newspapers are more likely to be violent and criminal than benign or sympathetic. A 1991 study of the content of United Press International stories, for example, found that the majority of newspaper stories dealing with psychiatric patients involved the commission of violent crimes.[27] Another study found that the most common traits of psychiatric patients presented in Canadian newspaper stories were dangerousness and unpredictability.[28] Again, the people with mental illnesses encountered by the public through the mass media are not only often dangerous madmen, but that image is more frequent than any other. The message conveyed is that those with mental illnesses are characteristically violent, dangerous, and unpredictable.

Within this pervasive depiction of dangerous insanity, there are a number of other noteworthy trends. First of all, the mentally ill killers portrayed are almost always male and their victims are usually female. These depictions thus take their place on the long list of images of violence (mostly male violence) directed toward females. The woman in jeopardy, the damsel in distress, is an almost archetypal image in storytelling and certainly a core feature of television and film drama. It is not surprising, then, that, in films and television, it is women who are most commonly terrorized by murderous madmen (and who must be saved by heroic males). Menace is established by a string of murdered women, and the heroines are stalked, attacked, threatened, and/or abused by the disturbed villains. So common is this plot that Michael Fleming and Roger Manvell note, in their examination of popular films: "There is . . . a genre of film whose singular purpose from its opening frame is solely to portray sadistic violence against women, and the exponential increase in such films warrants some attention. The plot line of such films almost always involves a mad murderer who, as evil incarnate, stalks his helpless victims [who are] almost always nubile females."[29] The image of male power and female helplessness, of course, has its own deep roots in our culture, and some would argue that films such as these function (to some extent deliberately) to strengthen these traditional roles, but with mental illness thrown in to make the currently unacceptable assertion of male dominance somewhat more disguised (it is mentally ill men, not all men, who display their power over women).

Thriller novels such as those mentioned earlier illustrate this trend, as well. The central character of such thrillers tends to be a socially isolated male whose multiple victims are usually young women, innocent and unacquainted with their killer. James Ellroy's *Blood on the Moon* is a typical offering. It focuses on a serial killer of women and the police officer who tracks him down. The killer in this novel is avenging his own adolescent rape and kills almost two dozen young women who remind him of his fantasy high school sweetheart. Passages such as "somehow, for some god-awful, hellish reason, his killer's insanity was peaking" make it clear that the criminal should be considered mentally ill and that mental illness is what motivates his murderous behavior.[30]

Spenser, the Boston private eye, tracks the Red Rose Killer in Robert B. Parker's *Crimson Joy*. The central character stalks and kills black women and leaves a red rose in their hands (presumably as a symbolic revenge on his own manipulative mother, Rose Mary Black). The killers of *Only When She Cries* by Edward Mathis describe their passions for killing women. One, "a goddamned psycho who'd killed maybe twenty-five, twenty-six girls," as the novel characterizes him,[31] explains: "I love to . . . to choke things . . . to feel them quiver, to watch their eyes. The girls . . . that's what blows me away . . . their eyes . . . the terror in their eyes, their sweet, sweet eyes."[32] The other, who is copying the crimes of the first, reveals his own passion: "Tears . . . I need tears. That first little bitch [whom he raped at age twelve] cried and I had this . . . this overwhelming urge to smash her, to rip her, see her blood."[33]

Once again, however, one does not have to complete such novels to absorb the image of mentally ill violence against women. Even a perusal of the cover and frontispiece advertising of these serial killer paperbacks is enough to confirm the extent to which women are the predominant victims. Elieba Levine's *Double Jeopardy* is said to feature "an elusive lady-killer with a grisly, insatiable hunger." In Herbert Lieberman's *Shadow Dancers*, "a ghoulish madman stalks the women of New York." For the murderer in Edward Mathis's *Only When She Cries*, "his victims are innocent young women with nothing in common except their red hair . . . and grisly fates." On the cover of *Rules of Prey*, by John Sandford, potential readers are told that the killer "left notes with every woman he killed." And in a 1979 Shane Stevens novel (released again more recently following the success of *The Silence of the Lambs*), the first page of the book proclaims that "his demons are women, all women. He is compelled to kill . . . and kill . . . and kill" while the title explains the motive—*By Reason of Insanity*.

As many of these descriptions suggest, the victims are innocent and unsuspecting. They typically have no relationship with the mentally ill killer, and their murders are presented as basically random and unpredictable. Victims have done nothing to the killer to warrant the destruction they suffer at his hands, but simply have the misfortune to be in the wrong place at the wrong time. The pathos of their deaths is made even more horrible by their complete innocence and vulnerability, and the tension of viewers is increased by the idea that the random violence of madmen can reach anyone, even people like themselves. The escaped psychiatric patient in Shane Stevens's *By Reason of Insanity* rents a room, disguised as a woman, in a rooming house exclusively for women and works his way down, door to door and floor to floor, killing any residents he can find. The killer in Thomas Harris's *Red Dragon* "murders entire families in hideous ways," as the back cover proclaims. The very title of Harris's *The Silence of the Lambs* suggests the slaughter of innocents, while the so-called psychopath of Robert Duncan's *The Serpent's Mark* explicitly seeks "an innocent, a child upon whom he can perform a miracle of death and resurrection." And Jeff Raines's novel, *Unbalanced Acts*, suggests that virtually all psychiatric patients engage in multiple murder of random victims. One patient in this book is said to have murdered fifteen teenagers with an assault rifle. Another killed seven "short" people, believing short people were out to get him. Still other patients escaping from Raines's fictional Q Wing of the New York State Prison for the Criminally Insane (where "untreatable" patients are kept) include a man "who may have abused and killed as many as five children," a "Loverboy Killer" who murdered fifteen women "for the hell of it," and a doctor at whose home "they found body parts of seventeen bodies buried in his backyard, and additional parts scattered around his house."

Innocent victims are also one of the components that make real-life crime stories "newsworthy." A 1979 study by Pamela Kalbfleisch examining newspaper homicide stories in the United States, for example, identified three basic ingredients for a "top story." They were (1) insanity, (2) unpredictability, and (3) victimization of ordinary people like the reader.[34] Novelists and scriptwriters create insane killers who prey on multiple innocent victims; newspaper editors highlight stories that have those same features.

As may be already apparent from some of the previous descriptions, it is the intensity as well as the number and objects of violence that also marks media portrayals of mentally ill killers. The violence is typically not the swift, distant death of guns or bombs, but up-close, mutilating, and graphically depicted attacks. In the growing market for psycho-killer films, the violence is ever-increasing. Fleming and Manvell observe: "Each consecutive film of this genre tries to outdo the previous one by making the sadistic attacks increasingly brutal."[35]

A prime example of this phenomenon is the *Friday the 13th* series. Plots do not vary much, and the exercise of creativity seems largely focused on finding new and more brutal ways to dispatch victims and increasingly realistic special effects through which to depict this. The body count for the seemingly endless parade of sequels is well over one hundred, with an average of fifteen or more grisly deaths per episode. The carnage has included slit throats, axes in the head, arrows in the eyes, strangulation with barbed wire, an ice pick in the head, spearing with a hot iron, a knitting needle through the mouth, a harpoon in the face, electrocution, and death by corkscrew, hacksaw, hedgeclippers, car flare, and even party favors. In the 1990s, Oliver Stone's controversial (but well-attended) film *Natural Born Killers* has stretched the limits of violent portrayal even further, with a mentally ill killer once again as its centerpiece.

Such brutality is a commonplace feature of thriller novels as well. Rex Miller's four-hundred-pound killer, Chaingang (appearing in *Slob* and reappearing in *Slice, Chaingang, Savant,* and *Butcher*), not only murders people without hesitation but occasionally rips out and eats their hearts. The killer of *Blood on the Moon* includes bludgeoning, evisceration, and dismemberment among his homicidal repertoire. The ritual killer of Gary Paulsen's *Night Rituals* cuts up his victims and ships their parts across the country, and William Heffernan's *Ritual* murderer removes and stores the heads of his victims. The psychotic murderer of Thomas Harris's *The Silence of the Lambs* is nicknamed "Buffalo Bill" because he skins his female victims, while Hannibal Lecter's nickname (the Cannibal) comes from his proclivity for biting and digesting his victims.

The epitome of such depictions is probably Brett Easton Ellis's 1991 novel, *American Psycho*. So offensive did people find the graphic descriptions of violence against women in this novel that employees of the scheduled publisher, Simon & Schuster, protested strongly, as did a number of feminist groups. Not only did the violence include torture (such as trapping a rat inside a woman's body so that it had to dig and eat its way out), dismemberment (often while the victim was still marginally alive to witness it), and cannibalism (as in a chapter titled "Tries to Cook and Eat Girl"), but these acts were described in vivid, extensive, and according to most reviewers, excessive detail. Simon & Schuster eventually refused to publish the book, despite having paid Ellis a substantial advance. The novel was quickly picked up and published by another company and had moderate sales amid continuing controversy and poor reviews. It is noteworthy that protests focused only on the issues of violence and its direction toward women; there was little if any apparent objection to the equation of mental illness with such violence.

It is also the case that sinister madmen of print and film fiction are characteristically advertised in threatening poses, conveying their message about the bestial violence of people with mental illnesses even without words. Book covers may show sharp, gleaming weapons and dead or terrified women; movie advertisements also visually underscore the painful, mutilating violence to be expected from the mentally ill characters featured in their films. The weapons of mutilation wielded threateningly in movie advertisements have included knives (for example, *Terror Train*), razors (*Dressed to Kill*), axes (*Prom Night*), meat cleavers (*Schizo*), and scissors (*Schizoid*). *Friday the 13th, Part 3* even featured an almost 3-D poster in which a huge knife pointed out at the viewer. Not to be outdone, *Maniac* was marketed with an ad showing a faceless male figure holding a bloodied knife and a mop of hair dripping blood. What is clearly communicated in all of these images

16. *Movies like this show mentally ill villains to be particularly violent and dangerous.*

is that people with mental illnesses are particularly to be feared; not only do they kill people, but they do so in strikingly gruesome ways.

17. *Movie ads communicate that those with mental illnesses are extremely violent.*

Even television, which lives by somewhat more rigid censorship standards, manages to make mentally ill villains fairly savage. A study by Brigitte Goldstein, for example, found that mentally ill villains on television police and detective shows are portrayed as even more dangerous than other, non–mentally ill criminals in those same shows.[36] Describing the findings of this research, one author writes: "The mentally ill offenders were not only shown to be dangerous but also portrayed in ways calculated to arouse fear in the audience. While the mentally ill were shown in deviant acts extremely harmful to others, they grimaced strangely, had glassy eyes, or giggled incongruously. . . . One bared his teeth and snarled as he jumped on his victims to suck blood from their jugular veins. Still another squeezed raw meat through his fingers and rubbed it on his gun as he prepared to kill his next victim. Unusual music often accompanied these scenes to enhance the effect. In some shows actions were timed to startle the audience."[37]

Yet another common facet of the criminal depiction of mentally ill characters is the suggestion that it is mental illness which makes people criminal. Such a suggestion protects us from a perhaps more troubling recognition that it could be our society, our neglect of those at risk for criminal development, our attitudes and policies toward weapons, alcohol, punishment, and so forth which foster criminality. Instead, fictional villains are presented who have been ordinary, law-abiding citizens—or even above-average contributors to society—but become villains when afflicted with a mental illness. Comic book villains, for example, often begin as well-intended scientists, but turn, à la Darth Vader, to the dark side when, for one reason or another, they become insane.

"Her real name was Crystal Frost," says a *Superman and Firestorm* comic book. "She was a scientist working on an arctic energy project called Mohole One. . . . Exposure to a supercooling system altered her molecular structure and drove her insane." Now she is a villain whom Superman and Firestorm must battle. The Thing and Black Bolt, heroes of a comic book by the same name, have similarly contended with another scientist who accidentally "absorbed an experimental anti-gravity element . . . one that enabled him to control the forces of gravity at will! Unfortunately, he lost control of his mind! He became obsessed with the roll [sic] of conqueror." Insanity has once again turned the good scientist into a villain.

Similar themes, of the transformation of well-meaning individuals into criminals and villains by mental illness are, of course, frequent in the mad scientist movies noted previously. Trekkers may recall a similar instance of this from their favorite television series, *Star Trek*. In one episode, an ambassador named the "Medusa" is transported by the Enterprise. No human can look at him with unprotected eyes without going mad, the viewer is informed. When, sure enough, a crew member does gaze upon the Medusa, the brilliant Vulcan science officer Spock questions the Medusa's blind guardian/companion: "Do you know whether he saw the Medusa?" he asks. "Yes, he did," is the reply, whereupon Spock pronounces, "Then insanity will surely be the result, Captain—dangerous insanity." The next scene shows the afflicted crew member attacking others on the Enterprise. Even in space in the future, mental illness appears to create violent tendencies.

Still another trait of mentally ill characters in the mass media is that, as Gerbner observes,[38] they are tinged with evil. They are more than just criminals. They are morally tainted. They are *bad* people. This connection of mental illness with moral taint, of course, has strong social and religious roots. Who but bad people would be afflicted with such pain as comes with mental illness? Thus people with mental illnesses tend to be depicted, as Fleming and Manvell put it, as "evil incarnate."[39]

Robert Duncan's *The Serpent's Mark*, in fact, asserts just that in its cover description: "He is evil incarnate. . . . Just beyond the reach of the glittering lights of Las Vegas, a psychopath who calls himself 'D' stalks his victims in the twilight of lonely desert roads. A sadistic murderer with religious visions, he tortures his victims before he kills them. And in the palm of each he has deeply carved his unmistakeable mark."[40] It is unmistakable also that "the serpent's mark" is the devil's mark and that the mentally ill killer of this novel is being presented as the ultimate evil one. An article in the February 10, 1991, *New York Times*, entitled "Cozying Up to the Psychopath That Lurks Deep Within," recognized the touch of evil attached to the character of Hannibal Lecter, declaring that "in the new movie, *The Silence of the Lambs*, a serial killer played by Anthony Hopkins illuminates the appeal of profound evil."[41] In Elieba Levine's *Double Jeopardy*, speculation about the disturbed killer's motives leads to the question, "Did you ever consider that it might have been an act of pure evil?"[42] Medical Examiner Kay Scarpetta, hero of Patricia Cornwell's novels, explains about the insane killer in *Post-Mortem*: "There are some people who are evil. . . . Like dogs. Some dogs bite people for no reason. There's something wrong with them. They're bad and will always be bad."[43]

Along with the notion that mentally disordered characters are fundamentally (and thus unchangeably) evil rather than ill, there is also the frequent suggestion that those with mental illnesses do not get better with treatment—and thus they remain violent and dangerous despite the best treatment efforts. *Halloween*'s Michael Meyers, for example, is portrayed as hopelessly insane; he will never recover. The mental hospital escapees who terrorize the public in books, films, and television programs demonstrate the ineffectiveness of psychiatric treatment for lessening the dangerousness of mentally disturbed individuals. Furthermore, newspaper headlines that emphasize the history of psychiatric treatment of killers and other law-breakers (ones like those in the May 9, 1982, *New York Post*: "Freed Mental Patient Kills Mom") provide what appears to be confirming evidence that even treated, *former* mental patients remain prone to violence. Often the expectation that individuals with mental illnesses cannot really be treated successfully is stated even more directly. Robert B. Parker's usually sensitive detective, Spenser, for instance, says of the Red Rose Killer he is seeking in *Crimson Joy*: "I assume he'll plead insanity, the court will believe him, and he'll go to Bridgewater State Hospital. Where he will not be cured."[44]

With the presentation of mentally ill characters as evil, villainous, and incurable, it follows logically that the main hope for safety from these dangerous criminals would be their permanent removal, and, indeed, the most common outcome for mentally ill villains in the media is death. There are few attempts to capture and treat the menacing villains of Hollywood slasher films; the unambiguous goal is solely their destruction—and this is usually achieved by the end of the movie (although, as noted, these villains are often resurrected for the purpose of sequels). The mentally ill killers and villains of television suffer similar fates. Gerbner's monitoring of television content has revealed not only a high level of violence in programs with mentally ill characters but a high level of violence *against* mentally ill characters. Mentally ill characters, Gerbner notes, "are most likely to be both violent and victimized." Eighty-one percent of mentally ill characters, according to his research, are victims of violence, and 23 percent (the same percentage as are portrayed as killers themselves) are killed. The treatment of

18. *Sensationalized news stories appear to confirm that even treated psychiatric patients are prone to violence.*

mentally ill characters on television, he suggests, is "a tooth for a tooth."[45]

The idea that killing mentally ill characters is justified is sometimes even more evident in thriller novels. These novels, in which death is again a common outcome for mentally ill characters, make it clear that it is okay, even desirable, to kill these villains—even if it involves breaking the law to do so. The police detectives in these novels, motivated by the apparently unacceptable possibility that the killer may plead insanity and escape punishment, frequently express their intention to see to it that the killer does not live. The detective Push Tinker, of *Night Rituals*, worries about the possibility of an insanity defense for his quarry ("He would get a fancy lawyer and plead insanity and spend a few weeks in a country club institution somewhere and he would skate") and decides that "he could not let Harvitt skate. Harvitt had to die."[46] When he finally catches up to the killer, he makes good on his pledge, strangling the man with his tie "until Harvitt's arms stopped moving, until Harvitt's legs quit kicking, until he could smell Harvitt's bowels release and knew, finally, that Harvitt was dead."[47] The pursuing detective of *Only When She Cries* promises: "Your run is over, animal! Wherever you are, I'll find you! Wherever you go, I'll hound you until you are dead, dead, dead!"[48] In *Slob*, a police detective fires a gun into the mouth of his injured and unconscious quarry to rid the world of someone he believes to be hopelessly insane and, therefore, irredeemably dangerous.[49] The detective hero of *Rules of Prey*, taunted by the killer's assertion that he will plead insanity, proceeds to kill the unarmed villain, noting, "It would be like losing, seeing you get away alive. I really couldn't stand that."[50] One subplot of *The Serpent's Mark* involves the detective hero's learning not to allow a mentally ill killer to live, as he once did with tragic consequences.[51] Again and again, readers and viewers are taught that the most fitting, indeed necessary, outcome for evil, vicious, insane murderers of innocents is death.

With all these portrayals of mentally disordered violence, including "factual" newspaper accounts of real-life incidents, one would think that psychotic killers lurk around every corner. Such a circumstance leads to questions about how true or accurate these depictions may be. How dangerous *are* people with mental illnesses? How likely *are* people who have been released from psychiatric hospitals to threaten or harm the public? As with many questions about mental illness, the answer is not a simple one, and, despite a substantial amount of research, unequivocal conclusions have been elusive.[52] Nevertheless, there are several clear conclusions that have emerged from research on the dangerousness of people with mental illnesses.

1. *Some people with mental illnesses* are *dangerous.* It cannot be denied that some individuals with mental illnesses have harmed others, occasionally in horrifying and headline-grabbing ways, and that sometimes their mental illnesses are contributing factors. The overwhelming nature of some of the symptoms of mental illness and the confusion and disorientation that can occur may make aggressive impulses more difficult to control. In addition, there are some people whose mental illnesses contribute more directly to their harming others. Some have hallucinations that command them to commit illegal and/or destructive acts. Some have delusions that they are being persecuted and act out aggressively against their perceived persecutors. It is this category of

people—people whose crimes are clearly the product of their mental illnesses—for whom the "not guilty by reason of insanity" legal defense is intended. These people, however, are extremely rare. The "not guilty by reason of insanity" defense is used in less than 1 percent of all felony cases in this country, and, in most (three-fourths) of those cases, the plea is unsuccessful.[53] In other words, it is very rare that a crime is found to be a product of a mental illness.

It should be noted, nevertheless, that recent studies have reported increased risk of violence associated with mental illness. That is, relative to nonpatients, individuals with psychiatric diagnoses have been found to have higher rates of crime and violence, particularly among those with active and untreated psychotic symptoms.[54] Those with diagnosed or diagnosable mental illnesses do appear to have higher rates of violent behavior.[55]

One must keep in mind, however, that these studies do not establish that mental illness itself accounts for the violence demonstrated. For some individuals who are both mentally ill and violent, the mental illness may be irrelevant to the violent or criminal behavior shown. Just as some non–mentally ill individuals rob, assault, or kill for profit or passion, those with mental illnesses may act out of those same "normal" motives. The fact that someone has a mental illness may have nothing to do with whether or not he holds up a convenience store to get money and shoots the owner in the process. Yet such a person would be counted in the statistics relating mental illness to violence. Because mental illness and violence both occur does not necessarily mean that the violence was caused by the mental illness.[56]

In addition, one must also consider the context in which dangerous behavior occurs. People treated in public hospitals, for example, come disproportionately from lower socioeconomic backgrounds, and lower socioeconomic status is itself strongly associated with most measures of crime and violence. The higher rates of violence among discharged patients may be showing only the effect of socioeconomic disadvantage, not mental illness. Furthermore, given the conditions under which many people with mental illnesses live—confronted daily with the frustrations of debilitating, long-term illnesses; experiencing fear, rejection, and devaluation in interactions with others; being poor or jobless or even homeless; facing the loss of privacy, legal rights, and independence that occurs in institutional settings—it would not be surprising to find them striking out angrily at others. But their doing so would not necessarily indicate that such actions were a product of mental illness; they could instead be a reaction to the provocative circumstances people with mental illnesses often encounter.

Even more important, we must recognize that current studies establish only a higher rate of violent behavior for people with mental illnesses than for people with no such illnesses; they do not establish that there is a high rate of violence. It is also the case that those with mental illnesses, overall, are a greater danger to themselves than to others—owing to high rates of suicide and to illnesses and injury as a result of inadequate self-care. Those who are involuntarily hospitalized are more likely to be committed as a danger to themselves than as a danger to others.

2. *The vast majority of people with mental illnesses are neither violent nor dangerous.* If epidemiological studies are correct that one out of every five Americans will experience a mental illness, it becomes obvious that most of these 40+ million people couldn't be violent and dangerous, or we would see crime rates that dwarf even our current unacceptably high levels. But what is also clear from research is that the statement above is true even for that smaller group of people whose severe mental illnesses correspond more closely to classical madness and from whom violence is most greatly feared. We are equally correct in saying that the vast majority of people with severe mental illnesses are neither violent nor dangerous. Whether studies look at assaults within the hospital, post-hospitalization arrests, or self-reports of aggressive actions, most come up with similar results: violent or dangerous behavior occurs in only about 10–12 percent (or less) of those with mental illnesses studied.[57] Turned around, this says that about 90 percent—nine out of ten—of those with mental illnesses, even the most severe illnesses, are not violent, dangerous, or criminal. "By all indications," John Monahan concludes in his 1992 review of the available research on violence and mental disorder, "the great majority of people who are currently disordered . . . are not violent."[58]

Studies examining the rates of mental illness among jail and offender populations, furthermore, have come up with similar conclusions. Estimates of rates of mental illness in offender populations tend to be around 20 percent—approximately the same as NIMH estimates for the population as a whole.[59] Moreover, severe disorders such as schizo-phrenia, major affective disorders, and other forms of psychosis ap-peared to be relatively rare among identified criminals, leading to the conclusion that "with the exception of alcoholism and drug dependence, prisoners do not appear to have higher rates of diagnosable mental illness than their class-matched peers in the open community."[60] In addition, psychiatric disorder appears to be a poor predictor of violent crime among released prisoners.[61] Mentally ill criminals are not more prone to crime and violence than other (non–mentally ill) lawbreakers.

Many other factors besides mental illness are far more clearly and more strongly associated with violence. Chief among these is substance abuse, but youth, male gender, and, as noted earlier, lower socioeco-nomic status are more predictive of violence as well. Monahan notes: "Compared to the magnitude of risk associated with the combination of male gender, young age, and lower socioeconomic status . . . the risk of violence presented by mental disorder is modest. Compared with the magnitude of risk associated with alcoholism and other drug abuse, the risk associated with major mental disorders such as schizo-phrenia and affective disorder is modest indeed. Clearly, mental health status makes at best a trivial contribution to the overall level of violence in society."[62]

One researcher has even suggested that investigation of the relation-ship between mental illness and violence has addressed the wrong question. The question we should be considering, as a concerned public, Saleem Shah suggests, is not how dangerous people with mental illnesses are. The question we should be asking, he says, is "which groups in American society pose the greatest threat to the community in terms of inflicting death and serious injury on others?" "The response," he goes on to note, "based on the evidence, would be that the seriously mentally ill (despite the shocking and headline grabbing nature of some of their violent acts) would clearly not be in top contention. In terms of sheer numbers and lethality involved, top place would go to persons with repeated arrests for driving under the influence of alcohol."[63] In a sad verification of his assessment, Shah, who had spent much of his life around psychiatric patients, died in 1992 from injuries suffered when his car was struck by a drunken driver.

Regardless of whom it may be appropriate to fear, it seems clear that it is not appropriate to anticipate violence from an individual just because he or she has a mental illness. The occasional violence of some individuals with mental illnesses, however dramatic, tragic, and frightening, does not warrant a blanket conclusion that people with a mental illnesses are dangerous or that any given individual with mental illness automatically has a high potential for violence. Just as the higher rate of violent crime in the United States does not justify Europeans' being afraid of Americans in general since the great majority of Americans are law-abiding and nonviolent, the higher rate of violent actions for people with mental illnesses does not warrant fear of the general population of people with mental illnesses since the great majority of them are law-abiding and nonviolent.

3. *Violence, when it does occur, is seldom directed at strangers.* When people with mental illnesses do strike out, it is typically at those whom they know—those who have frustrated or frightened or challenged them, those with whom they have frequent contact, those to whom they are emotionally attached—just as is the case for homicides in general. According to a 1985 review by Kenneth Tardiff, there were 23,000 people murdered in the United States in 1981 and "in most of the murders, the victim and perpetrator were friends, acquaintances, or family members."[64] The pattern is similar for the rare person with a mental illness who attacks or kills others. Random attacks upon innocent victims are unusual events even among those with severe mental illnesses. Likewise, serial killers who prey upon multiple, randomly selected victims are extremely rare. We can probably count fewer than a hundred serial killers over the last fifty years and, while that is far more than we would wish (indeed, even one is too many for comfort), those multiple murderers account for a tiny percentage of the 23,000 or so homicides that occur each year and represent an even smaller percentage of the millions of people with mental illnesses in this country.

4. *The insanity defense has not resulted in the release of large numbers of dangerous individuals into the community.* To begin with, the insanity defense is a very specialized and rarely invoked legal defense. The idea behind this defense is that people whose alleged criminal actions are a product of a mental disorder should not be held to the same level of responsibility as those who commit criminal acts with clear minds. Treatment rather than punishment is seen as the appropriate social

response to crimes committed because one has a mental disorder. Legal definitions of insanity attempt to articulate the circumstances under which a judgment of diminished responsibility and application of treatment alternatives are appropriate.

Although definitions of legal insanity can differ from state to state, the majority of states have similar standards. In particular, most require evidence of a diagnosable mental disorder of a nature that impairs the person's capacity to appreciate the wrongfulness (criminality) of his/her actions and/or the person's capacity to conform his/her behavior to the requirements of the law. A person who possesses the delusional belief that he is Jesus Christ and steals food from a grocery store in order to feed the masses may meet the criterion of not knowing right from wrong; he does not understand how redistributing the largess God, his father, has provided can be wrong. Someone who hallucinates screams and moans coming from the house next door and burns down her neighbor's house in order to save neighborhood children from that neighbor's suspected basement torture chamber may be convinced that her actions are right and necessary. A person who hears persistent and frightening voices commanding him to destroy all automobiles because they spew poison into the air might be compelled to act on those persistent directions and thus might meet the criterion of being unable to conform his behavior to the requirements of the law; the voices that are a product of his illness compel him to illegal actions.

It is important to note here that a person may have a mental illness and commit a crime and *not* be considered legally insane. Not all disorders, even severe or psychotic ones, render people unable to understand the nature of their actions or unable to control their actions. Conversely, when individuals seem to have difficulty controlling their actions (as in a temper outburst), it does not mean that they have a mental illness; criminal actions as a result of impulse or emotion are therefore not necessarily eligible for an insanity defense. In addition, disorders that are manifest primarily in antisocial or criminal behavior (Antisocial Personality Disorder/Psychopathy) are explicitly excluded from an insanity defense by the laws in many states. Thus it is hardly a given that someone with a mental illness will be absolved of blame for criminal actions "by reason of insanity."

As pointed out earlier, the insanity plea is rarely used, and John Hinckley, Jr., aside, infrequently succeeds. The majority of our most infamous serial killers, assassins, and mass murders—Charles Manson, Charles Starkweather, John Wayne Gacy, Sirhan Sirhan, Ken Bianchi, Ted Bundy, Jeffrey Dahmer—either did not plead insanity or were unsuccessful in their insanity pleas; they all went to prison. Moreover, according to the American Psychiatric Association Insanity Defense Work Group, "the majority of such successful defenses, rather than being awarded by juries after criminal trials, occur instead by concurrence between the prosecution and defense."[65] Most of the time, the prosecution and the defense are in agreement that the not guilty by reason of insanity plea is appropriate. Furthermore, it is not only serious crimes, such as homicide, for which the insanity plea is granted. It is estimated that only about 14 percent of those using an insanity defense are alleged murderers, while approximately 30 percent have come to the attention of the criminal justice system for crimes involving no violence at all.[66]

In addition, it is untrue that people who achieve not guilty by reason of insanity judgments find those verdicts a speedy route to freedom. Typically, they remain incarcerated for long periods of time, often for periods longer than they would have been imprisoned if found guilty of the crime with which they had been charged. Particularly if one is male and charged with a serious crime involving physical harm to someone else (homicide, aggravated assault, rape), one can expect a lengthy hospital incarceration.

5. *Given the above facts, it becomes clear that the portrayal of mental illness in the media is highly inaccurate.* The proportion of characters shown or portrayed as violent is far greater than the proportion of violent patients in reality. The figure of 72 percent who commit violent acts on prime-time television, for example, is enormously divergent from the 12 percent or less found in carefully conducted studies. Television and films suggest that most people with mental illnesses are dangerous when the reality is that most are not dangerous. The number of serial killers found in popular novels is probably greater than the number of serial killers who have emerged in reality during the time frame of their publication. The risk that mentally ill killers will "get off" with an insanity plea and thus be free to prey on an unsuspecting public—an idea emphasized in the media and used in fictional portrayals as justification for killing mentally ill characters—does not accurately

reflect the rarity of insanity pleas, the low likelihood of their success, and the extended enforced hospitalization that usually follows.

Further, newspaper stories of murders and other crimes committed by individuals with mental illnesses, however "factual," are highly selective. Sanford Sherizan reminds us in his 1978 examination of crime news: "Printed crime stories are not a summary of all the crimes which have occurred during the previous 24 hours. . . . The newspaper reader is offered certain newsworthy crime events prepared as news stories about crime. These news stories contain specialized images of crime, images which have little to do with the realities or complexities of crime."[67] Only a small proportion of crimes committed are ever reported in the news, but homicides are more likely to be reported than other crimes. And even those homicides are carefully selected. Peter Carlson, writing for the *Washington Post Magazine*, comments: "The news media revel in every juicy detail of certain murders. But the coverage is inevitably misleading because those cases are by definition unusual—mass killings, serial killings, the murder of the powerful or the rich and famous. Barely mentioned are the most common homicides—the killing of poor and obscure people by their friends or relatives during arguments fueled by booze or drugs."[68] As I have noted, a suspect with a history of mental illness often appears to make a story even juicier and thus even more likely to be selected for publication. Selective presentation of those homicides creates a spurious connection between mental illness and murder.

Also, it should be remembered that, just as a small number of crime stories are selected for presentation, only a small number of possible stories about people with mental illnesses are ever reported in the news. The many instances of individuals with mental illnesses leaving a hospital, recovering from their illnesses, and getting on with their lives are less likely to be reported; the rare instance of a dramatic crime committed by a person with mental illness, however, is highly likely to make the papers—probably with a large headline to call attention to the story. This selective presentation of people with mental illnesses mainly in the context of crime stories gives a decidedly inaccurate picture, making these rare events seem much more characteristic of those with mental illnesses than they really are.

The consistent, strong mass media association of mental illness with violence and criminality, which occurs in both entertainment and news media, remains a grossly inaccurate representation of people with mental illnesses. The stereotype that emerges from the media is in marked contrast to the reality. The great majority of people with mental illnesses, including those with the most dramatic forms of madness, are not the violent, dangerous, evil, and untreatable villains they appear to be in the mass media.

Chapter Five

So
What?

It is time to pose a simple but important question. So what? What is the practical significance, the meaningfulness of the facts I have presented so far? Media portrayals are inaccurate. They depict people with mental illnesses as different, dangerous, and laughable. They misuse or casually use psychiatric terms. So what? What difference does this make? What are the real-life consequences of these media images of mental illness, and are they sufficient to warrant extended attention to them? The answer to this last question is an unqualified "yes"; the media depictions of mental illness examined in previous chapters do have important and wide-ranging consequences for the lives of those with mental illnesses and for the ways people act toward others with psychiatric disorders.

To begin with, the mass media convey information to the public. Viewers and readers pick up specific knowledge through the media. They learn, for instance, about health issues—AIDS, cancer, addictions—through their media portrayals. They learn about history, about science, about legal issues. Few people had even heard of Munchausen's by proxy, for example, until it became a movie-of-the-week topic. It is probably also true that more people have learned about "Miranda rights" by watching police shows in which suspects are routinely advised of those rights than through any other source. The situation is similar for mental illnesses. People learn about mental illnesses from what they see and hear in the mass media. As noted earlier, the public identifies the mass media as their primary source of information about mental illness[1] (although, since that information is frequently inaccurate, it may be more appropriate to say that the mass media are a primary source of the public's *mis*information about mental illness).

Furthermore, consumers of mass media indicate that they tend to believe what they see and hear in the mass media about mental illness. A number of years ago, I wrote a short piece on inaccurate presentations of psychiatric material on television for *TV Guide*.[2] I received numerous letters from readers in response to the article, and many of them indicated surprise that there should be such inaccuracies in the presentation of psychiatric disorders. One person wrote: "I am one of the many viewers Dr. Wahl mentioned whose only exposure to mental illness is television. As I watched these shows, I immediately concluded that the writers of these programs must know what they are talking about." Another reader confessed, "I had just assumed the scripts were checked with a professional for accuracy of symptoms, etc."

As is apparent from these responses, many people do make the assumption that information about psychiatric disorders is checked with an expert consultant, just as is commonly done with medical disorders, to ensure accuracy. In reality, such expert consultation on psychiatric matters is more the exception than the rule. Nevertheless, viewers and readers tend to expect information to be accurate and thus tend to believe what they encounter. Their reliance on the media tends to create misconceptions and misunderstanding concerning many of the basic facts about mental illnesses, as was shown in an early study by Jum Nunnally.

Nunnally compared three sets of "ideas" about mental illness—the ideas reported by members of the lay public, the ideas presented in the mass media, and the ideas stressed by psychiatric experts. He found that the ideas of the public tended, in almost all cases, to fall *between* those of the experts and those of the media.[3] Such results, others have suggested, demonstrate the pull of the media, with public notions of mental illness being drawn away from those of the experts and toward the inaccurate information presented in the mass media.[4]

Understanding (or misunderstanding) about schizophrenia is a perfect example. We have noted that schizophrenia is frequently presented, in the mass media, as equivalent to multiple personality. That almost two-thirds (62 percent) of the lay respondents to a 1987 survey about the symptoms, causes, and treatments of schizophrenia identified multiple personality as a common or very common symptom of schizophrenia suggests that the public has effectively picked up what the media convey.[5] There is widespread misunderstanding of schizophrenia as multiple personality, and it is no accident that the erroneous idea shared by the public corresponds to the one put forward so frequently by the media.

Another example of the spread of misinformation is the public's view of the insanity defense. Recent studies have explored the public's views of the insanity plea and found it to be highly inaccurate. The misconceptions, moreover, are consistent with the media depiction of insanity pleas noted in previous chapters. The public overestimates the use of this defense (seeing it as thirty times more common than it is), overestimates the likelihood that a defendant will be acquitted with an insanity plea, and underestimates the time successful insanity defendants will spend confined.[6] As do authorities in films and novels, members of the public express fear that the insanity defense will allow dangerous killers to return to the streets and further menace themselves and their families.[7]

This misinformation is of more than academic concern. It is not simply a matter of considering error bad and insisting on accuracy for accuracy's sake (although even the Television Code of the National Association of Broadcasters urges that "no program shall be presented in a manner which through artifice or simulation would mislead the audience as to any material fact").[8] Misinformation and the resulting misunderstandings about mental illnesses have significant practical consequences. Misconceptions about schizophrenia, for example, may lead to confusion, false expectations, and conflict. The family whose relative shows no sign of multiple personalities may be puzzled (and their confidence in the diagnosing clinician lessened) when their relative receives a diagnosis of schizophrenia. Their ability to recognize the onset of schizophrenia may be impaired by their misunderstanding of the symptoms involved, and their attempts to help their relatives may be frustrated by the symptoms and behaviors which appear but which, in their minds, are not ones associated with the "schizophrenia" label. Those suffering from the disorder, and harboring the same misconceptions, may be equally confused and frustrated.

That this confusion does indeed occur is evidenced by the remarks of Nancy Schiller, the mother of Lori Schiller, whose book, *The Quiet*

Room, describes Lori's struggle with and recovery from a mental illness. Mrs. Schiller writes of her reaction when she is given the information that her daughter has schizophrenia: "Schizophrenia? What did that word mean? I didn't understand it. . . . Schizophrenia meant split personality, didn't it? I had heard about schizophrenia, and I had seen some movies about it. To me, schizophrenia was *The Three Faces of Eve*, the film starring Joanne Woodward about a woman who had three different personalities that came and went without warning. How many personalities did they think Lori had? Was the girl who told us she could fly a different personality from the personality of the Lori we knew and loved? Where had this other person come from and how could we make her go away and get our Lori back?"[9]

In addition patients and their families who have achieved an accurate understanding of the disorder may be discouraged and hurt by the public's apparent lack of understanding. One comfort in struggling with a painful disorder is the knowledge that others may appreciate what you are going through; but when you are reminded, by repeated misrepresentations of your disorder, how little others understand, that comfort may be replaced by frustration, anger, and discouragement.

We asked earlier how jurors on a case involving a psychiatric defense, a case such as that of Ricardo Caputo, might arrive at a verdict and where they would get the information on which to base their decisions. If those jurors are like other laypersons who have picked up their knowledge of the insanity defense and its consequences from the media—and it is likely that they are—it will probably be difficult to convince them to risk a not guilty by reason of insanity verdict (which may well be one of the reasons why such defenses rarely succeed). Again, the misinformation conveyed in the mass media has very meaningful real-life consequences.

Media portrayals, however, do more than simply provide discrete pieces of information. They influence broader conceptions and create and support general stereotypes. Media that are such integral parts of our lives, numerous observers and researchers have noted, shape our ideas of what the world and its members are like. "It is no exaggeration," writes Robert P. Snow, "to say that we live presently in a media culture. It means that nearly every institution—including religion, government, criminal justice, health care, education, and even the family—is influenced by the mass communication process. It seems," he concludes, "that the character of the American culture and individual action is being developed more and more through media experience."[10]

What social scientists like Snow are observing is that attitudes and impressions of the public are indeed being shaped by persistent patterns of media portrayal. Our ideas about the world and its members—what George Gerbner refers to as conceptions of "social reality"[11]—are influenced by those persistent and consistent patterns. We come to see the world and other people as they are portrayed in the mass media.

Gerbner's work, for example, has established that the rate of violent crime on television far exceeds the occurrence of violence in real life. Television police officers and private detectives are far more likely to be shot or killed and far more likely to fire their own weapons than are real police officers or detectives. Citizens are much more likely to be assaulted, threatened, or murdered on television than they are in real life. This presentation of the world as a dangerous, violence-ridden place appears to be picked up by consumers of television images. In Gerbner's research, those who were heavy viewers (that is, who reported viewing more than four hours a day) were significantly more likely to expect to be victims of violence than were those who viewed television for fewer hours. Heavier viewers were also significantly more likely to express greater fear of crime and greater overall mistrust of others.[12] In other words, those who have more extensive exposure to the exaggerated rates of violence on television tend to perceive the world as a more violent and threatening place—that is, as it is portrayed on television.

Television, Gerbner further argues, accomplishes what he calls the "mainstreaming of America." Although the American public is remarkably diverse in many of its sources of influence—educational level, socioeconomic status, cultural background, religion—there is one source, he notes, that is common to all. Television is a part of over 90 percent of the households in this country, and those televisions are on an average of over seven hours a day. Whatever their differing backgrounds, Americans are being exposed to similar steady diets of television images and stories. Their views of the world and of various groups of people (women, minorities, elderly people, doctors, lawyers, police officers) are homogenized by their common exposure to the (often inaccurate) stereotypes of this ubiquitous medium.

Perception of violence, furthermore, is only one aspect of television influence. Considerable research has pointed to similar television contributions to inaccurate beliefs about older people, occupational roles, gender roles, and other components of society.[13] Children who were heavy television viewers, for example, ascribed occupations and activities to men and women that were closer to identified television stereotypes than did children who viewed less television. Asked about the frequency of various occupations, children gave responses consistent with television's narrow range of occupations (dominated by law enforcement professions such as police officer, judge, lawyer, and so forth). Heavy viewing has been associated with inaccurate beliefs that the number of older people is declining and that older people are less open-minded and adaptable than other people, consistent with television stereotypes. Robert Snow suggests, "Gradually the reality presented by television is becoming the paramount reality in society."[14]

It is likely that the same process occurs with respect to images of mental illness presented in television and other mass media. Depictions of mental illness, we have seen, are pervasive and consistent in the stereotypes they present. There is every reason to expect that they, like the media stereotypes of other groups, will shape the public's views, and that consumers of mass media will come to see people with mental illnesses as they are depicted in the media.

That media images of mental illness may contribute to unfavorable stereotypes, moreover, is not simply inferred from parallels to other depicted groups. Colleagues and I have completed several studies in our own laboratory that more directly demonstrate the media's influence on attitudes toward mental illness. In one study, we looked at the impact of a TV movie entitled *Murder: By Reason of Insanity* on expressed attitudes toward mental illness in general and toward community care of people with mental illnesses in particular.[15] The movie was based on a real-life incident in which a man, Adam Berwid, on a day pass from a psychiatric hospital, killed his wife as he had threatened to do numerous times. The film chronicled the man's breakdown and hospitalization, his wife's (and her lawyer's) frightened attempts to keep him from leaving the hospital, and the (graphically depicted) tragic results when he did leave the hospital. It concluded with an impassioned plea by the lawyer to the hospital board to never let such a thing happen again—that is, to keep patients in the hospital so that they would not be free to harm others.

This seemed exactly the kind of film—showing graphically and dramatically the violence of a person with a mental illness and containing an explicit message that the public needs vigilant protection from mental patients—that might contribute to the dangerousness stereotype. Indeed, mental health advocacy groups, the National Alliance for the Mentally Ill in particular, were very concerned that this film would encourage fear of those with mental illnesses and further fuel resistance to the community care of psychiatric patients. Accordingly, we attempted to assess the impact on public thinking that the film did have.

One group of college students was shown the film while another group watched a different movie involving murder but not mental illness. Following the films, both sets of viewers filled out questionnaires assessing attitudes toward mental illness and mental health care. Participants who saw the film depiction of a violent mentally ill person were more likely to express concerns about the potential dangerousness of people with mental illnesses and less likely to find community care for such people acceptable than were those who saw the other film. *Murder: By Reason of Insanity*, in short, appeared to have encouraged harsher attitudes toward mental illness, just as mental health advocates had feared.

A similar study with a newspaper article about violence committed by a psychiatric patient produced similar results. We asked individuals to read a real-life newspaper article concerning a psychiatric hospital patient who killed a young girl in full view of her parents and other onlookers at an outdoor fair in Connecticut. The article was introduced with a bold headline—"Girl, 9, Stabbed to Death at Fair: Mental patient Charged"—and contained all those elements discussed earlier as typical of such stories—a psychiatric patient, an innocent victim, and grisly details. Compared with a comparable group of students who read a neutral article, those who read the target article expressed many more negative stereotypes of mental illness. They indicated that people with mental illnesses were more dangerous, more in need of supervision and restriction, less acceptable to have in the community, and more a source of fear and anxiety than did those who did not read the target article.[16] Once again, exposure to even a single shocking media image of violent mental illness seemed to increase the expectation that those labeled as mentally ill are particularly likely to do physical harm to others and to make the media consumer more fearful of those so labeled.

Moreover, these studies involved only single exposures—viewing one movie and reading one article. As established in previous chapters, the kinds of depictions used in these studies are pervasive and recurrent in mass media. The average consumer will have multiple, perhaps even daily, exposures to such images. It seems reasonable to expect that the detectable effects of single exposures will be magnified many times by the steady diet provided by the mass media.

We can expect that the image of people with mental illnesses as violent and dangerous, dominating television portrayals of mental illness and pervasive across almost all forms of media, will lead media consumers to a belief that those with psychiatric disorders are likely to attack and harm others in their communities. Such a belief will, in turn, create discomfort and fear in the presence of those with identified mental disorders. Indeed, in a 1991 Louis Harris poll, mental illness was the disability with which the smallest proportion of respondents (19 percent) reported feeling comfortable.[17] The expectation that those with mental illnesses are a threat to one's safety will lead people to cross the street or exit buses or move away when they encounter others showing signs of or admitting to a mental illness. "At a bus stop once," wrote a recovering patient, "I struck up a conversation with a woman. The inevitable question arose: 'What do you do?' I hesitated but finally said that I was 'retired' and that I had been in a psychiatric hospital. The woman's reaction was immediate and unforgettable. She gasped, then looked quickly for an approaching bus; seeing none, she flagged down a passing cab."[18]

The stereotype of psychiatric patients as violent and dangerous may also increase the reluctance of many people to visit friends, relatives, or colleagues in psychiatric hospitals. They will not be eager to expose themselves to the uncontrolled aggressive urges they expect from the population of those hospitals. Stereotypes of the dangerous mental patient, furthermore, may contribute to the unavailability of needed resources for recovery by fueling opposition to the presence of individuals with mental disorders in the community. The citizens standing up at group home placement hearings to voice their concerns about being attacked by the former mental patients to be housed near them are expressing quite reasonable fears based upon the media images of dangerous insanity with which they have been inundated. These citizens, having been shown repeatedly that people with psychiatric disorders, treated or not, represent a threat to their safety, are quite naturally reluctant to tolerate the care or presence of those individuals within their communities. It is estimated that as many as 50 percent of the attempts to establish group homes for discharged psychiatric patients in residential neighborhoods have failed because of community opposition based on such fears.[19]

And once people do leave psychiatric hospitals—people whose need for support and acceptance may be particularly acute—they are likely to be met instead with suspicion and fear. Moreover, when they encounter those who believe that people with mental illnesses are as dangerous as media presentations suggest, any behavior, however objectively harmless, that clearly suggests a mental illness (for example, hearing voices) will likely frighten others, who may then seek the ex-patient's rehospitalization in order to protect themselves and their communities. The end result is that large numbers of people with serious mental illnesses either remain unnecessarily in isolated hospital environments or add to our growing homeless population because there are too few communities or too few affordable residences in which they are allowed to live.

Acceptance of the media stereotype of people with mental illnesses as fundamentally different from others likewise has significant practical consequences. When we perceive those with mental illnesses as a "different" group or kind of people, it creates barriers to communication and understanding. Such a perception leads us to expect that it will be hard to relate to, to understand, or to appreciate those who are so different from the rest of us. In addition, as social scientists have repeatedly observed, the notion that a group of people is "different" is the cornerstone of rejection. The idea that someone is "different" often carries with it the connotation that he or she is also in some way "inferior," an idea certainly bolstered, with respect to mental illness, by the jokes and slang references to mental disorder found in the media. The image of people with mental illnesses as both different and unworthy lessens our desire for contact with such individuals and thus contributes to the social rejection commonly experienced by those with psychiatric disorders.

It is even possible for rejection to progress to persecution. There is historical precedent for the use of the idea that those with mental illnesses are different from others, along with the companion notions that they are also inferior, unworthy, and even evil, to justify deliberate attempts to purge these individuals from society. In particular, Nazi Germany included people with mental illnesses on its list of "degenerates" to be exterminated for the purification of the German race.[20] Other eugenics movements have implicitly or explicitly suggested that it would be beneficial for those with mental disabilities to be "selected out," and even now many states still have laws permitting the involuntary sterilization of people with mental illnesses.

In addition, the belief that mental illnesses strike *other* people may be a contributing factor to the current inadequacy of mental health care in this country. Even when people hold compassionate views about mental illnesses and the people who suffer from them, their inclination to improve the situation or prospects of people with mental illnesses is diminished when the problem is not perceived as personally relevant. With so many problems to worry about, so many groups in need of assistance of one form or another, there is a natural tendency to focus mainly on those problems with some personal meaning for ourselves and our loved ones. Mental illness, when viewed as a rare phenomenon that happens only to a special group of (flawed) individuals unlike ourselves, would not be one of those "relevant" problems.

People who inaccurately believe mental illness to be someone else's problem are not likely to be avid advocates for increased resources and research for mental illness. If they do not recognize that it could be their sons or daughters or spouses or co-workers who might suffer from a mental illness, they are less prepared to argue that more of their tax dollars should be directed to the problems of "the mentally ill," particularly if they also believe that those with psychiatric disorders are dangerous, morally flawed, and thus undeserving of public support. If they believe that those people who become lost and homeless following discharge from psychiatric hospitals are anonymous aberrations and have difficulty recognizing them as the loved one of someone much like themselves, they are less likely to insist on adequate housing for "the homeless." Funds, programs, and facilities for treatment of mental illnesses remain strikingly inadequate and money for research into the causes and treatment of mental illness lags far behind almost any other significant health problem one could name. The federal funding for research on muscular dystrophy, for example, is estimated to be about $1,000 per patient; for heart disease, it is about $130 per patient; but for a mental illness as devastating as schizophrenia, the per-patient expenditure amounts to only about $14.[21]

There is even a subtle but significant influence on the care and protection people provide for themselves. People choosing health insurance policies seldom scrutinize, or even consider at all, the extent of coverage for mental health problems. It is likely that many readers, unless they have already had the misfortune to struggle with a mental illness in their families, do not even know what mental health coverage their current insurance policy provides, and it is even more likely that they did not ask about mental health coverage when deciding on a policy. Why not? Because it never occurs to them that they or their loved ones might need mental health care; mental illnesses, after all, happen to other people. Thus the public has not attended well to the mental health care provisions of health insurance, with the further result that health insurance coverage for mental illnesses has decreased steadily over the past decade or more.

Media images that present those with mental illnesses as different, dangerous, and unworthy of respect and empathy contribute not only to broad stereotypes but to even more global attitudes. Media depictions show us that individuals with psychiatric disorders are villains, failures, and deviates, possessing few positive traits. Those with mental illnesses become perceived as generally bad, undesirable, and unlikable. Pervasive and persistent images of psychiatric patients in unfavorable and disrespectful ways will, in short, contribute to the overall unfavorable public attitudes toward mental illness that are collectively referred to as "stigma."

Those who have experienced mental illness strongly agree. In a 1989 survey, we asked members of NAMI, the National Alliance for the Mentally Ill (mostly relatives of persons with severe mental illnesses), about their perceptions of stigma. Most participants (77 percent of the 487 respondents) indicated that their mentally ill relative had been much or very much affected by the stigma of mental illness. Over half (56 percent) felt that non-ill family members were also affected by that stigma. In addition, most felt that media features were among the most significant contributors to stigma: 86 percent identified "popular movies about mentally ill killers" as a major contributor; also frequently cited were news coverage (82 percent), casual use of terms like "crazy" and "psycho" (74 percent), jokes about mental illness (71 percent), and references to mental illness on commercial products such as t-shirts and coffee cups (63 percent).[22]

Stigma is defined in the dictionary as a "mark of shame or discredit."[23] It has also been defined by one social scientist as a "trait which is deeply discrediting."[24] There is little doubt that these definitions fit mental illness. Mental illness is viewed as a shameful and discrediting characteristic. Early studies of public attitudes toward mental illness, for example, showed that the personal characteristics attributed to people with mental illnesses tended to be much less favorable than those attributed to other groups of people. Jum Nunnally described the findings of one study: "The mentally ill are regarded with fear, distrust, and dislike by the general public. . . . Old people and young people, highly educated people and people with no formal training— all tend to regard the mentally ill as relatively dangerous, dirty, unpredictable, and worthless."[25] Even ex-convicts fared better when another researcher asked people to describe their reactions to various disability groups; those with mental illnesses were rated lowest of all twenty-one disability groups included in that study.[26]

It is also apparent that the general public sees those with mental illnesses as so undesirable as to warrant avoidance and exclusion. In one study, less than half of the participants indicated that they would be willing to work with an individual identified as having a mental illness.[27] In another, one out of five residents of a rural community indicated that they agreed with the advice that "it is best not to associate with people who have been in mental hospitals."[28]

What is even more significant in studies of public attitudes toward mental illness is that the rejection expressed by the public is based not on any real knowledge of the individual's specific disorder or psychiatric symptoms, but simply on the knowledge that the person had an unspecified "mental illness" or even that he or she had been to see a mental health professional about an unspecified problem.[29] One study, for example, had undergraduate students read vignettes that portrayed a person as having either cancer or schizophrenia and then asked them to rate the person with respect to a number of traits. The person identified as having schizophrenia was perceived as less desirable as a friend, less acceptable as a club member or neighbor, and less able to function in the community than the cancer patient despite the fact that the vignette descriptions (apart from the disorder suggested) were identical.[30] In other words, it is the public's negative image of mental illness and not the person or specific disordered behavior to which they respond with discomfort and rejection. They are responding not to what they observe directly about the person with a mental illness, not to the actions or emotions of the psychiatric patients they encounter, but to their stereotypes, their expectations, their acquired images of people with mental illnesses.

Thus part of the answer to the "so what" question is that media images contribute to mental illness stigma—that is, to unfavorable ideas and attitudes toward those with mental illnesses. The "so what" question can be carried a step further, however, to consider the consequences of stigma.

Stigma is burdensome. Added to the weight of already painful, and sometimes overwhelming, psychiatric disorders is the hurt of other people's disdain, dislike, and avoidance. Eighty percent of a 1991 survey sample of members of a Staten Island patient support group, for example, reported being burdened by mental illness stigma.[31] When individuals describe their personal experiences with mental illness, stigma is often prominently mentioned. "How can I work and be a part of a society that I feel hates me?" asked one writer.[32] Another reflected: "Most mental health consumers with whom I have talked agree that the stigma is worse than the illness itself . . . the discomfort of [my] nine months of hospitalization was not nearly as bad as dealing with the stigma for the last forty years."[33]

Not only is it difficult for those with mental disorders to face a world that misunderstands and devalues them, but it is isolating. Strangers and casual acquaintances keep their distance, and even friends may reduce their availability when they learn of one's psychiatric label. "I know the shame, humiliation, rejection, and confusion that occur when people find out that you have a mental illness," noted one woman in describing her experiences of multiple hospitalizations. "One girlfriend refused to see me after I got out of the hospital. She said she saw no potential in me and that I had no future."[34] Another former patient who wrote to me a number of years ago put it quite simply and powerfully: "To be an ex-mental patient for the past 22 years is one of the heaviest burdens in my life. It gave me and my relatives a lot of unpleasant memories.

I had to learn not to tell anybody about it, for the simple reason, to avoid being treated as crazy and to be able to keep my friends." Sixty-one percent of surveyed NAMI members reported that mental illness stigma had made it difficult for their ill relatives to make and keep friends.[35]

Fear of unfavorable public responses and of losing friends, furthermore, often leads to an additional burden—the burden of keeping one's illness a secret, of bearing it silently, of fearing disclosure. Those with mental illnesses quickly learn that it is not wise to disclose their illnesses to others, as anecdotes like the following, from a leader in the mental health consumer movement, indicate: "At first I did not appreciate the stigma involved in having a psychiatric label. This quickly changed. While strolling down a corridor on a pass during my first hospitalization, I met a surgeon who was a colleague of my father's and whom I had known since childhood. He asked me what brought me to the hospital. When I told him I was a patient on the psychiatric unit, a look of horror gripped his face momentarily. This expression was too quickly replaced by forced humor. 'That's a good one Danny,' he laughed too loudly and briskly walked on. I knew from that time on I was branded and should not lightly share information about my hospitalization."[36] Another patient echoed these same sentiments in her personal account: "I learned to speak about my illness only when I'm asked about it. I rarely volunteer my 'confession' of sins as a mental patient."[37]

Disclosure is more the exception than the rule among those with psychiatric illnesses. Eighty-nine percent of the respondents in the Staten Island patient support group survey reported that they withhold information about their condition because they fear negative reactions. One quarter of them said that they revealed their illnesses only to close family members. And 7 percent indicated that not even close family members knew of their disorders.[38] Tellingly, a large number of the "First Person Accounts" that have been provided in the *Schizophrenia Bulletin* and elsewhere have been anonymous. One author explained: "After careful consideration, I have decided to publish this article anonymously, in the hope that by doing so, I will protect my family, my friends, and myself from further embarrassment and discrimination. Protection against stigmatization is needed because our society does not feel 'safe' for those of us who have been hospitalized for mental illness."[39]

So potent is the fear of the consequences of disclosure of mental illness that mental health professionals have long structured parts of their practices to accommodate the need for secret-keeping. One of the important features of mental health intervention, confidentiality, is predicated in part on the need to protect patients from stigma. Therapists, from Freudian times to the present, have scheduled their clients or structured their offices so that patients will not meet other patients as they come or go and have thus helped to protect them from feared exposure as a psychiatric patient. Enoch Calloway, a psychiatrist who has himself experienced mental illness, could be speaking for most mental health professionals when he observes: "I have treated a lot of very productive people, including prominent doctors, lawyers, scientists, and psychotherapists. To a person, all of them want their illnesses kept secret. And I know that my experience in my practice is not unique. Secrets are kept. And stigma remains a staple in the common wisdom."[40]

Stigma, by discouraging disclosure of one's psychiatric disorder, also perpetuates itself. Individuals who have recovered from mental illnesses or who cope well enough with their mental illnesses to be able to conceal them successfully are less likely to be seen by the public (or to be accessible to the media). Those more visible, then, are people who have been so overwhelmed by their illnesses that they cannot be concealed—those with dramatic symptoms, those who wander our streets and subways, those who commit crimes. Because of the stigma of mental illness, our neighbors and co-workers and even friends are careful about revealing their psychiatric status, and mental illness remains an alien and frightening phenomenon associated mainly with the extremes we do get to see.

The need to conceal information about one's psychiatric disorder leads further to an uncomfortable, guilty secrecy. Mental illness becomes a person's hidden shame, and the effort to maintain that secret, the caution and deception that might be involved, is awkward, unpleasant, and unhealthy for most people. In addition, secrecy isolates individuals from valuable social and emotional support. Disclosure of medical problems usually leads to an outpouring of support from friends and colleagues. When one has surgery or develops a physical illness, people come to visit, to express sympathy, to raise spirits, and to encourage recovery. Such support, we know, has therapeutic value, as does the opportunity to share troubling experiences with others. When an individual has a mental disorder and fears the effects of disclosure, however, he or she does not have the same access to, or expectation of, empathic support.

Fear of disclosure may lead those with mental illnesses to themselves increase their distance from others, as demonstrated in a study by Bruce Link and his colleagues.[41] Psychiatric patients, in this study, indicated that they indeed feared disclosure and that they *selected* strategies of withdrawal from social contact to protect themselves from the rejection they feared. As a result, their social networks were more restricted, with those showing most fear of rejection having less social contact outside their own families. Mental illness stigma undermines recovery both by adding a burden of secrecy and by isolating psychiatric patients from needed social and emotional support.

Stigma also undermines the search for treatment. Those who are reluctant to acknowledge their disorders are also likely to delay (or avoid altogether) seeking appropriate (psychiatric) help, because that treatment will itself mark them as undesirable. The NIMH Epidemiological Catchment Area Study, as readers will recall, found one in every five people they interviewed to be suffering from a mental disorder. It also found that less than half were actually in treatment, despite the availability of proven, effective treatments for most of the identified disorders.[42] It is probable that mental illness stigma, which discourages people from disclosing their socially disapproved disorders, contributes to this situation. Indeed, over 80 percent of our NAMI sample indicated that stigma had contributed at least somewhat to their relative's reluctance to admit his or her mental illness. Forty percent indicated that stigma had lessened their own willingness to acknowledge that their relative had a mental illness.[43]

In addition, many people are reluctant to use insurance coverage, which would help pay for psychiatric treatment, because using it would increase the possibility that others (employers, insurance company staff) will learn of their psychiatric difficulties. They will forgo treatment or take on additional financial burdens rather than have their need for mental health care known. As a result, many people go untreated or wait so long to get treatment that their difficulties are much more severe or ingrained and hence harder to treat successfully. For some, like the presidential aide Vincent Foster, who committed suicide after struggling many years with unacknowledged depression, stigma-fueled reluctance to seek treatment may prove fatal.

Mental illness stigma also leads to discrimination and reduced opportunities. It is clear from both research and observation that people with mental illnesses experience significant discrimination because of their disabilities—or, more accurately, because of what is incorrectly believed about their disabilities. In one study, for example, a researcher posed as a job applicant and obtained an interview at a number of different manufacturing firms. Half the time he represented himself as having been traveling during the previous several months; in the other interviews, he indicated he had been in a psychiatric hospital. Job offers were less likely with the latter.[44] In a similar study, job applicants to a Veteran's Administration hospital were evaluated by workers at the hospital. The applicant was less likely to get a job recommendation when he was presented as a former mental patient than when he was identified as a former surgical patient.[45] In yet another study, directors of graduate medical training programs were asked to evaluate potential applicants. Applicants with a history of psychological counseling (but otherwise identical to other applicants) were judged less likely than other applicants to be invited for an interview and less likely to be accepted into the training program.[46] It is small wonder that 64 percent of our sample of NAMI respondents reported that mental illness stigma had unfavorably affected their ill relative's success in getting a job[47] and that the advice of some mental health counselors to job-seeking psychiatric patients is to lie about their psychiatric history.

Discrimination in housing also occurs for those with mental illnesses. Female callers responding to rental ads, for example, were found to have more difficulty obtaining housing (being accepted as a tenant) when they revealed that they were former mental hospital patients than when they did not report a psychiatric history.[48] Again, these different outcomes occurred despite the fact that the person's manner, history, and approach were the same except for the information about psychiatric history. Potential landlords respond on the basis of unfavorable stereotypes of mental illness, not to the person or the person's current behavior. Such unfounded refusal to rent a person a room is discrimination, and, according to families of those with mental illnesses, such discrimination with respect to housing has been experienced by about 65 percent of their ill relatives.[49]

Stigma-based discrimination, moreover, may be perpetuated at higher levels—through government neglect of issues relating to a population as threatening and unworthy as those with mental illnesses are perceived to be. "Besides directly preserving the stigma of mental disability," one set of observers has asserted, "the states commonly have neglected to protect mentally disabled people from violation of their civil rights by private parties. The majority of states still fail to protect mentally disabled people from discrimination in housing, employment, and public accommodations, and many of the states have not guaranteed mentally disabled people access to health and life insurance."[50] There are high hopes that the newly enacted Americans with Disabilities Act (in which mental health advocates had to fight for inclusion of mental illness) will make such discrimination more difficult (although, thanks to stigma, its usefulness may still be limited, since people must disclose their mental illness to get some of the benefits). Meanwhile, as Judith Rabkin concludes in her review of the research literature on public attitudes toward mental illness: "Even now, former mental patients who continue to be identified as such by their behavior or history are not treated in a way comparable to former medical patients when it comes to housing, school admission, some employment, or general good will."[51]

This differential, discriminatory treatment, furthermore, is not only offensive, burdensome, and unfair, but countertherapeutic. Employment is very important to people's self-esteem. Being able to identify oneself as a productive member of the community, to establish oneself as valued enough to be hired and salaried, contributes enormously to the average person's feelings of worth, confidence, and self-respect. Those with mental illnesses are no exception. When return to a productive life as a contributing member of the community is denied because of stigma-based discrimination, self-esteem and recovery are undermined for those with mental illnesses. One recovering patient comments: "For most of us, the workplace is the primary source of ego strength. . . . Without a job, we lack meaning. We become parasites on society by chance rather than by choice. Worst of all, we have no self-worth."[52] Housing discrimination has similarly antitherapeutic effects. Lack of affordable, available housing contributes to homelessness, which then adds to the burden of mental illness the challenge of daily survival. Inadequate, unhealthy living conditions and increased stress are hardly conducive to improved mental functioning.

All of the previously described effects of media images are important ones. However, there are also some effects that are even more direct and personal. Media images of mental illness such as those reviewed in earlier chapters are painful and offensive to people who suffer from those illnesses and to others who are intimately connected to them. People with mental illnesses are consumers of mass media just like everybody else (another way they are *not* different from others). Some research has shown that patients in psychiatric hospitals watch even more television on an average day than does the rest of the heavy-viewing public.[53] And among the effects of viewing oneself portrayed again and again in demeaning and unfavorable ways are hurt and anger.

It is emotionally painful to see yourself or those you love consistently portrayed as villains and buffoons. One becomes aware that, as one former patient put it, "the worst insult people can think of is 'You ought to be in a mental hospital where crazy people live.' "[54] With the hurt may also come anger. It is offensive to see trivialized the conditions that devastate your life. It is frustrating to strive for acceptance and witness comic portrayals that suggest that you are someone who is not to be taken seriously. It is infuriating to hear people like yourself, suffering through no fault of their own, demeaned by names like "nut," "loony," and "fruitcake." One woman who wrote to me when I first began writing about the problems of media images of mental illness showed very clearly the reaction such images can provoke. She wrote: "It is about time someone spoke up regarding TV shows depicting a false image regarding emotional illness and psychiatry. . . . I'm one of those people TV seems to enjoy reveling in writing scripts about. I'm 27 and have been in therapy for close to 8 years. . . . Why. . . . Why. . . . Why. . . . are my compatriots portrayed with so much evil and evil-ness. . . ??? Are we not made of the same stuff the rest of humanity is made of??? Don't we cry and bleed and love??? I want to scream . . . we're not all crazies . . . psychopathic killers . . . not all disturbed men are rapists . . . not all disturbed women want to be hurt or molested . . . or lie . . . I'm lucky in a way, I guess; people react with surprise [that I am a patient]. 'But you don't look or act that way.' I become so enraged and want to scream . . . what am I and others with difficulties supposed to look like, with horns on our heads . . . drooling monsters? I guess my letter is a little 'emotional.' It's just that I've wanted so long to speak up . . . but to who and where?"

Furthermore, being routinely confronted with unfavorable media images of oneself, along with the experience and anticipation of the negative public attitudes illustrated by such depictions, likely contributes to lowered self-esteem. People who are bombarded with unfavorable information about themselves, social scientists have established, begin to internalize such images, to doubt themselves, to conceive of themselves in the same distorted and demeaning ways that others appear to.[55] It is difficult to feel good about yourself when confronted by constant messages that people such as yourself are flawed, disapproved of, and disliked. Moreover, it must be recognized that, before the onset of illness, patients are likely themselves a part of the psychiatrically misinformed and inexperienced general public and are persuaded by the same images of mental illness as others. They too may start out with views of people with mental illnesses as dirty, dangerous, different, and so forth. When they then become mentally ill, they are already primed to feel self-loathing. Damage to self-esteem, in fact, was the most commonly reported result of stigma among our 1989 NAMI sample, by 95 percent of the respondents.[56]

It seems clear, then, that media images may contribute to stigma which, in turn, has many damaging effects. Further discussion is probably not necessary to confirm that media images of mental illness do have meaningful consequences. Before leaving discussion of these consequences, however, there are a few more points that must be considered. First of all, the concerns expressed about media impact are not, strictly speaking, about individual portrayals, but about a pervasive and persistent *pattern* of portrayal. Individual instances are of concern in that they contribute to those patterns. It is the accumulated effect of consistent, repeated depictions over time that does the damage.

Second, I do not mean to suggest that the mass media have single-handedly created the negative attitudes toward mental illness that exist. Such attitudes have been around for a long time and have many sources. Mass media presentations, however, help to perpetuate those inaccurate and unfavorable beliefs in their depictions of mental illness. They do so by strengthening the unfavorable beliefs that may already exist, a process Gerbner refers to as "resonance,"[57] and by passing on to new generations the incorrect beliefs of previous ones.

Third, the effects of media images of mental illness are not lessened by their appearance in entertainment media. Although some have argued that images in entertainment sources will inevitably have less influence because consumers will recognize them as clearly fictional, the reverse may actually be true. It is possible that those entertainment images (again, when repeated and pervasive) may have even more impact than nonfictional ones. Documentary-type programs or films, books by mental health professionals and advocates, talk shows that focus on psychiatric topics are likely to be viewed critically, with an eye toward identifying biases and thinking about and discussing the issues. In entertainment contexts, when the film, novel, or television show is not about mental illness, readers and viewers may give the mental illness depiction very little critical thought. They may merely absorb the images and have their already inaccurate views reinforced without even being particularly aware that they are learning about mental illness. As one film critic comments, "It may be mindless, but that doesn't mean it isn't affecting minds."[58]

Moreover, entertainment images, if well crafted, have the advantage of being emotionally arousing. Not only do they provide information, as documentary or talk shows might do, but they manipulate emotions in skillful, deliberate, and effective ways through the use of cinematography, music, and evocative prose. Take, for example, the shocking shower scene from Alfred Hitchcock's *Psycho*. Viewers knew that the film was fictional and that no real carnage took place (even the "blood" shown was merely chocolate syrup). Nevertheless, many viewers still— more than thirty years later—are nervous about taking showers when they are alone in the house, as a result of this movie.

The power of emotion-inducing entertainment over information was apparent, with respect to mental illness depictions, in our study of the television movie *Murder: By Reason of Insanity*. The movie was shown to viewers both with and without an information trailer that representatives from the National Alliance for the Mentally Ill had been successful in persuading network executives to include. The trailer,

presented verbally and visually at three different points in the movie—
at the beginnning, at the first commercial break, and at the end—
stated that the portrayal was "not intended to be a general reflection
of the mentally ill, the vast majority of whom never commit a violent
act."[59] Although intended to lessen the potentially stigmatizing effect
of the film portrayal of a violent psychiatric patient, the information
trailer could not compete with the dramatic visual depiction; all viewers
who saw the film—with or without the trailer—showed the same
unfavorable attitudes compared with those who saw a different film.[60]
The effect of the vivid, emotionally involving film could not be overcome
by the mere addition of corrective information. Images of mental illness
in entertainment contexts may be even *more* powerful than those from
nonfictional sources.

Finally, all of this calls for further comment about the issue of
"political correctness." One of the implications in criticisms of political
correctness is that the objections expressed by those demanding such
correctness are trivial and even ridiculous. Were those objections coming from groups with status and respect or for whom the offending
depiction is likely to have little effect, that implication might be support-
able.[61] People with mental illnesses, however, do not have the same
status and respect as others do. They are devalued, misunderstood,
and discriminated against. And there is clear evidence that unfavorable
media images contribute to continued devaluation, misunderstanding,
and discrimination. Those with mental illnesses cannot afford to tolerate
the demeaning terms and disparaging portrayals that perpetuate the
public's perception of them as undesirable and unworthy of respect.
"Political correctness," under such circumstances, becomes not just an
acquiescence to petty sensitivities but a means to help a long-stigmatized
group achieve needed—and deserved—acceptance and respect.

Inaccurate and unfavorable images of people with mental illnesses
lead to misconceptions and stigma. They contribute to confusion and
misunderstanding about mental illness which, in turn, influence both
the individual and the collective treatment of those with mental illnesses.
Media depictions, in their persistent and pervasive inaccurate stereotypes, perpetuate the negative attitudes of the public toward people
who experience mental disorders and thus help to maintain the stigma,
rejection, and discrimination that has added to their burden. Furthermore, the consistent demeaning portrayals of individuals with psychiat-

ric disorders in the mass media undermine the self-esteem and recovery of those who so often encounter these damning representations of themselves. For people with mental illnesses—many of whom are our neighbors, our friends, our loved ones—the images of mental illness that media currently present have very important, very personal, and very painful consequences.

Chapter Six

So, Why?

It is clear that media images of mental illness tend to be both inaccurate and harmful. So why do such images persist? Why has the portrayal of mental illness become and remained so far removed from the available facts? Why are people with mental illnesses depicted in such consistently unfavorable ways—as different, dangerous, and laughable? The answers to such questions are predictably complex, and I cannot claim to have the definitive response to them. However, I would suggest that, among the many factors, are the following.

1. *Profit.* There is no question that one of the driving forces in media selection of what to present to the public is the financial bottom line. The mass media operate for profit, and they must present what the public will buy in order to ensure reasonable profits for themselves and their shareholders. And in terms of profits, mental illness produces.

Phenomena that are dramatic and puzzling have always been attractive to audiences. Mental illness is such a phenomenon. Fleming and Manvell comment: "Madness appears as a condition that stands in opposition to reason and sanity. It provokes fundamental questions about our place in, and understanding of, the world. It makes us look more closely at our definitions of the nature of things and at our expectations of what should follow. Madness therefore has profound implications for our interpretation of ourselves and of our environment and eventually leads us to question who we are and what we are."[1]

These fundamental questions make mental illness an ideal topic for engaging audiences.

Interacting with the attraction of the philosophical/existential challenge presented by madness is the public's appetite for arousal and excitement, its desire to be frightened and titillated. Stories about crime and violence provide that titillation. I have already noted that crime news takes up a disproportionate amount of newspaper space. Homicides are more likely to be reported, more likely to receive large headlines, and more likely to be found on the front page. Those are the stories that attract viewer attention and interest. Homicides involving mental illness are even more terrifying, more morbidly fascinating to the public, more likely to receive splashy coverage, and, most important, more likely to sell newspapers than other kinds of homicides. Pamela Kalbfleisch concludes in her study of the kind of homicide story that makes the news, "Nothing sells newspapers like an insane, unpredictable, undetectable, gory killer on the loose who has caused a great deal of pain and anguish to the friends and relatives of the victim—all of high moral character."[2]

Lou Grant, a drama series about newspapers, widely hailed for its realistic presentation of news topics and editorial issues, acknowledged this draw in an episode involving the murder of a young woman by the mentally ill nephew of the associate editor, Art Donovan. Lou Grant, in a conference with the newspaper's editor-in-chief and its owner, questions the decision being made to give the story of the nephew's actions substantial coverage: "If it had nothing to do with Art Donovan, would we even be considering it?" asks Grant. The reply of his editor-in-chief recognizes the sales appeal of such a story: "You bet we would. A coed, an art student, killed in her apartment by a guy just released from a state hospital. You bet your rear end we'd cover it. We would be all over it!"

Mentally ill killers are equally profitable in movies. The public's thirst for excitement and fascination with violence is taken into account here too. Audiences like to be kept on the edge of their seats, and current audiences, especially youthful ones, seem to have an increasing appetite for blood and gore. Psycho-killer movies seem to satisfy these desires. People go to see these movies or rent them at the videotape store or watch them on television in astounding numbers. Furthermore, although big-budget blockbusters are often necessary to produce big box-office bucks, a somewhat safer bet, one often preferred by beginning (and less well funded) filmmakers, is the "slasher" film. These horror films typically do not bring in as large audiences or as many box-office dollars, but they are usually much cheaper to produce, without big name stars, with limited numbers of sets, and a simple script—young people, usually female, menaced by a disturbed stalker who kills many victims in gruesome ways. The biggest budget item is the special effects used to make the killings more graphic and shocking. Thus these psycho-slasher films can turn a good profit without the huge audiences that blockbusters require.

In addition, there is a certain creative economy that figures in to the frequent appearance of mentally ill killers in all forms of fictional entertainment. As noted, suspense and thrills are attractive to audiences. Murder and threat help to provide suspense. Someone who is at risk—being stalked, plotted against, targeted by villains—is also a typical component of successful suspense. To provide a situation and rationale for such elements can require a substantial amount of creative plotting. To provide and explain the motives of fictional killers can be a difficult task. That hard work can be minimized, however, by the insertion of a mentally ill villain whose motives don't need careful explanation—the killer kills, the villain threatens because he is mentally ill, and no other motive is needed. It is not surprising to find that scriptwriters, particularly television writers who must grind out scripts for series week after week, year after year, take frequent advantage of this short-cut to suspense. Similarly, where there is limited time in which to establish a plot—as in one-hour television programs—a story that does not have to spend time setting up the suspenseful situation with background and motive is quite handy.

There are also the general requirements of entertainment itself. In order to be "entertaining" (and thus in order to attract and hold a paying audience seeking to be entertained), presentations must involve characters who are both larger than life and easily identifiable.[3] Mass media, therefore, rely on exaggerated stereotypes that are both striking and quickly recognized by consumers. The stereotypes of people with mental illnesses have just these qualities—they are extremely danger-ous, outstandingly different, and/or excessively ridiculous. They are, in other words, entertaining and profitable.

Finally, there is the tendency of investors in media products to repeat what has proved profitable in the past. Financial investments in mass media are often enormous, and those risking their money naturally want to increase the likelihood that they will, at the very least, recover their investment. One way to do so is to re-use what has worked in the past, to stick with proven money-makers. We have thus seen the endless sequels to *Friday the 13th* and *Nightmare on Elm Street* (and their translation into television series). John Sandford has produced numerous books in his serial killer *Prey* series; Rex Miller's Chaingang has murdered his way through multiple novels, without signs of retiring. And few doubt that Thomas Harris's immensely popular Hannibal Lecter will return for additional novels and films. Public response to such fare has made these media depictions of mentally ill killers consistently profitable. As long as they remain so profitable, they are likely to continue to appear in mass media driven largely by economic considerations.

2. *Ignorance.* Media personnel—writers, editors, filmmakers, publishers—are often ignorant regarding the facts of mental illness, and here the word ignorant is not intended with any pejorative connotations. It is used simply to denote that there is likely much that media professionals do not know about mental illness, just as there are many aspects of media operations about which mental health professionals are ignorant. Those who work in the media to produce scripts, books, articles, and other fare for the general public are not mental health professionals. There is no reason that they should be as knowledgeable about mental illnesses as mental health professionals (particularly when, as noted below, mental health professionals themselves have often given out inaccurate information). In fact, there is no reason to expect that media professionals will be any more informed about mental illnesses than other members of the general population. The misconceptions that abound within the general population are probably shared by writers, directors, and editors as well. When they put together their portrayals, when they depict people with mental illnesses as different and dangerous, they are often unaware that these depictions are inaccurate.

Media professionals are also often unaware of the frequency and consistency of their portrayals of psychiatric patients. Just as some readers of this book may have been surprised at how frequently portrayals of mental illness appear in the media and at how consistently these portrayals present mental illness as an object of fear or humor, media people may be similarly surprised. In addition, focusing on a specific instance of mental illness portrayal with which the writer, editor, or producer has been involved may make it difficult to appreciate the overall problem. Those with mental illnesses do sometimes kill others; they do sometimes behave in ways that others find humorous. How is it inaccurate to portray this? The answer, once again, is that the specific work is only one contributor to a pervasive pattern of portrayals that together create an inaccurate stereotype.[4] Without awareness of the pattern of depictions throughout their own and other media (recognizing, for example, that mentally ill characters are almost always portrayed as villains), media professionals may not perceive a problem in stereotyping. It is my experience that many media professionals are indeed ignorant in this respect and are both surprised and alarmed when I have demonstrated this pattern to them through material such as I have presented here. Without such exposure, however, there is again no reason to expect that media people will be any more cognizant of a widespread pattern of inaccurate stereotyping of people with mental illnesses than any other member of the general public.

3. *History*. The images of mental illness that appear in today's mass media reflect conceptualizations and representations of people with mental illnesses that have been around for centuries. The creative professionals of today's media are, in some ways, just carrying on traditional depictions of the past. Many of today's images are repetitions or residuals of long-standing popular beliefs. The connection of mental illness with evil, for example, mirrors early explanations of disordered behavior. Early societies often saw madness as a manifestation of "possession" by evil spirits of some sort and adopted a number of severe treatments, including starvation and beatings, to drive out these demons.

The Greeks, too, saw mentally disturbed people as tainted with evil and viewed madness as punishment by their gods for some transgression. Take, for example, the story of Hercules in Greek mythology. Hercules, according to one version of the story, was one of Zeus' many out-of-wedlock children. He had great strength and extreme self-confidence and even dared to challenge the Olympian gods if he disagreed with them. His arrogance annoyed the gods, especially Hera,

Zeus' wife, who already disliked Hercules as a product of her husband's infidelity. Accordingly, Hera sought to punish and humble the great Hercules and did so by "sending madness upon him" and causing him to kill his own wife and children.[5]

The Bible also suggests that madness is a godly punishment: "The Lord shall smite thee with madness, and blindness, and astonishment of heart" (Deuteronomy 28:28), and in Christian countries of the Middle Ages, people who showed what today would be seen as symptoms of mental illness were seen as "in league with" or possessed by the Devil and thus as having committed one of the gravest of sins. *Malleus Maleficarum*, a book published during the Inquisition as a guide for witch hunters, identified sudden loss of reason as one of the many signs of demon possession. As in Greek mythology, people who were mad had obviously done something wrong to bring this condition upon themselves.

The idea of moral lapses as precipitants, if not causes, of mental illness continued even into the mid-nineteenth century, according to Gerald Grob's history of psychiatric care in the United States. "Insanity," he writes, was believed to be "provoked by willful violation of certain natural laws that governed human behavior. . . . Psychiatrists tended to interpret insanity as an inevitable consequence of behavioral patterns that departed from their own normative model of behavior. . . . Disease—irrespective of its particular manifestations—was perceived to follow violation of natural, that is conventional, behavior, and was therefore seen to be related in part to immorality, vice, and filth."[6] The notion we see today in our media that people with mental illnesses are the embodiment of evil is a residual of this recurring type of thinking.[7]

Even some of the scientific ideas and terminology of the past have contributed to negative moral views of mental illness. Early understandings of the human body's nervous system led medical experts to theorize that some people had weaker or more unstable nervous systems than others. Those people with less stable nervous systems were believed to be prone to mental illness when the weak nervous system began to deteriorate further. The deterioration of the nervous system was referred to as "degeneration" and was thought to be precipitated by any number of factors, including the person's own intemperate behavior. Those with mental illnesses were quite literally "degenerates," with all the morally unfavorable undertones attached to that label. Today's media portrayals of people with mental illnesses as evil maintain the negative aura that has long been attached to mental illness.

The influence of (now disproved) scientific thinking can be seen in notions of the physical distinctiveness of people with psychiatric disorders, as well. In the early 1800s, increasing belief that the brain is a complicated organ that controls thinking and behavior (and accounts for mental disorders) led to theories like those of the phrenologists. They argued that different parts of the brain were involved with different personality traits and behaviors, and that traits and behaviors which were pronounced reflected excess growth of the parts of the brain thought to control those functions. Thus the size of different parts of the brain—and the resultant shape of the skull—would differ from person to person in ways corresponding to differences in their psychological functioning. Different kinds of psychiatric symptoms, then, would be associated with different and distinctive brain and skull shapes. In other words, "abnormal" people would look different from "normal" people in consistent ways. Considerable effort was devoted to studying skull shapes and variations and to articulating the special appearance of insane patients.

Similar searches for distinctive physical characteristics were motivated by scientists/philosophers who argued that the eyes are the window to the soul and that one's personality, including whether or not one is mentally stable, is revealed through the eyes. A variation of this was the later focus on facial expressions as mirrors of one's psyche. From these beliefs came the images of wild-eyed, grimacing madmen whose outward appearance reveals their inner disorder. There even evolved a (no longer used) psychological test based on notions of the physical distinctiveness of various forms of mental illness. In the Szondi Test, people were asked to look at photographs of faces and to indicate which ones they liked most and least. The photographs were of patients with different psychiatric disorders, and the preferences of test subjects were said to reveal their own underlying pathologies (reflecting unconscious identification with the specific mental illnesses of the faces they preferred).[8]

The idea that people with mental illnesses look different from others relates also to artistic conventions that have evolved for depicting mental illness. Early artists seeking to depict those with mental illnesses were presented with an interesting challenge—namely, how to represent visually what is basically an unobservable mental phenomenon. Sander Gilman suggests, in his work on artistic representation of mental illness, *Seeing the Insane*, that artists latched on to what he calls "icons of madness"—outward symbols that were associated with insanity and that could then be used to indicate madness in a drawn figure.[9] Early (fourteenth-century) icons came from a failure to distinguish between individuals with mental illnesses and hermits (or "wild men") of the forests. Both were artistically depicted as having disheveled hair and tattered clothing.[10] Dishevelment became a key icon of madness, and drawings and paintings of insane persons invariably showed them with matted, unkempt hair and torn and tattered clothing.

Other external features used to suggest mental illness are also noted by Gilman. "Melancholic" people—those we would refer to today as depressed—were shown in characteristic poses that included downcast eyes and little muscular tension. They also tended to be drawn as dark in complexion, in keeping with the views, introduced by the Greek physician Hippocrates, that melancholia was the end result of an excess of black bile in the victim's body (thus lending a darkness to one's overall physical appearance). In contrast, muscular tension and an arched back were added to dishevelment in depicting frenzied madness.

As Gilman observes, such depictions are not necessarily accurate, and certainly not literal, representations of mentally ill subjects. They reflect the artistic need to find some way to represent madness visually so that the intended audience can recognize that madness is what is being portrayed. The current media presentation of those with psychiatric disorders as distinctive in physical appearance reflects a convention that has become accepted and uncritically utilized—not only by painters and sculptors of earlier centuries but also by filmmakers, television producers, and illustrators of the twentieth century—to depict mental illness.

The idea that those with mental illnesses are dangerous also has been part of public, and even professional, thinking for centuries. Sixteenth-century blending of madman and hermit made for an easy equation of madman with forest beast—primitive, savage, and threatening. Early "treatment"—in hospitals such as London's Bethlehem Hospital—was colored by the view that insanity rendered people incompetent, insensate, and bestial.[11] Insane people, it was believed, would never recover but grow steadily worse until they were so mentally incapacitated as to be little more than animals. They were accordingly treated as such, often kept in cells, naked and chained, with the public invited to visit and view them (for a small fee) just as we now visit zoos. There was little thought that these visits would trouble the patients, because they were (presumably) completely unaware of their situation. The notion that those with mental illnesses were like animals, with no understanding or appreciation of their surroundings, much less the rules of polite society, of course contributed to fears that these patients were dangerous and, without the enforced control of the hospital, liable to run amok, like wild animals, and ravage the community.

In addition, there was, in early psychiatry, little or no differentiation of types of mental illness and no known treatment. "Insane" people were thought to be basically all alike, with little hope of recovery and, in fact, a high likelihood that they would grow steadily worse. Some of these "insane" people were violent and aggressive and, since there was but one kind of insanity, mental health professionals tended to believe (and to convey to the general population) that all similarly "insane" persons were potentially violent.

Janet Colaizzi points out in her 1989 book, *Homicidal Insanity*, that mental health professionals have contributed to the inaccurate public image of people with mental illnesses as dangerous in a variety of ways.[12] She reports that dangerousness originally played little role in decisions to confine people in psychiatric asylums (the need to protect and provide for those with mental illnesses, as a parent would for a child, being the primary motivation for early mental institutions), but that hospital superintendents came to exaggerate the dangerousness of their patient charges in order to maintain and expand their authority. The argument that mental hospital patients were violent and dangerous gave superintendents and hospital staff justification for whatever form of restraint and control they might deem "necessary." It also allowed them to assert the central importance of hospital treatment for people with mental illnesses; insane people were, after all, dangerous and needed the security and control institutions could provide. Moreover, hospital superintendents (with the support of others in the field) argued that dangerous patients remained dangerous no matter how long their confinement, and that, therefore, release from their hospitals (and into the hands of other types of mental health practitioners) would be too risky.

As Colaizzi also reports, these assertions even ran counter to what little objective evidence was at hand at the time. She cites, for example, an experimental treatment program begun in Massachusetts in 1883 through which patients were "boarded out" with area families rather than remaining in the hospital. Even after reviewing the results of this experiment, in which there were no homicides and only two suicides among 762 patients boarded out over twenty years of the program, the executive officer of the Massachusetts State Board of Insanity was able to declare: "The potentiality of danger is inherent, as in all other dealings with the insane, who are unstable and may veil vicious motives and tendencies in apparently harmless guises."[13] Although the assertions of these hospital officials may have been motivated more by self-interest than by objective observations, their communications certainly lent further support to the notion that those with mental illnesses are dangerous. Media professionals have been misled no less than the rest of the general public by such assertions.

The idea that psychiatric patients are dangerous and violent is maintained also, Colaizzi suggests, by a number of legislative and judicial rulings in recent years. First of all, as individual civil rights and public awareness of those rights expanded, particularly in the 1960s, the rights of people with mental illnesses came under scrutiny. Among other things, the proper circumstances under which the government could bypass certain individual liberties and confine a person to a mental hospital against his or her will were questioned. Courts eventually decreed that involuntary hospitalization was a form of incarceration and that having a mental illness was not sufficient justification to deny people's basic rights to freedom by confining them against their will, however benign the intention. Numerous state laws relating to psychiatric hospitalization were struck down as unconstitutional because their criteria for involuntary commitment were judged to be unclear or inadequate. Eventually there emerged the criterion of dangerousness: it was decided that only those patients who were a danger to themselves or others truly needed hospital care enough to warrant the massive curtailment of liberty associated with involuntary commitment. Those who did not need the confinement and supervision provided by a total care institution—who were not likely to harm themselves or someone else without such attention—could (and should, the courts ruled) be treated in other, less restrictive settings. Thus the statutory standard for commitment, in most states, has become dangerousness to self or others. Although the majority of all hospitalized patients are voluntary admissions (and thus not committed under a dangerousness statute) and the majority of those involuntarily committed are hospitalized on the basis of their dangerousness to themselves, not to others (they may be suicidal, neglect their health, be confused and careless), the dangerousness standard encourages people to believe that those in mental hospitals must indeed be dangerous to have found their way to such institutions.

A second legal thrust involved consumer demands for greater accountability of health professionals for their decisions and actions. Increasingly, health professionals, mental health professionals included, were brought to court and judged liable for mistakes they may have made. One of the most egregious errors a psychiatric professional could make was to decide that a patient was not dangerous, discharge the patient from the hospital, and have that patient harm someone. It was far safer to overpredict dangerousness and to keep the patient in the hospital or to discharge the patient with cautions and warnings about his or her potential dangerousness. In doing so, professionals once again encouraged views of people with mental illnesses as violent and dangerous. Under the circumstances, it is understandable if the public and the media have picked up the idea that mental illness and violence go hand in hand.

A final contribution of history is the influence of past writing on current creations. It is sometimes said that there are few new plot lines, that all current plots are basically some variation of previous ones, going back to the Greeks or at least to Shakespeare. The creative community of authors, playwrights, and screenwriters naturally calls upon, however unconsciously, the stories with which they have grown up to create current entertainment fare. When that history includes Greek myths like that of Hercules, Elizabethan tragedies that mix madness and murder, Edgar Allan Poe tales of homicidal instability, and other such memorable stories of disordered violence, it is not surprising to find similar images in current creations.

4. *Socialization.* Cultures and societies pass on to their members their knowledge of the world and their understanding of the nature of the world through the stories they present to their people. The mass media are the storytellers of today, and, as such, they function as a primary socializing agent, ensuring that all members of our society are given the information and taught the lessons that form the shared basis of our culture.

Many media depictions, for example, reflect attempts to convey to the public what is known or believed about mental disorder. As beliefs about mental illness, its causes, and its treatments have changed, so has media depiction of mental illness (although, as noted previously, residuals of earlier thinking often remain despite changes). When knowledge is limited or beliefs incorrect, inaccurate stereotypes emerge.

The Greeks, believing that the Olympian gods had a hand in most of the events in their human lives, naturally concluded that the gods were involved in a phenomenon so dramatic as madness. When someone had been functioning normally for many years of life and then suddenly seemed afflicted with madness, some divine hand, the Greeks reasoned, must be at work. And for what reason would the gods bring something as painful and debilitating as madness upon someone other than some offense to which the gods were responding? Storied presentation of madness as punishment from the gods helped to explain to the public the otherwise mysterious phenomenon of mental illness.

Other societies, at other times, have viewed mental illness differently and have thus conveyed different information through their stories. In seventeenth-century Europe, the idea that mental illness was merely a product of sinfulness or a sudden incurable disease of the brain was supplemented by notions that insanity might be one unpleasant result of accumulating misfortunes in life. Many of Shakespeare's plays convey the idea that madness is a product of life stresses—Lear's betrayal, Ophelia's losses, and Lady Macbeth's guilt, for example. Elizabethans were given evidence, in popular dramas, of the emerging contemporary belief that mental illness might be a reaction to life events. Those plays were serving, in part, the function of providing the public with updated views of mental illness.[14]

Current films, television programs, novels, and other mass media entertainment perform the same function. They convey current knowledge—or, equally often, current theories—about the nature and causes of mental illness. Fleming and Manvell's extensive analysis of films about mental illness demonstrates the relationship between social and psychiatric views of mental disorder and the artistic depictions of madness that precede and follow promotion of these views.[15] They note, for example, the increase of psychodynamic explanations of mental disorder in films following the rise of psychoanalytic theories that stressed the impact of parental child-rearing practices on the development of psychopathology. Mothers, of course, were believed to be at fault, and the mother-obsessed villain, driven to madness by parental neglect and abuse, became a common feature of theatrical films.

Fleming and Manvell also note that the frequency of "battle fatigue" during World War II led to a greater portrayal of madness as a consequence of wartime trauma. The Vietnam War and psychiatric delineation of Post-Traumatic Stress Disorder (a disorder that follows extreme stressors and is characterized by anxiety and psychological reexperiencing of the traumatic circumstances[16]) similarly led to many films and television programs with this disorder as a focus. The popular consensus that people with mental illnesses are dangerous—a belief often supported by professional pronouncements—is likewise disseminated through mass media to all members of society.

It is not only knowledge and theory, however, that are conveyed through stories. The stories we pass on are also frequently intended as moral lessons, conveying to current and future members of a given culture certain basic, shared moral beliefs by which that culture operates. The Greeks, in portraying mental illness as a punishment of the gods, were also urging obedience to their gods and avoidance of the kinds of behaviors that, in their tales, brought on the wrath of the gods. Their epics and plays were illustrations that such unacceptable behavior was folly; indeed, it was madness, as its consequences showed. Thus the notion of mental illness as a reflection of personal transgression or of evil was part of a moral lesson to the culture.

The insistence on providing moral lessons through mass media has helped to shape media portrayals of mental illness in the modern era, as well, and to produce the images examined in previous chapters. George Gerbner and Percy Tannebaum have noted some of the ways moral concerns have influenced television and film depictions of mental illness.[17] Television, radio, and films, they point out, are governed by industry-generated codes that specify acceptable and unacceptable practices. These codes have had a number of provisions that directly relate to the presentation of psychiatric disorders and/or have indirectly influenced such portrayals. One provision of the early Hollywood Production Code had to do with the presentation of evil. According to Gerbner and Tannenbaum, the code was concerned about the moral implications of entertaining depictions of evil and therefore required that evil was to be clearly shown as wrong, unappealing, and ultimately punished. "One way to show wrong as wrong and evil as repellant," the authors note, "is by showing it to be insane."[18] Murderers who are ordinary citizens were morally unacceptable; killers who were insane or who were punished by being or becoming insane were less objectionable. Suicide also was not an acceptable action—indeed it was seen as sinful—unless the character was mentally ill. Gerbner and Tannenbaum conclude: "Preoccupations with the Code's standards of conventional morality enhances the probability of morbid, unsavory, and criminal associations attaching to the mentally ill on screen."[19]

Another example involves provisions concerning the treatment of professions. Basically, the code specified that one should avoid portraying any professional group in consistently unfavorable ways. Since mental illness was seen as unfavorable, care was taken to avoid showing mentally ill characters as professionals, thus avoiding attachment of this negative characteristic to any professional group. Consequently there was little information provided about the professions of mentally ill characters. One reason, then, that mentally ill characters tend to have little or no social identity in media depictions is to ensure that no one (or at least no one influential) will be offended. At the same time, if a professional (for example, a doctor) were to be portrayed in an unfavorable way—as a criminal, as violent, or as merely inept— the character was likely to be shown as insane to make clear that he or she was an atypical member of that profession. Villainous scientists and doctors became mad scientists and mad doctors to protect the overall reputation of these professions in line with the industry codes governing such matters.

5. *Psychological reassurance.* Presenting mentally ill characters as different and dangerous may serve a psychologically self-protective function. Mental illnesses are frightening conditions. They attack and damage the very faculties that constitute the core of our human experience, our thoughts and feelings. To think that we could suffer from such devastating illnesses, or that our loved ones might someday experience the pain of such illnesses, is very discomforting.

I have often encouraged students to visit psychiatric hospitals in order to go beyond textbook descriptions of mental illnesses. On their first visit, students typically focus on whatever deviant behavior they may observe—patients talking to themselves, pacing the halls, rocking back and forth in chairs—and they are struck by how odd and "different" these people are. After they have visited regularly (as I urge them to do), however, they begin to see striking similarities between themselves and the same patients they viewed earlier. They see only occasional bizarreness, and instead the common human desires for interaction, affection, security, achievement, and approval become much more apparent. They begin to perceive that these individuals are not all that different from themselves or from their families and friends; some even find other college students inhabiting psychiatric hospital wards. And then they begin to get very anxious. Their struggle to cope with their learning becomes very obvious in class discussions, which increasingly have a "how can this be?" theme.

The discovery that "patients" are not all that different from themselves proves both enlightening and frightening for students. The reality that mental illnesses occur in one out of every five people, that even severe disorders like schizophrenia afflict one out of every one hundred, is equally disconcerting. Knowing that education, loving parents, wealth, and other advantages may not be enough to spare one from mental illness is even more threatening. It is also frightening to recognize that those we rely on for the well-being of ourselves and our loved ones—doctors, dentists, teachers, airline pilots, police officers—are vulnerable to mental disorders that can impair their effectiveness. So people do what is often done with frightening realities; they try to deny them. For example, they try to convince themselves that mental illnesses happen only to "other" people, to people who are somehow fundamentally different from themselves and from their own circle of friends and loved ones. A sociological study by David Kantor and Victor Gelineau showed that such denial can occur even among those who work in the mental health field. They observed that staff of a psychiatric hospital, although outwardly committed to helping patients recover from their mental illnesses, actually encouraged continued symptom expression in subtle ways of which they themselves were not even aware. Such encouragement of continued deviance, it was suggested, helped to maintain a clear—and psychologically needed—distinction between patient and helper, a distinction that became uncomfortably blurred when patients behaved more "normally."[20]

Media depictions of people with mental illnesses as distinctly different from others, even in physical appearance, provide a reassuring message to the public that mental illness won't happen to them or to people like them. Sander Gilman expresses the need for this message in his book *Disease and Representation*: "The banality of mental illness comes in conflict with our need to have the mad be identifiable, different from ourselves. Our shock is always that they are really just like us. This moment, when we say, 'they are just like us,' is most upsetting. Then we no longer know where lies the line that divides our normal, reliable world, a world that minimizes our fear, from that world in which lurks the fearful, the terrifying, the aggressive. We want—no, we need—the 'mad' to be different, so we create out of the stuff of their reality myths that make them different."[21]

How powerful this need for those with mental illnesses to be different was brought home to me when I read *The Quiet Room* and found that I was both inspired and terrified by the description of Lori Schiller's experience of and recovery from schizophrenia. In particular, as I read Lori's mother's description of her daughter as an excellent student, an obedient daughter, and an enjoyable companion prior to her mental breakdown in her high school and college years, I could not help but think of my own daughter, whom I would describe in very similar ways and who was just leaving home to begin her college years. To believe that it was even remotely possible for someone much like my daughter to come back from college with such a devastating disorder was profoundly anxiety-provoking, and I found myself searching for evidence that my daughter was very different from (and thus less vulnerable than) the daughter described in that book.

The "differentness" ascribed to mentally ill characters by the media is thus in part a reflection of what media people often claim they do— give the public what it wants. In this case, what the members of the general public want is support for their denial of vulnerability to something as potentially devastating as mental illnesses. Gilman notes: "Society, which defines itself as sane, must be able to localize and confine the mad, if only visually, in order to create a separation between the sane and the insane."[22] Mass media representations help to create and verify that separation and to reassure us that we and our loved ones are safe from such a frightening outcome as madness.

The notion that those with psychiatric disorders are dangerous involves similar kinds of self-protective thinking. It is somewhat reassuring to believe, for example, that acts of extreme violence are committed only by a rare group of psychotic individuals—not by ordinary citizens whom we might encounter on a daily basis (discounting, of course, that individuals with mental illnesses *are* people we are likely to encounter on a daily basis). Data which suggest that one is most likely to be injured or killed by someone he or she knows (for instance, in the course of a domestic argument) are very threatening. We would like to feel safe with others except for extraordinary circumstances; thus we attribute violence to the extraordinary (though, in reality, not so extraordinary) circumstance of mental illness.

Again, Gilman describes this most eloquently: "The mad, especially in the incarnation of the aggressive mad, are one of the most common focuses for the general anxiety felt by all members of society, an anxiety tied to the perceived tenuousness of life. If I am afraid that I am to be attacked, have my goods stolen, lose my status in society, I do not want this fear to be universal, pervading every moment of my life. I want to know who is going to steal my hard-won status. So each society selects a certain number of categories onto which it projects its anxieties. . . . [in Western society, these categories include] Jews, Blacks, Women, Homosexuals, Madmen, Gypsies, and others we designate as 'different' . . . Our response to the perceived aggressiveness of the mad . . . reassures us. We have localized the source of our fear. We know who is dangerous. We respond correctly and we have control over our world."[23]

Acknowledgment that most violence is not a by-product of mental illness is troubling in other ways, as well. For example, it is more demanding. Without madness as a simple cause, violence requires more difficult explanations. If not mental illness, then what accounts for a murderous action? Certainly, psychologists, sociologists, and other observers of U.S. culture have identified many possible factors that contribute to the United States' leading the world in homicides and other violent crimes. This country is one in which handguns are freely available (and are used in the majority of homicides), in which media heroes like Arnold Schwarzenegger, Steven Seagal, and Jean-Claude Van Damme—and John Wayne and Clint Eastwood before them— reflect the cultural acceptance of aggression as verification of masculinity, in which family and social supports have been steadily weakened, in which poverty and unequal opportunity have created breeding grounds for crime and violence, and in which recognition, if not celebrity, may sometimes be established more quickly by destructive acts than by continued good works. Any or all of these features may contribute to the increasing violence that plagues our society. Understanding the multiple and complex factors that may contribute to individual violent acts, however, requires substantial effort; far easier is to accept the simple explanation that violence is merely a by-product of an individual's deteriorated mental condition.

Solutions, too, become much more difficult when we look beyond mental status to account for violence. As long as the locus of the violence is seen as an aberration within the individual, it can be taken care of simply by dealing with the individual; the "disordered" individual can be eliminated or incarcerated. Recognition of the complex social issues involved beyond the individual requires more complex, more prolonged, and usually more expensive interventions. Society can be spared the effort and expense by using mental illness as a scapegoat to account for its unwanted violence.

In addition, admission that violence may be due to factors outside the individual is guilt-producing. Such an admission implies an indictment of our society and of ourselves as its members and shapers. To look beyond the individual's mental state is to admit that, as members of this society, as ones who have roles in maintaining or changing the structure of our society, we bear some responsibility for violent outcomes. No one, however, likes to think that he or she is to blame, even indirectly, for undesirable events, and focus on the aberrant and unusual characteristics of the individuals involved helps us to avoid such thoughts. The media tendency to associate mental illness with violence and murder and to assume or imply mental illness when violence occurs thus serves to meet the needs of the public for relief from "blame."

Finally, as Gerbner suggests, current portrayals of mental illness may help to assuage our guilt about our own inadequate response to the needs of people with mental illnesses, while at the same time maintaining the status quo. Because of both our misconceptions and our apathy, we, as a society, have feared and shunned people with mental disorders. We have largely failed to provide adequate money and services for their care. Historically, we have abused and discriminated against those with psychiatric disorders. And what justification can there be that could allow us, first, to remain complacent and guilt-free and, second, not to have to spend additional money and effort to change the situation? Mass media portrayals of mental illness help to provide such justification.[24]

People with mental illnesses, we are reassured in media depictions, are different and dangerous. They are not like us and their plight is not relevant to us. It is not in the best interest of ourselves and our families to deplete our emotional resources caring about a group of deviant and undeserving strangers. Indeed, whatever inadequacies of treatment those with mental illnesses have experienced are only what they deserve. They are evil and deserving of punishment, and we have no reason to feel bad if they are treated harshly. Such is the message of media portrayals of people with mental illnesses as different, danger-ous, and evil. It is no accident that so many of the mentally ill characters in modern fiction are killed in the end. The message is that they deserve such fates. And that message, argues Gerbner, persists because it allows us to remain comfortable with our continued indifference to and poor treatment of people with mental illnesses.

6. *Lack of consumer feedback.* Change is generated by both education and challenge, and there has been relatively little of either with respect to media images of mental illness. Media personnel (who, again, are not mental health professionals) cannot always be expected to know

when their depictions are inaccurate or objectionable, without feedback from their audiences. Moreover, mass media are consumer-driven industries. Unless there is a clear demand for change from their consumers and some widespread indication of dissatisfaction with their product, media personnel are unlikely to make significant modifications in their presentations. Most people who are aware of and concerned about the patterns of negative stereotyping in the media, however, have generally not communicated to media personnel about their concerns and have not been assertive about their desire to see change, especially relative to the complaints filed by many other groups.

Until recently, for example, the number of mental health professionals addressing the issue of media images of mental illness was quite small. Mental health professionals tended to view involvement with mass (particularly entertainment) media as less central to their work as scientists and practitioners and to focus their attention on what were perceived to be "more substantive" scientific and clinical issues. Mental health professionals today show better recognition of media images of mental illness as a topic warranting their attention; many more write and speak about the subject than in the past. More also now write or call editors and program directors and advertisers to point out inaccuracies and provide accurate information about mental illnesses. Such action takes time and energy as well as recognition of a problem, however, and risks accusations of political correctness and censorship. Thus, like other consumers of mass media, most mental health professionals are still unlikely to take the time and effort to formally convey their reactions and concerns to appropriate media personnel.

Mental health professionals are often reluctant to provide feedback to the media even when called upon to do so. In a 1985 study conducted by myself and Gary Axelson (a clinical psychologist who is himself a former television newscaster), we surveyed both television news staff and mental health professionals concerning their views of news coverage of mental illness.[25] Both news staff and clinicians agreed that mental health professionals are often hesitant to comment publicly on stories involving mental illness. News personnel may desire psychiatric comment to add to their stories, but mental health professionals are typically wary of becoming involved in such stories, often fearing that they will be misquoted or have their statements taken out of context. In addition, there was agreement from both groups that psychiatric professionals often do a poor job when expressing themselves to and through the mass media, finding it difficult to explain facts about mental illness simply, briefly, and in language that is clear and understandable to nonprofessionals (for example, without using psychiatric jargon).

Those with mental illnesses or with relatives suffering from mental illnesses have not, until recently, provided much corrective feedback to media personnel either. Those with mental illnesses have had their hands full attending to more basic issues of coping and recovery; their struggle with mental illness has typically left them with little energy to respond to the less immediate issues of media depiction. In addition, many have been inhibited from speaking up about troubling portrayals by the expectation that their opinions would probably be ignored anyway as the ramblings and/or neurotic sensitivities of "crazy" people. Relatives of those with mental illnesses likewise have focused initially (and understandably) on more immediate personal issues—dealing with the stresses attendant to having a mentally ill person in the family, finding and fighting for improved treatment for ill relatives, struggling with the financial burden of treatment costs, and improving their own understanding of mental illness. Although often offended by media portrayals, families have only recently begun to monitor and respond to these portrayals.

Lack of response from people with personal and professional knowledge of mental illnesses has thus contributed to the continued lack of knowledge of media personnel about mental illnesses and about the problems in their presentations. When few people appear to object to media depictions (as has been the case for most of the past twenty or thirty years), there is little reason for media professionals to perceive a problem. Without corrective feedback, inaccurate images, reflecting the misconceptions media professionals share with the general public, persist. Without demand for change from consumers of mass media, change is less likely to occur.

The persistence of inaccurate and damaging stereotypes of people with mental illnesses in mass media cannot be simplistically attributed to the malevolence and insensitivity of the media professionals responsible for the production and dissemination of these images. There are many complicated forces that shape the media images of mental illness that appear today, with the list presented here probably far from exhaustive. Moreover, most of these factors operate in subtle ways outside our own awareness and, consequently, exert their influence unrecognized and unchallenged. To overcome these forces and to produce change in the troublesome stereotypes that result from them, therefore, will require deliberate, thoughtful, and concentrated effort.

Chapter Seven

Future
Images

That media images of mental illness are frequent, generally inaccurate, and potentially damaging is of great concern to those with mental illnesses, their families, and mental health care professionals. Such concern has led naturally to questions about what can be done to improve this situation. How can the inaccurate and unfavorable media images of mental illness be changed? If they cannot be changed, how can their harmful impact on the thinking and attitudes of the public be minimized? In this chapter I will be discussing some of the strategies adopted by mental health advocates concerned with stigma and with media contributions to stigma. I will also provide specific examples of what is being done to bring about improvement in the mass media portrayal of mental illness and to reduce media-fostered misconceptions.

First of all, there are many organizations dedicated to increasing public understanding of mental illnesses. Numerous studies indicate that the public is, in general, not well informed about even some of the basic facts about mental illnesses. In the Robert Wood Johnson national survey, U.S. citizens described themselves as knowing relatively little about mental illness. Only one in four felt "very well informed" about mental illness, while six of ten agreed that they should know more about it. The survey concluded that "Americans feel better informed about all other health problems tested"—alcoholism, cancer, drug abuse, heart disease, and even AIDS—than about mental illness.[1] It is likely that the public's lack of knowledge about mental illness makes them more vulnerable to media stereotypes and that widespread access to accurate information about mental illnesses would make them less dependent on the inaccurate information provided in entertainment media and less prone to misconceptions. Mental health advocates have therefore reasoned that public education about mental illness itself— straightforward factual information from knowledgeable sources— should at least help to limit the impact of otherwise misleading media images.

Considerable efforts are under way to provide such information to the public. The National Mental Health Association (NMHA), for instance, has made public education about mental illness one of its primary goals since its beginnings in 1909 as the National Committee for Mental Hygiene. A largely volunteer organization with a network of state and local affiliates, the NMHA develops and distributes information booklets, posters, and brochures about mental illnesses (an estimated 350,000 annually). The organization has also established May of each year as Mental Health Month, during which state and local mental health associations launch public education campaigns and stage media events to highlight mental health information and concerns.

The American Mental Health Fund (AMHF), founded by John Hinckley, Sr., and now joined with the NMHA, also has set public education about mental illness as one of its priorities. The initial thrust of the AMHF's efforts was to encourage people to be alert to the warning signs of mental illness. No doubt related to the Hinckleys' own experience with their mentally ill son, the education materials for the AMHF's first public education campaign, begun in 1989, stressed the idea that much personal and family pain can be avoided by early identification of serious psychiatric disorders and by appropriate intervention. The AMHF produced posters, brochures, and public service announcements (PSAs) urging people to "Learn to see the sickness; learning is the key to healing." People seeing these posters and ads could write or call the AMHF to receive additional information, such as a brochure that spells out some of the warning signs of mental illness. Other materials attacked common misinterpretations of early signs of mental illness, for example suggesting the inappropriateness of responding to a young adult's increasing withdrawal and uncommunicativeness with the attitude "All he needs is a swift kick in the pants" (as one of the group's posters was headlined). Still other materials have focused on stigma and emphasized that attitudes about mental illness are "still in the dark ages" (another poster heading). By the end of 1989, according to the American Mental Health Fund's 1990 Annual Report, more than 330,000 copies of its educational booklet had been distributed, most of them in response to requests from the public, and its print and broadcast advertisements had been sent to over 20,000 media outlets.

The National Institute of Mental Health (NIMH), a federal agency that overseas treatment and research programs for mental illness, launched its own multiyear, multimedia public education campaign in May 1987, choosing depression as its focus. The reason for this focus was based on several findings of NIMH-sponsored research. First of all, epidemiological research had established depression as one of the most commonly occurring psychiatric disorders. That same research also found, however, that most of those suffering depression were not receiving psychiatric treatment despite other research showing that available treatments were highly effective in relieving the disorder.[2] These findings led to the conclusion that literally millions of people continue to suffer needlessly from depression because they are not taking advantage of the successful treatments available. Furthermore, it was believed that many people were not seeking, or being referred for, appropriate psychiatric treatment because of ignorance of the basic facts about depression, misunderstanding of some of the common symptoms (which are often mistaken for physical ailments—fatigue, sleep disturbance, loss of energy, somatic complaints), lack of knowledge about what treatments are effective for such problems, and the stigma that acknowledgment of such a psychiatric disorder would involve.

NIMH decided that public education about depression (as well as education of primary care physicians, who are often the first to see individuals with depression) was a needed task, and the D/ART (Depression Awareness, Recognition, and Treatment) program was begun. The intention was to continue the campaign over several years and to shower the public with information about the frequency, symptoms, and treatment of depression. The program has been successful in disseminating information through national and local media and through its toll-free information number, responding to more than 125,000 requests for information between July 1991 and May 1992 alone. NIMH has now expanded its public efforts to a similar extensive campaign focusing on anxiety disorders.

The National Alliance for the Mentally Ill (NAMI) has also been very active in trying to provide the public with better information about mental illnesses. A grass-roots organization founded in the late 1970s, the National Alliance has over 130,000 members and over 1,000 affiliate groups throughout the United States. Most members are individuals with relatives who suffer from severe mental illnesses such as schizophrenia and manic-depression. NAMI has developed a variety of information materials to inform people about mental illnesses and has recently undertaken an extensive public education campaign to let people know that "the most shocking thing about mental illness is how little we understand it" (as NAMI posters and brochures proclaim). In 1985 NAMI joined with the American Psychiatric Association in launching Mental Illness Awareness Week, which now takes place across the country in October of every year. During this week, advocates arrange a variety of activities, from government proclamations to public lectures to candlelight marches, to make people more aware of mental illness and its consequences.

A slightly different public education strategy has involved education not just about the facts of mental illness but also about the issues of media stigmatization of those with mental illnesses. As noted in Chapter 5, those being entertained by media depictions involving mental illness are often unaware that they are being informed and influenced; they give little thought to the images of mental illness they are absorbing. When they do think about it, they often assume that the portrayal is an accurate one, developed and/or approved by expert psychiatric consultants. By informing consumers of mass media about the inaccuracies and biases in the depiction of mental illness, we create viewers and readers who may be less likely to accept uncritically the depictions of mental illness to which they are exposed.

That such a strategy can be effective is borne out by both anecdotal observations and controlled research. My own teaching experience, for example, supports the idea that alerting people to the pervasiveness and inaccuracy of media stereotypes of mental illness helps them to become more critical viewers, listeners, and readers and to recognize and question stereotypes rather than simply assimilate them. One piece of feedback I often get from students to whom I have given presentations about media stereotyping of mental illness is that they no longer can view mass media in the same way. They report that they now see things that they never really noticed before and that they can't watch television or films anymore without noticing the stereotypes of mental illness discussed with them.

In addition, I have already described a study of the impact of a stigmatizing newspaper story about a murder committed by a psychiatric patient. People reading that story reported less favorable attitudes toward mental illness and toward community care of people with mental illnesses. In that study, we also tested the effectiveness of providing corrective (actually, prophylactic) information to readers prior to their reading of the stigmatizing (target) story and found that the impact of the target article was indeed lessened by such information. If the participants in our study first read an article that presented information about the rarity of violence among those with mental illnesses or an article about the media stereotyping of mental illness (in particular, about selective reporting of violent incidents), they were less likely (than those who read the target article without first reading one of these other articles) to express fear about mental illness and resistance to community care. Educating readers to be aware of inaccuracies and possible biases in the homicide article did appear to have a mitigating effect on their responses to the negative media depiction.[3]

Public education strategies, however, have significant limitations. It is difficult, first of all, actually to get information about mental illness to the general public. Distribution of mental health education information through affordable channels—for example, via displays in post offices, banks, libraries, and so forth—will reach only a small portion of the population. To reach a large general audience, one needs mass media, but access to those media tends to be both very expensive and very restricted. Many mental health education efforts, for example, have involved the development of public service announcements to be presented on television and radio. Prime-time airing, however, is prohibitively expensive for most mental health advocacy organizations (and too profitable for stations to give away). Mental health education PSAs usually end up "in rotation" with scores of other PSAs and are aired when audiences are smaller—primarily during the late night and early morning hours.

Moreover, even when such information appears in public places, those who attend to or utilize it are mainly those already sensitized to mental health issues. Those who have experienced a mental illness or whose relatives have had mental illnesses respond to such presentations. The majority of the population, who do not perceive the information as relevant to themselves, may barely notice.

In addition, public education strategies are up against heavy competition. It seems highly unlikely that public education campaigns alone, however successful their dissemination of accurate information about mental illnesses or appropriate cautions about media biases, will be able to compete with the steady flow of polished and powerful media portrayals of individuals with mental illnesses as odd, evil, and laughable. The hundreds of thousands who have seen and responded to NAMI, American Mental Health Fund, or NIMH information are still a relatively limited audience compared with the 180 million people who *Entertainment Weekly* estimates have viewed *The Silence of the Lambs*[4] or the millions more who watch television's daily parade of stereotypes. The impact of the relatively small flow of positive information to limited audiences is likely undone by the more pervasive pattern of negative images already in mass media. Mental health advocates have thus also sought ways to reduce the number and frequency of negative stereotypes being presented.

One approach is to provide education specifically for that special segment of the population responsible for media depictions. As we have seen, one of the reasons for the occurrence and persistence of inaccurate media stereotypes is media ignorance. Media professionals have the same limited knowledge of mental illness as do others outside the mental health field. They are also similarly unaware of the inaccuracy, prevalence, and potential harm of their psychiatric depictions. Furthermore, even when they are aware of the problem, they are often uncertain as to how best to fix it. Many efforts, therefore, are being made to reach and teach media professionals.

In 1980 the Mental Health Association of Hawaii developed a resource guide specifically for writers and editors. Positively titled *Building New Links of Understanding*, the guide began with a description of the issues of concern—stigma and media contributions to it—and presented statistics about mental health problems in Hawaii. A second section juxtaposed common myths (for example, that people with mental illnesses are dangerous) with facts concerning those myths. Still another section provided specific suggestions as to how media might avoid stereotyping communications, including words and phrasing to avoid and other terms to substitute for offensive ones. It advised, for example, that writers avoid words like "psycho" or "maniac" and avoid emphasizing a person's history of emotional disorder or psychiatric hospitalization if it was not essential to the situation being described.

More recently, NAMI has produced similar guides. One is a several-page brochure for writers, which begins: "Serious mental illnesses like schizophrenia and manic-depressive illness are often in the news, and are frequently the subjects of dramatic films or television programs. As a writer for film, television, radio, or print media, you have an opportunity to bring understanding to a topic that is widely misunderstood."[5] Inside the brochure is information about specific disorders such as schizophrenia and depression, about violence, and about the burden of stigma. There is also a section on language, noting the unacceptability of terms like "crazy," "wacko," and so forth and urging the use of more humanizing references to "people with mental illnesses." Along with this guide, NAMI has produced a smaller, single-page summary of the language section of the brochure that can be pasted in any writer's notebook or on a reference pad for a brief and easy reminder of NAMI concerns. These guides have been mailed to thousands of writers and producers in the national and local media.

The Carter Center of Emory University, as part of its ongoing commitment to mental health, has recently started its own Mental Illness and Entertainment Media Initiative. Its plan is to use the status and prestige of former President Jimmy Carter and his wife, Rosalynn Carter, to reach influential people in the entertainment media and to encourage the production of more accurate and more humane portrayals of mental illness and its treatment. A major element of the Media Initiative involves the education of the creative community in the entertainment media, communicating concerns about the portrayal of mental illness to appropriate decisionmakers and providing educational seminars for the writers and producers of popular entertainment.

Still another educational strategy, one not yet as actively pursued as the ones already mentioned, is to try to reach future writers, editors, and producers through their training curricula. Literature, journalism, and filmmaking programs often include not only technical training but

LANGUAGE

Mental illnesses are frequently the subject of news stories, or of dramatic films or television programs. The National Alliance for the Mentally Ill offers the following guidelines for use of medical and slang terms about mental illnesses:

- words like "crazy," "nuts," "wacko," "sicko," "psycho," "lunatic," "demented" and "loony" are offensive

- terms like "insane" are inappropriate except when used in a specific medical or legal context (e.g., the term "criminally insane" in a courtroom scene)

- referring to a "mentally ill person" or a "person with a severe mental illness" is preferable to "the mentally ill," which depersonalizes — highlighting the illness, not the person

- terms like "schizophrenia" and "manic depressive illness" have very specific meanings and apply only to certain groups of ill people; such scientific labels need to be checked carefully for accuracy; they should not be used to refer to "schizophrenic weather" or other uses unrelated to the illnesses themselves

■ ■ ■ ■ ■ ■ ■

For more information, contact the National Alliance for the Mentally Ill, a self-help organization providing mutual support, public education, research and advocacy for people with serious mental illnesses:

Public Relations Department
National Alliance for the Mentally Ill
2101 Wilson Boulevard, Suite 302
Arlington, VA 22201
703/524-7600

⟨ONAMI⟩

ABOUT MENTAL ILLNESS

19. *NAMI has attempted to provide language guidelines for media professionals.*

also the exploration of issues in the field. Coverage of the issue of social influence and stereotyping could well include consideration of media images of mental illness, just as it now includes examination of the images of women and minorities. If the creators of media images can be sensitized early in their careers to the problems of mental illness stereotypes in mass media and to the facts about mental illnesses, there will be less to overcome later. Mental health advocates have begun exploring ways to participate in the education of future media professionals and to influence the faculty of mass communications training programs to add to their curricula discussions of the stereotyping of mental illness.

Another, somewhat more aggressive, approach to changing current and future images is to create pressure for change by communicating concerns and complaints to media professionals about specific presentations whenever they occur. This approach recognizes that mass media are consumer-oriented industries. They are businesses, run for profit, and their profits depend greatly on consumer satisfaction. They consequently tend to take consumer concerns very seriously. Furthermore, most mass media have stated commitments to social responsibility and have industry standards that urge responsible treatment of sensitive subjects. Concerns communicated by consumers to whom media presentations are being marketed can create a demand for change.

Consumer complaints about media stereotyping of mental illness have proved to be effective mechanisms for change.[6] One media presentation reacted to by the National Alliance for the Mentally Ill was the advertising of the Georgia peanuts named "Certifiably Nuts." As readers may recall, this involved a sack of peanuts wrapped in a straitjacket, with commitment papers and a string to pull to produce maniacal laughter. Not surprisingly, the product was seen as particularly offensive by many mental health advocacy groups. NAMI urged its affiliates and members to write to the creators and the distributor of the product as well as to the CLIO awards committee that had given the product one of its awards for creative advertising. Representatives from NAMI contacted these individuals, as well, to express their concerns about the exploitative use of mental illness to market the product, while others approached local department stores and other sales outlets where the peanuts were being sold. In addition, Rosalynn Carter, a longtime advocate for mental health, wrote a letter to the distributor indicating her distress that a Georgia product with which the Carter family had long been associated—peanuts—should be so presented. As a result of these actions, many local outlets stopped selling the gift peanuts, the product was eventually withdrawn, and the president of the CLIO awards apologized, promising: "I will do everything in my power to see that this never happens again. I have instructed our public relations department and the staff of CLIO not to promote this winner and to be on the lookout for any submissions in the future that may be similarly offensive."

Another example of effective consumer response concerned the advertising for the movie *Crazy People*. Although there were some differences of opinion about the acceptability or unacceptability of the comic content of the film, most mental health advocates were in agreement that many of the promotional elements for the movie were objectionable. The original newspaper and poster ads for this comedy, for example, showed a cracked egg with hand and arms making a silly gesture and declared, somewhat ominously: "Warning: Crazy People Are Coming." Representatives from a variety of mental health advocacy groups wrote to executives at Paramount, the film's producer, about what they perceived as a totally unnecessary suggestion (and one incon-sistent with the content of the film) of menace from "crazy people." As a result, advertising for the film was changed, with new ads saying simply "You wanna laugh tonight?" and showing a picture of stars Dudley Moore and Daryl Hannah.

On a local level, a newspaper in Philadelphia, where the film was to open, ran a promotion offering free tickets to a screening of the movie for anyone who could prove that he or she was "crazy." Represen-tatives from the Mental Health Association of Southeastern Pennsylva-nia, from the Philadelphia Mental Health Care Corporation, and from Project SHARE (a self-help organization for people with mental illnesses) wrote letters, marched in the street outside the paper's offices, and arranged for a meeting with the paper's editor and publisher in order to convey how troubling it was to have the paper treat "being crazy" as a joke. The paper responded favorably and published an apology for the ad, saying: "This was part of a promotional campaign. We picked up on the spirit of the campaign, and on reflection, that spirit was mean-spirited and wrong." The paper also reportedly decided not to run any further ads for the movie, to learn more about Project

20. *The original ads for this movie implied that one should be afraid because "crazy people are coming."*

21. *After consumer protest, the ads were changed so as not to suggest* ➤ *threats from "crazy people."*

"You wanna laugh tonight?

See 'Crazy People' - it's a funny, funny movie."

—Susan Granger, WICC-AM/NEW YORK

"Dudley Moore...is perfect... Lots of laughs..."

— Jeffrey Lyons, WCBS RADIO/WESTWOOD ONE

"★★★ ½ Irresistible."

— Gary Arnold, WASHINGTON TIMES

DUDLEY MOORE · DARYL HANNAH

Crazy People

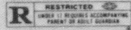

SHARE, and to attempt to run more stories that presented other views of mental illness.[7]

A number of mental health organizations have made reduction of stigmatizing presentations about mental illness one of their priorities and routinely respond to problematic media depictions. One of the strategies taken by such organizations to increase their effectiveness in identifying and responding to stigmatizing media material involves what has sometimes been referred to as a "media watch" or "stigma clearinghouse" model. This model calls for participants/members to be alert to media presentations about mental illness and to call to the organization's attention any depiction for which they think action would be appropriate. Organization representatives then respond to as many depictions as possible, contacting media personnel and conveying their concerns on behalf of their members. Media watchers are also urged to take individual action and to write or call themselves to express their concerns about depictions directly to the media involved. In addition, media watch sponsors sometimes call upon their members for concentrated and coordinated response to specific depictions— for instance, they organize letter-writing campaigns—when a more powerful response is deemed necessary.

An excellent example of this kind of media watch operation is the National Stigma Clearinghouse (NSC).[8] The NSC was begun in 1990 under the auspices of the Alliance for the Mentally Ill of New York State. It collects material (some identified by its small staff, much sent in by participants from across the country using standardized reporting forms distributed by the NSC) that pertains to mental illness from television, radio, advertising, films, and other mass media. Staff members write letters and make phone calls to appropriate media sources explaining the concerns about the identified material and passing on more accurate information about mental illness. They also urge members/contributors to take action on their own and distribute a monthly report summarizing NSC activities. In particular, the monthly report describes all the media references/portrayals submitted by staff and participants (which serves to educate newsletter recipients about the pervasiveness and nature of media depiction of mental illness) and includes the text of letters sent in response to individual items (providing not only information on what has been done but also models for others to use). Occasionally, the report will call for a more concerted effort from recipients, requesting multiple letters and calls concerning particularly troublesome items or even orchestrating demonstrations and boycotts.

One of the NSC's most successful efforts involved the much-publicized death of Superman. In the November 1992 issue of Superman comics, the longtime superhero was killed. Well before his actual demise, however, there was massive publicity about the upcoming tragedy. Included in that publicity was a report, from one of the editors, that Superman's killer, Doomsday, would be "an escapee from an interplanetary insane asylum."[9] Worried that the depiction of the killer of such a beloved comic book hero as a mentally ill person would contribute substantially to the image of psychiatric patients as evil and violent, Stigma Clearinghouse representatives quickly obtained the addresses and phone numbers of D.C. Comics, its editors, and its parent company, Time Warner. They then proceeded to distribute this information, as a "Stigma Alert," to attendees at the annual conference of the National Alliance for the Mentally Ill, urging people to write or call with their concerns and to take the material back to their home organizations and ask their members to write as well. In addition, a protest demonstration was organized and carried out in front of the corporate headquarters of D.C. Comics in New York City during Mental Illness Awareness Week in October.

The outcome of these efforts was that, when the death issue of Superman comics hit the newsstands (and sold out immediately), it contained no reference to Doomsday as an escaped mental patient. Superman's killer was simply, as mental health advocates had urged, a powerful and destructive individual. Interestingly, D.C. Comics did not acknowledge that the story line had been changed. In fact, the company asserted that there had never been any intention to portray Doomsday as an asylum escapee, despite the news story quotes about such plans (and despite July 1992 storyboard summaries, obtained by mental health advocates, that described Doomsday as wearing the remnants of a straitjacket in his battles with Superman and being identified by other characters as a "cosmic lunatic"). Whatever D.C. Comics' intention had been, it was clear that its representatives became sensitized to the issues involved, leading to a statement from Jeanette Kahn, president and editor-in-chief of D.C. Comics, that "D.C. Comics is extremely sensitive to prejudicial portrayals of any group and would never consciously promote anything that could be construed as a negative characterization." In addition, the controversy was picked up by the press, and articles in the *Boston Globe* and the *New York Post*, among others, contributed to wider public education about the issues of stigmatization and media depictions of mental illness.[10]

Critics of the media watch/stigma clearinghouse approach argue that it is too negative and reactive. Complaints about media portrayals after they have already occurred, they suggest, do little to change them. Those portrayals, after all, have already been seen. Moreover, such protests create bad feeling and strained relationships with media professionals rather than sympathetic understanding. And some media professionals do indeed perceive stigma clearinghouse efforts unfavorably—as coercive, as censorship, as attempts to infringe on First Amendment rights of freedom of speech and press.[11] Media watch organizers, however, emphasize that their primary goal is education, not coercion,[12] that they are eager for good relationships with media professionals, and that their approach is an effective blend of both proactive and reactive features.

As I have pointed out, lack of consumer feedback leads media professionals to assume that there are no problems in their portrayals. Writers, editors, producers, and sponsors need to be informed that there is a problem and that there are people in their audience who are concerned about and/or hurt by their portrayals of mental illness. Media professionals can respond to problems only if they are recognized. Consumer reactions serve to bring issues, such as the stereotyping of mental illness, to their attention. In fact, media watch advocates suggest, consumer reactions to *specific* portrayals educate media professionals in ways that other, purely proactive (that is, before-the-fact) educational efforts cannot.

As with public education efforts, attempts to educate media professionals about mental illnesses may be undermined by their perceptions of mental health information as less relevant to their lives and careers. Media professionals may not recognize the problems in mental illness depiction in their works or in their medium. Why should they spend valuable time reading articles or attending workshops about mental illness when they see the depiction of mental illness as such a trivial part of what they do? It is the reactive aspect of media watch efforts that gives relevance to the information being offered to the media professionals and enhances its educational effectiveness. It is not advice and guidance offered without a context, as part of general education about mental illness in case the media professional needs to use it sometime in the future. It involves a response to a specific product to which that media professional has contributed (and from which he or she likely hopes for both monetary and personal gain). It involves input from consumers, from the audience who must be satisfied if profits and acclaim are to be achieved and/or maintained. And it involves a specific instance rather than a harder-to-grasp general concept. When information is provided in the context of a specific work, it indeed becomes more relevant and more likely to gain the thoughtful attention of the media professionals involved.

The reactively provided information then becomes proactive when it sensitizes media personnel to the issues of mental illness stigma and public portrayal of mental illness and to the reactions of audiences to that portrayal. The response to a current instance of portrayal of mental illness will, it is hoped, influence the writer, editor, producer in his or her next presentation. It is possible that change will come because the creative agents are more aware that there are consumers in the audience who will protest, perhaps even vigorously, if they persist in the challenged depictions. Ideally, however, the change will come because the media professionals contacted will better understand and share the concerns of mental health advocates.

Those involved in media watch/stigma clearinghouse approaches have expressed their eagerness to develop more positive relationships with media personnel and to recruit them as allies in the effort to reduce stigmatizing portrayals of mental illness. This goal is explicit, for example, in a media watch kit, developed by NAMI, that provides guidelines for people wishing to communicate with media representatives. It urges potential respondents, for example, to approach their communication with the assumption that media people are not malicious, just ignorant, and to keep in mind that the purpose of their communication is both education and recruitment to their cause. They are advised also to show respect, to avoid being rude, threatening, or self-righteous, and to try to build relationships with media personnel even while confronting them. This recommended attitude of respect and recruitment has produced occasional remarkable successes.

In 1984 Hasbro Bradley Toys produced, as part of its G.I. Joe action-figure series, a villain named Zartan. His special characteristic was that he had two faces and two identities, and he was described on the toy box as an "extreme paranoid schizophrenic." For mental health advocates, this represented a classic example of stigmatizing communication to children, suggesting a connection between mental illness and criminality as well as reinforcing the confusion of schizophrenia with multiple personality. Hasbro received numerous letters expressing concern about the stigmatizing effect of the toy description, and representatives from NAMI contacted the company and asked for the opportunity to sit down with the company's officers to discuss their concerns. Not only were Hasbro's executives genuinely apologetic about their inadvertent stigmatizing, but the company's president, Alan G. Hassenfeld, responded with a promise to change future packaging and a substantial donation to NAMI (with which NAMI hired a public relations person to coordinate future antistigma efforts). Mr. Hassenfeld and Hasbro Bradley Toys became a continued strong supporter of NAMI's overall efforts, donating toys to be distributed to children with mental illnesses at Christmas and providing scholarships for affiliate members to attend NAMI's annual conventions.

In another instance, the Stigma Clearinghouse contacted the John Deere Company after NSC members discovered an ad for the "world's first schizophrenic lawnmower" (one that can be several different mowers—a mulching mower, a mower that bags the grass as it is cut, or one that discharges cut grass on the side) in the company's sales catalog. When contacted by NSC representatives and apprised of both the NSC's concerns about the misuse of the term "schizophrenic" and their overall concerns about stigmatization and public misunderstanding of mental illness, John Deere was quite sympathetic. The company not only pulled the ad but included a large antistigma advertisement about mental illness in its Summer 1991 catalog of products.

I do not mean to suggest, in the selection of these examples, that only large organizations or mass action can be effective in obtaining cooperative responses from mass media. It is true that an organization such as NAMI, representing many members with presumably similar views, often has more persuasive influence. That is one reason why such organizations are formed. Sometimes, when individuals consider

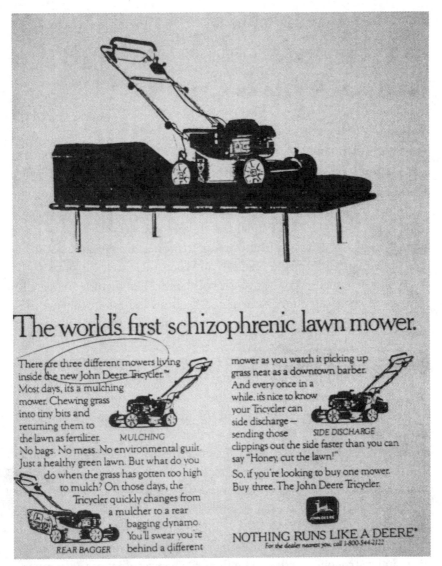

The world's first schizophrenic lawn mower.

There are three different mowers living inside the new John Deere Tricycler.™ Most days, it's a mulching mower. Chewing grass into tiny bits and returning them to the lawn as fertilizer. MULCHING No bags. No mess. No environmental guilt. Just a healthy green lawn. But what do you do when the grass has gotten too high to mulch? On those days, the Tricycler quickly changes from a mulcher to a rear bagging dynamo. You'll swear you're REAR BAGGER behind a different

mower as you watch it picking up grass neat as a downtown barber. And every once in a while, it's nice to know your Tricycler can side discharge — sending those SIDE DISCHARGE clippings out the side faster than you can say "Honey, cut the lawn!"

So, if you're looking to buy one mower. Buy three. The John Deere Tricycler.

NOTHING RUNS LIKE A DEERE®
For the dealer nearest you, call 1-800-544-2122

22. *John Deere replaced this ad with an antistigma poster after being contacted by concerned consumers.*

writing to large corporations, businesses, or bureaucracies, they are discouraged by the expectation that their single voice will be ignored and without impact. Indeed, sometimes the replies received when letters are sent (if they are acknowledged at all) are extremely unsympathetic and could easily lead writers to believe that they have wasted their time. Nevertheless, feedback to media from individuals can be—and has been—effective.

When a May 1990 episode of *Dallas* presented unfavorable stereotypes of patients in a psychiatric institution, along with references to those patients as "nut cases" and "fruitcakes," one woman wrote to the executives of CBS-TV, not only pointing out the offensive nature of the portrayal but noting the damage done by such depiction (in this case, citing a state senator's amendment to cut off funding for group homes for patients with mental illnesses). She received an immediate response from the executive in charge of the Program Practices Department at the network that included this assurance: "We are working with several organizations in an attempt to more carefully and sensitively craft our depictions of the mentally ill when they are necessary to the storyline. To that end, I have recently issued a memo to the CBS programmers in an effort to heighten their awareness in this area."

On another occasion, a listener was troubled by the implied connection of mental illness with violence in the advertisement of a broadcast segment on a Syracuse, New York, radio station as "armed and dangerous and off our medication." He promptly called the station manager, and, after forty-five minutes on the phone, the manager reportedly agreed to take the offending ad off the air, stating that it was not the station's intent to offend anyone and that it was not worth the risk of alienating listeners. In a similar instance described to me by Charles Harman, former director of communications for NAMI, a NAMI member reacted to a Volkswagen ad showing a person in a straitjacket and the tag line "you're crazy if you don't take advantage of this deal." The member called the Volkswagen company, asked for the name of its president, and wrote a letter to him describing his concerns as a person in a family struggling with mental illness. The president of the company called the member after receiving the letter, indicated that he understood and sympathized with the man's concerns, and discontinued the troubling ad campaign. Individual actions have produced results.

Sometimes the individual, personal approach has actually been more effective than a group or organizational effort. According to an example described by Demitri and Janice Papolos in their book, *Overcoming Depression*, an organizational response (by the public relations director of NAMI) to a coffee mug that said "kiss me twice . . . I'm schizophrenic" brought only a defensive reply. The giftware company producing the mug reportedly conferred with its lawyers, and, falling back on First Amendment protections of free speech, announced: "Our plans are to continue the 'kiss me twice—I'm schizophrenic' mug." An individual member of NAMI, a father with two mentally ill sons, subsequently called the president of the company and described to him what it was like to live with serious mental illness and the damage products like the coffee mug could do by undermining public understanding and acceptance. The company was reportedly persuaded by this individual and personal plea to suspend manufacturing of the mug.[13]

Communication of concerns about stigmatization to media professionals, then, particularly rapid response to specific instances, whether from individuals or organizations, has proved an effective strategy for changing media images. Negative images are already being reduced by such actions. Moreover, the use of the media watch approach is expanding. When the Stigma Clearinghouse first began in New York State in 1990, the majority of its contributors were from the New York and New Jersey area. By 1993 the NSC had received items from several hundred different contributors in twenty-six different states, and the National Alliance for the Mentally Ill was attempting to set up an Anti-Stigma Network among its hundreds of nationwide affiliates using a similar media watch model.

While reduction of negative images of mental illness is central to the media watch strategy, the increase of accurate and sympathetic portrayals is also a goal. Included with efforts to reduce unfavorable images of mental illness, therefore, have been strategies for increasing accurate and sympathetic portrayals. One obvious strategy is for mental health advocates themselves to create/produce more positive portrayals of mental illness. Rather than wait to respond to planned or completed media depictions, some advocates have attempted to provide ones of their own. Some have noted, for example, that newspapers and magazines have space to fill on a monthly, weekly, or even daily basis and that those media sources sometimes fall short in doing so with immediate news or previously planned material. If other material, such as mental health material, were available to fill those gaps, it might well be used.

The Mental Health Association of Northern Virginia, operating on this philosophy, recruited volunteer mental health professionals to write brief articles on mental health topics such as schizophrenia and panic disorders and provided local papers with camera-ready copy of those articles in three different lengths—750 words, 500 words, and 250 words. The newspapers were thus able to print whichever version of the articles fit the specific space needs that occurred. Every six months a different set of three articles was sent to the targeted papers. The newspapers made no commitment to use the material, and the Mental Health Association did not press for publication; nevertheless, many of the articles found their way into print simply because they were available at the right time.

One of the public affairs campaigns earning a 1992 award from the American Psychiatric Association involved a similar approach.[14] The program, called Media Briefs, involved the development, by the Northern California Psychiatric Society, of a series of one- to two-page "briefs" on current mental health topics, often topics that related to current major news events (for instance, the emotional effects of the Gulf War and the psychological effects of the 1989 California earthquake on children). Each brief addressed several aspects of the chosen topic in two to three short paragraphs and included the name of a mental health professional willing to be contacted and/or interviewed about the topic. These briefs were distributed to media throughout California, with the result that many of the briefs, or portions of them, were used by media sources. In addition, the mental health professionals listed were often called for further information, and the Northern California Psychiatric Society was contacted by media people asking if it could provide similar information on other mental health topics about which the newspaper or news station was considering doing a story.

Books, magazine articles, and newspaper pieces that provide personal stories of mental illness are seen as particularly valuable in correcting the public image of mental illness, and increasing numbers of these have appeared in recent years. The *Wall Street Journal* ran a lengthy article on the mental illness and inspirational recovery of Lori Schiller, an article that was expanded into *The Quiet Room*, a book then promoted by mental health advocates. Other personal reflections on their mental illnesses have been provided by presidential aide Robert Boorstin, psychologist Fred Frese, lawyer Theresa Collier, and others in publications such as the *Boston Globe*, *Newsweek*, and the Ohio *Beacon Journal*.[15]

Future Images   153

Recollections by author Susanna Kaysen of her psychiatric hospitalization as a teenager—*Girl, Interrupted*—even reached the *New York Times* best-seller list.[16] One of the appeals of Peter Kramer's highly successful book, *Listening to Prozac*, is its descriptions of individual patients and their growth following the prescription of Prozac.[17] The number of such publications—and their success in attracting audiences and returning profits to their publishers—is definitely increasing, meaning that more and more people are reading true-life stories of experience and recovery that can counteract the problematic stereotypes found elsewhere in the mass media.

Some in the mental health field have even tried their hands at video production. The American Psychiatric Association commissioned the production of three films about mental disorders as part of its "Let's Talk about Mental Illness" education campaign. The first film, *The Panic Prison*, about panic disorders, was released in 1989, the second film, *Faces of Anxiety*, in 1990. Through cable and television broadcasts and showings at schools and community events, these two films have been viewed by an estimated two million people. The third film, *Depression: The Storm Within*, was produced in South Carolina and uses Hurricane Hugo as a metaphor for the devastation and turmoil produced by depression. It aired on PBS in the Fall of 1991, and copies of it have been given to the Blockbuster video store chain in South Carolina, from which it can be borrowed without charge. A similar creative effort by parents whose child suffered from schizophrenia resulted in a July 1989 HBO documentary, *Into Madness: America Undercover*, which movingly examined the lives of three families struggling with schizophrenia.

Rutgers University, with the encouragement of the Alliance for the Mentally Ill of New York State, produced a one-hour program on mental illness stigma as part of its Symposium series. The program, *Mental Illness: Unraveling the Myths*, aired originally on NET in New York on March 25, 1990, and featured several individuals who had themselves experienced serious mental illnesses, as well as an expert in mental health law and myself as an observer of media contributions to stigma. According to feedback from the show's producers, this program generated more mail and phone calls than any other show in their series' history.

Other efforts are also currently under way to produce videos on the topic of mental illness stigma and media images of mental illness.

A consortium headed by the Virginia Treatment Center for Children has applied for funding to develop a PBS-intended video on media images of mental illness. According to its grant proposal, "much of the video will be devoted to letting consumers speak for themselves, telling untold stories" and would juxtapose media footage and images of print clips with interviews with mental health consumers, mental health professionals, and media personnel. In addition, other individuals, on both the East and the West coasts, are undertaking similar video projects on their own, with the hopes of having their work picked up by public television.

Those interested in increasing positive portrayals of mental illness, but recognizing their own limited ability to produce such portrayals, have attempted to further their goal by facilitating media use of positive material. Newspapers, magazines, and even entertainment media are frequently on the lookout for good "human interest" stories with which to engage their readers or viewers—sympathetic stories about people and their struggles and accomplishments. Thomas Backer, president of the Human Interaction Research Institute in Los Angeles, points out that "TV movies have become common ground for covering social problems, what programmers refer to sarcastically as the 'disease of the week' trend."[18] People involved with mental health—professionals, consumers, families of people with mental illnesses—probably know any number of stories of caring, coping, and recovery that might appeal to reporters and scriptwriters. One way to increase the presence of positive portrayals of mental illness is to provide positive materials such as these personal stories to appropriate media. The Mental Health Association in Hawaii used this reasoning in establishing what it called its "Success Story Project." The group distributed reporting forms to volunteers, asking them to identify or suggest mental health successes that could be forwarded to the media. It is undoubtedly true that most unsolicited material will never be used; however, some may be. Moreover, potential "good" stories will certainly not be used if media people are not aware of them in the first place.

Improved portrayals have been encouraged, as well, by acknowledging and applauding the more favorable depictions that already appear. There are positive images of mental illness to be found in the mass media, and advocates realize that such accomplishments must be acknowledged and applauded if they are to remain and increase. Most media watch organizations include communication of praise as well as criticism in their feedback to media professionals. The National Stigma Clearinghouse, for instance, explicitly urges its participants (after being urged by respondents to a 1992 evaluation poll) toward a greater focus on positive depictions. Between 1992 and 1993, the proportion of items submitted for praise increased from 12 percent to 32 percent of all submissions, and NSC reports came to include a special section for kudos. Among the items selected for praise and encouragement were the *Wall Street Journal* story on Lori Schiller's recovery from schizophrenia; a 1994 CBS television movie, *For the Love of Aaron*, about a character with schizophrenia; a *Boston Globe* article on stigma by Robert Boorstin; and a March 1994 *Nightline* discussion with Washington Bureau Chief George Watson about his depression.

Those interested in media change also have not overlooked the importance of the more direct participation of media professionals in this effort. It is clear, for example, that access to mass media is essential for public education strategies. To reach a mass audience, one needs mass media. And media professionals control access to those media. Efforts to reach a mass audience must involve the goodwill, if not the active participation, of media gatekeepers. Furthermore, media professionals have special expertise in producing polished, influential, and audience-grabbing material. If we wish to have destigmatizing materials presented that can compete successfully with the powerful images that currently pervade the media, those materials will have to be polished and professional. Filmmakers and scriptwriters, editors and reporters are far more likely to be able to produce effective counterimages than mental health advocates who, however talented and determined, are typically unschooled and inexperienced in the development of successful mass media depictions. Media professionals need to be included in efforts to develop new and more accurate images of people with mental illnesses.

It is important also that interaction between mental health and media professionals be a two-way process. The idea is not simply to approach media professionals to gain access to their power circles or to exploit their creative expertise. What is needed is cooperation. As the NAMI media watch guide urges, media professionals need to be approached as potential partners in efforts to change media images of mental illness.

Constructive interaction with media professionals requires viewing them as something more than villains or power brokers. Once again, it is important to recognize that most media professionals are not malicious or insensitive profiteers who stigmatize people with mental illnesses solely for their own evil ends. Many media representatives are eager to help change the stereotyping that occurs. Gary Axelson and I found in our survey of Washington, D.C., television news staff that most expressed very favorable attitudes about mental illness—views comparable to those of mental health professionals at a local mental health center. In addition, news staff were very critical of their own work covering mental health topics, stating that television news does an inadequate job of reporting on mental illness and agreeing that their news stories tended to stereotype people with mental illnesses as dangerous and unpredictable. Moreover, they did not use identified limitations inherent in broadcast news (for example, limited preparation and presentation time) to justify their coverage and indicated that improvements were possible despite such limitations. Overall, the study results suggested that there is much common ground between mental health advocates and media professionals such as news broadcasters on which to build cooperative efforts to change media images of mental illness.[19]

In addition, there are many reasons for media people to want interaction with individuals in the mental health field. They need and desire, for example, expert consultants. News reporters frequently seek comments from mental health professionals concerning stories with mental health components. Panel discussions at a 1984 conference involving both media and mental health professionals identified a number of reasons why people in the entertainment media would want consultation from mental health professionals. They included the following: to avoid being sued; to avoid making big mistakes that cost money in the production process; for purposes of accuracy and social responsibility; to have sufficient accurate understanding of mental illness to provide creative direction for writers, actors, directors, and so forth; and to avoid embarrassment among one's professional peers, sponsors, and the public. Participants also identified several kinds of input mental health consultants might be asked to provide, including accurate statistics, a sense of what the new and "hot" topics in psychiatry might be, aid in creating an accurate character who shows the "typical" symptoms of a particular mental illness, and access to real-life psychiatric settings or patients.[20]

A common lament of people in the news media also is that, with mental health stories, they lack people to put with their facts in order to make stories more interesting and appealing to readers or viewers. Martella Walsh, of the Wheeling, West Virginia, *News Register*, noted in a 1991 teleconference on the topic of mental illness stigma: "Consumers of media learn more from personal stories from people. When there's a name and a face telling a story, then they begin to understand, 'Hey, this is a lot like me, this is somebody that lives down my street.' " Walsh even described an occasion when a major finding about schizophrenia had received minimal coverage in her newspaper because the paper was unable to get disclosure stories, from individuals with schizophrenia or from their families, to accompany it.[21] News personnel desire to have those who have experience with mental illnesses available to add a human face to their news reports. Without personal stories, other stories may never even be seen.

Despite the mutual needs of media professionals and mental health advocates for more consultative interaction, it is clear that there are still many barriers to be overcome. Both news staff and mental health professionals agreed in our 1985 survey that "mental health professionals often appear reluctant to comment publicly on sensational stories involving psychopathology."[22] There is widespread discomfort and distrust among mental health professionals concerning their lack of control over which words of theirs may actually be reflected in the media. Knowing that media professionals will likely select from and edit what they have provided, mental health professionals fear that they will be misquoted or be misrepresented by remarks taken out of context in news stories. They fear that their input to entertainment media may ultimately be ignored or distorted for dramatic or comedic effect. Those with mental illnesses are, because of stigma, reluctant to reveal themselves publicly as having psychiatric disorders. In addition, the difficulty of translating one's knowledge or experience into language understandable to the general public and presenting it in a clear, concise manner within the time and space limitations of the mass media can be daunting. For both mental health advocates and psychiatric patients, there is anxiety about embarrassing oneself in front of thousands, if not millions, of others.

From their perspective, media professionals also have some hesitations about working with mental health professionals. They too are concerned about the possible inability of interviewees to convey information to their audiences in clear, concise, and useful ways, to avoid confusing jargon and frequent qualifications. They worry that the egos of experts and the passion of advocates may lead to insistence rather than advice when they are employed as consultants. They worry about the intrusiveness of consultants from the mental health field who do not understand the creative processes or business concerns of media enterprises.

The end result is that, despite the desire of news and entertainment personnel to have mental health professionals and consumers available to them and the parallel desire of mental health advocates to educate the public about mental illnesses, mental health/media cooperation has been limited. Efforts to reduce the barriers and establish increased trust, understanding, and cooperation between the two fields as one step toward improving media images of mental illness are needed and, in fact, are under way.

One way that mental health advocates have attempted to foster this cooperation is by inclusion of media professionals in conferences and workshops on stigma—and not just as members of the press from whom news coverage is sought or as an audience to be preached to, but as active participants in the problem-solving process. Such participation is expected to help media professionals to better understand mental health concerns about their images and to help mental health advocates to better understand how media operate in presentation of mental health topics and what media need from those in the mental health field to improve their depictions. The basic premise is that valuable learning can occur on both sides of the mental health/ mass media interaction.

A good example of how media and mental health professionals have attempted to cooperate in this way is the 1984 conference sponsored by the National Institute of Mental Health entitled "Portraying Mentally Ill People in Films and Television Shows."[23] People from the creative community were invited to attend this workshop along with representatives from nine mental health organizations cosponsoring the event. The workshop began with appropriate reminders from Thomas Backer that the cooperative engagement of media professionals in fighting stigma requires that mental health advocates recognize media's interests as well: "Attitude change and informational efforts will only be successful if the commercial media are asked to do things that are also in their own interest. Many public information and change campaigns have failed in the past because human service professionals tried to get the media to work 'in the public interest' or 'because the message is good.' This has little effect in a profit-making business, however real may be individual and corporate feelings of responsibility. The solution lies in finding the common ground between commercial considerations and the needs of mentally ill people with regard to stigma."[24]

The NIMH workshop included presentations by mental health advocates on the realities of stigma and on studies of media portrayal of mental illness, panel discussions of the advantages and tensions of having mental health consultants to the media, and description of a successful model of media—mental health collaboration in the creation of a drug abuse education television program. In addition, workshop participants reviewed a draft of a booklet of guidelines and informational resources for use by local media professionals. Finally, participants discussed possible follow-up activities, one being the creation of an ongoing Coalition on Portraying Mentally Ill People, consisting of all workshop participants as initial members.

I had the opportunity to be involved in what I believe was also a successful interface between media and mental health professionals in a 1989 conference, "Overcoming Stigma," in Westchester County, New York. At this conference, I participated in a panel presentation and a workshop on media images of mental illness along with the executive editor of the Westchester/Rockland newspapers, Lawrence Beaupre. Not only did Mr. Beaupre get to hear firsthand concerns about stigma and media contributions to it, but other participants, including myself, got to hear firsthand a newpaperman's account of the decisions he must make about stories with mental health content and of the processes by which such decisions are made. There was also extended discussion of how the news media could help to reduce stigma and how mental health advocates could help the news media in its job. In an editorial following the conference, Mr. Beaupre passed on what he had learned to his readers, noting that "the conference accomplished its purpose, at least for me, in sensitizing me once again to the need to be diligent about avoiding stereotypes, labeling and unsupported generalities about groups of people."[25]

Through conferences such as these, media professionals are becoming more aware of the issues of stigmatization within their media and becoming allies in the efforts to reduce stigma. Mental health advocates are learning more about media processes and about what they can give to media professionals. Furthermore, the personal interactions that occur at such conferences are helping to break down barriers of mistrust and misunderstanding.

Mental health advocates and media professionals have also been able to act on overlapping interests in the promotion of desirable depictions of mental illness. There have been positive portrayals of mental illness by mass media. And, when there are, mental health advocates have not only recognized them but helped to publicize them. When the NBC television movie *Strange Voices*, about the schizophrenic breakdown of a young woman played by Nancy McKeon, was developed, the producers provided an advance showing of the film at the annual convention of the National Alliance for the Mentally Ill. The thousands of participants who saw and were moved (many to tears) by the film returned to their home states and became unpaid publicists for the show, praising it in their organization newsletters and urging others to tune in and see it when it was shown in October 1987. The expanded audience for a sympathetic portrayal of mental illness was beneficial both to the makers of the movie and to those wishing to increase public understanding of mental illness.

Mental health groups similarly assisted in the promotion of television films such as *Promise*, a 1986 CBS Hallmark presentation with James Woods as a man struggling with schizophrenia and James Garner as the brother who must fulfill his promise to care for him when their mother dies. Mental health advocacy groups not only applauded and publicized this film as an excellent, accurate, and moving portrayal of mental illness and the painful dilemmas produced by it but also helped CBS and Hallmark put together a fact sheet about schizophrenia to accompany the promotional materials already developed by the producers. More recently, NAMI helped to publicize *Out of Darkness*, a 1994

23. *Mental health advocates have helped to promote sympathetic por-trayals of mental illness such as this one.*

television movie of a woman's recovery from severe schizophrenia, starring Diana Ross—and, in return, had its 800 number presented at the end of the film, resulting in thousands of calls for further information about mental illness.

In the fall of 1992, National Public Radio aired a documentary titled "Manic Depression: Voices of an Illness." The program, narrated by Patty Duke (herself a sufferer of manic-depressive disorder), featured interviews with individuals with bipolar illness and with their spouses, as well as expert discussion of the illness and its treatment. The program produced substantial listener response, and the NIMH D/ART program helped to fund and prepare a repackaging of the program into an educational kit that they and other mental health organizations helped to market. A sequel to that program, "Schizophrenia: Voices of an Illness," narrated by Jason Robards (whose first wife suffered from schizophrenia), was aired in October 1994, with additional cooperation and promotion from NAMI and NIMH. Such cooperative efforts between media and mental health advocates enable positive images to be more widely seen, encourage media professionals to produce more such portrayals, and provide an opportunity for additional public education about mental illnesses.

One final strategy is that which those in academia have undertaken—the accomplishment of research to help to better understand the issues involved in media depiction and change. Although I have cited numerous studies relating to these issues, systematic investigations of the frequency, nature, and impact of media images are small in number relative to most other topics in the mental health field. In addition, as I discovered in a recent review of the research literature, currently available studies have numerous limitations, not the least of which is the age of most of them, and they leave many gaps, particularly in firmly establishing the overall impact of media portrayals of mental illness.[26]

We also will need research to assess the extent to which the strategies being used to alter media depictions of mental illness are (or are not) effective. How will we know whether negative images of mental illness are increasing or decreasing? What strategies will turn out to be most effective in reducing negative images and increasing positive ones? What strategies will prove best in allowing media and mental health professionals to work cooperatively toward improved images? Researchers are now beginning to collect data that may answer these questions. It is clear from the examples provided in this chapter that there have been some striking individual successes. How successful mental health advocates will be in changing the overall patterns of media portrayal of mental illness, however, requires more systematic and long-term research.

Chapter Eight

Exit
Lines

Public sensibilities about the ways groups of people are characterized and referred to have grown along with the rise of feminism, civil rights, and ethnic pride. Although some disparage aspects of the movement toward "political correctness," most recognize and accept the important idea behind it—the idea that all people deserve to be treated with respect and dignity. At the same time, both social scientists and the general public have become increasingly convinced of the power of the mass media to shape attitudes and perceptions. As a result, the mass media have become much more careful in their portrayals of different groups, particularly disadvantaged and historically devalued groups. Considerable progress has been made in the reduction of negative stereotypes of women, racial minorities, immigrants, and other diverse groups.

Media images of mental illness are just as inaccurate and defaming as the worst stereotypes of any of these other groups. The depictions of mental illness that have found their way into almost every medium consumed by the public remain largely unfavorable and inaccurate. As we have seen, the public continues to be exposed to repeated presentations of people with mental illnesses as comical, different, and dangerous—images that perpetuate unfavorable stereotypes which, in turn, lead to the rejection and neglect of those with psychiatric disorders. Until recently, however, there has not been the same sensitivity to media stereotyping of those with mental illnesses. Those with psychiatric disorders, in fact, are one of the only groups of people for whom unchecked media defamation continues to occur. It is time for that to change.

I have warned readers previously that I am not unbiased. I will confess further now that I am quite passionate in my bias. I agree strongly with a 1992 position paper drafted by the U.S. President's Commission on Employment of People with Disabilities as part of an effort to establish a coalition of the major mental health advocacy groups to address the stigmatization of those with mental illnesses: "The prejudice, ignorance, fear, and continued negative stereotyping of people with mental disabilities continue to be a major barrier which denies them opportunities for employment, civil rights, housing, and the chance to be important, valued members of their communities. The media has continued to dehumanize people with mental illness by its flawed portrayal of them in movies, printed materials, and on television. The media continues to miseducate the public. This is not acceptable."[1] Regardless of who or what may be to blame for the preponderance of negative images of mental illness in the mass media, current patterns of portrayal are not acceptable.

Fortunately, there is now considerable momentum building for change. The consumer movement in mental health, which has sought to empower those with mental illnesses, has been and will continue to be a strong force in that change. As consumers of mental health services who should and do have much to say about the ways they are treated, people with mental illnesses have begun to speak out and to make clear what is hurtful and harmful in media depictions (as well as in public attitudes and professional conduct). The family movement likewise promises to be a strong contributor to improved public images of mental illness. Relatives of individuals with mental illnesses, by joining with one another and rejecting outdated theories that held them to blame for their family member's illness, have become a potent social and political influence. Organizations such as NAMI have moved from a fairly exclusive focus on mutual support and direct care concerns to an expanded agenda that includes stigma reduction and, hence, attention to media depictions of mental illness.

I am encouraged by the fact that, since I began work on the topic of media images of mental illness in the 1970s, I have seen dramatic growth in the number of organizations and individuals who have made change in media portrayal one of their major goals. The U.S. President's

Commission on Employment of People with Disabilities, the National Alliance for the Mentally Ill, the National Mental Health Association, the American Psychiatric Association, the National Mental Health Consumers' Association, the Carter Center, and the National Stigma Clearinghouse, to name just a few, now have strong commitments to reducing mental illness stigma and to altering the media images that contribute to it. Efforts to respond to unfavorable media images are both more numerous and more sophisticated than even ten years ago (although, as noted earlier, those efforts have been slowed a bit in the 1990s as mental health advocates have turned their attention to the compelling issue of health care coverage for mental illness).

Moreover, it is increasingly possible to find more positive images of mental illness in today's media. Sympathetic personal accounts of people with mental illnesses, which were virtually impossible to find in mass media in the late 1970s or early 1980s, are now appearing even in the *Wall Street Journal*. Press coverage of mental illness today includes discussions of the issues of stigma and mental health advocates' concerns about media depictions of mental illness. The entertainment industry is discovering that stories about real people recovering from serious mental illnesses make successful films, such as *Out of Darkness*, which mental health advocates are eager to promote. The ranks of the detective novel now include mentally ill heroes as well as disturbed villains—for example, Abigail Padgett's child abuse investigator whose struggles with manic-depressive disorder play as large a role in the story as do crime and violence.[2]

Such gains are encouraging and exciting. There is still much to be done, however, as even these many small successes remain overshadowed by the more frequent negative portrayals. Fuller success will depend on fuller commitment—of individuals as well as organizations—toward change in media images. Concerned citizens need to speak up more frequently, more forcefully, and in even greater numbers—as they have in response to unfavorable stereotypes of other groups—for change to be achieved, sustained, and expanded.

And all citizens should be concerned, for mental illnesses affect virtually all of us. It is unlikely that any of us will go through life without experiencing a mental illness or knowing someone close to us who does. To ignore the harmful media depictions of mental illness is to increase the suffering and confusion that we or our loved ones will experience when afflicted with a mental illness. Attention to such depictions is not merely a chore for mental health professionals or an act of altruism offered in support of other unfortunates, but a matter of self-interest. By acting to reduce the negative public images of mental illness and lessen the stigma associated with mental disorder, we may be lessening the burden faced by our future selves or by those about whom we care deeply.

Those who would like to contribute to efforts to improve media portrayal of mental illness or who would simply like more information about mental illness, may find the following organizations good places to start:

The National Stigma Clearinghouse
275 Seventh Avenue, 16th floor
New York, NY 10001
(212) 255–4411

The National Alliance for the Mentally Ill (NAMI)
200 North Glebe Road, Suite 10150
Arlington, VA 22203
(703) 524–7600 or (800) 950–NAMI

The National Mental Health Association
1021 Prince Street
Alexandria, VA 22314–2971
(703) 684–7722

National Mental Health Consumers' Self-Help Clearinghouse
1211 Chestnut Street, 11th floor
Philadelphia, PA 19107
(215) 751–1800

The National Depressive and Manic-Depressive Association
730 North Franklin Street, Suite 501
Chicago, IL 60610
(312) 642–0049 or (800) 826–3632

Depression Awareness, Recognition and Treatment Program (D/ART)
5600 Fishers Lane, Room 10-85
Rockville, MD 20857
(301) 443–4140 or (800) 421–4211

It is my hope that readers of this book will have an expanded understanding of the problems of media images of mental illness and be motivated to become part of current efforts toward change. It is my hope that each reader will be able to take some action, however small, to contribute to improved images of mental illness. It is my hope that someday, in the not too distant future, efforts for change will have been so effective that I will be able to refer to the troubling media images described in this book by a variation of the famous concluding line of Walter Cronkite, himself a symbol of the public's trust in the media, and say simply: "That's the way it *was*."

Appendix A

Films about Mental Illness

In order to provide a more complete idea of the variety of contemporary films with mental illness themes, this appendix provides descriptions of films shown on television with release dates of 1985 or later. The descriptions have been taken verbatim from the television guide section of the *Washington Post*. Some of the films are made-for-TV movies, but many are movies originally released for theatrical showing.

In order for a film to be included in this listing, some character must have been described, in the television guide, by a term clearly connoting mental illness—that is, by a term such as mentally ill, insane, mentally unstable, schizophrenic, mental hospital patient, deranged, psychotic, psychopathic, and so forth—or have similar terms in the title. Films set in psychiatric hospitals or described as focusing on patients in treatment were also included. Films described as dealing with alcoholism, drug abuse, or mental retardation, however, were not included; nor were films focused on psychiatrists or other kinds of psychotherapists even though these probably involved some presentation of psychiatric patients. The list also does not include over three hundred additional films released before 1985 which have also been shown on television in recent years. Finally, there are probably many additional films which involve psychiatric portrayals but which were not described as such and which, therefore, could not be included in this list.

After Dark, My Sweet (1990): A mentally unstable former prizefighter becomes embroiled in a kidnap plot engineered by a seductive widow and her shady cohort.

American Gothic (1988): A camping vacation turns deadly after three couples take refuge on an island populated by two elderly eccentrics and their demented offspring.

Anguish (1988): A horror film triggers a deadly response from a mentally unbalanced movie-goer in this "movie within a movie" from Spain's Bigas Luna.

Arachnophobia (1990): A country doctor's fear of arachnids becomes a terrifying reality when an army of lethal Venezuelan spiders invades his community.

Backdraft (1991): Spectacular pyrotechnics highlight this story of two quarreling brothers on the Chicago Fire Department and an arson investigator's search for a madman.

Backstreet Dreams (1990): A child psychologist attempts to convince a small-time gangster that his life of crime is threatening his autistic son's future.

Bates Motel (1987): The Psycho saga gets a darkly humorous reworking in this story of a recently released mental patient who inherits the late Norman Bates' hotel.

Bloodfist II (1990): A champion kickboxer is spirited away to a madman's island for a series of gladiatorial death matches.

Blood Relations (1988): A huge inheritance, a beautiful fiancee, and a mad doctor's operating table complicate a man's plot to avenge his mother's death.

Blue Desert (1991): A comic-book artist's flight from urban violence leads her to a desert community and a frightening encounter with a madman.

Blue Steel (1990): A rookie New York City policewoman hunts for the psychopath who has implicated her in a series of nocturnal killings.

Boris and Natasha (1992): The Russian agents who gave Rocky and Bullwinkle fits tangle with a mad scientist in this live-action adventure inspired by the popular cartoon series.

The Boy Who Could Fly (1986): Friendship develops between a teenager coping with family problems and her neighbor, an autistic boy who seems to live in a world of his own.

Cage (1986): Two Vietnam veterans—a mentally impaired brute and his former commanding officer—find themselves trapped in a bare-knuckle boxing tournament in L.A.'s Oriental underworld.

Call Me Anna (1990): An adaptation of Patty Duke's autobiography that traces her rise from child star to respected actress and her battle with mental illness.

Cassandra (1987): An escaped lunatic is reunited with his twin sister, an emotionally disturbed woman with psychic ability.

Chattahoochie (1989): Horrible conditions at a mental institution inspire a patient's campaign for hospital reform.

Cheerleader Camp (1988): A mentally unstable cheerleader becomes a murder suspect when her teammates take a bloody tumble.

The China Lake Murders (1989): A desert community is terrorized by a clever serial killer who hides behind a Los Angeles police badge.

Chopper Chicks in Zombietown (1990): An insane funeral director's experiments in re-animation are thwarted by a nomadic band of motorcycle mamas.

City Streets (1985): Driven out of her home by her mother, a teenager ends up working the streets of New York for a mentally unstable pimp.

Class of Nuke 'em High, Part II: Subhumanoid Meltdown (1991): A campus reporter uncovers a madwoman's plot to toxically transform Tromaville's student body.

Clownhouse (1989): Three escaped lunatics disguise themselves as circus clowns and embark on a rampage of terror.

Cobra (1986): A serial killer who's claimed 16 victims in a month is targeted by a determined Los Angeles police officer who specializes in tracking down and eliminating psychopaths.

Committed (1990): An emotionally distraught nurse struggles for her life after being mistaken for a patient at her new employer's insane asylum.

The Couch Trip (1987): An escaped mental patient becomes a popular Beverly Hills radio psychologist.

Crawlspace (1986): The demented son of a Nazi war criminal uses an elaborate network of air shafts to prey on female tenants at his boarding home.

Crazy People (1990): A new campaign involving honesty in advertising lands a burnt-out executive in an asylum for the mentally ill.

Creator (1985): With the help of a free-spirited young woman, a brilliant but daft scientist tries to recreate his long-dead wife from cells he's preserved for 30 years.

Cries from the Heart (1994): Two strong-willed women must put aside their differences to help an autistic child face a horrible secret.

Criminal Law (1988): A psychotic, but clever, serial killer manipulates a defense attorney into providing him with the legal loophole that will set him free.

Critical Condition (1987): A con man confined to a mental ward is mistaken for a doctor when a raging hurricane leaves the Staten Island hospital powerless.

Cutting Class (1989): A former mental patient becomes a prime suspect when his return to high school coincides with a rash of grisly murders.

Danger Zone II: Reaper's Revenge (1988): The psychotic leader of a motorcycle gang is released from prison and seeks revenge against the police detective who arrested him.

Darlings of the Gods (1989): Laurence Olivier's fairy-tale marriage to Vivien Leigh crumbles beneath the pressures of infidelity and insanity in this dramatization of their relationship.

David's Mother (1994): A woman makes personal sacrifices to care for and strengthen her relationship with her mentally challenged son.

Dead Again (1991): An amnesiac learns her nightmares may stem from a 40-year-old murder in this tale of reincarnation.

Deadly Game (1991): A deranged millionaire hunts seven houseguests in a game of revenge at his island retreat.

Deadly Innocents (1988): A sheriff learns that a dangerous schizophrenic is tutoring a young woman in the fine art of murder.

Deadly Intentions (1985): The wife of a doctor fears for her life when her husband shows signs of mental instability.

The Dead Pool (1988): A psychotic film buff and an imprisoned mobster cause dangerous complications for San Francisco detective Dirty Harry Callahan in his fifth cinematic outing.

Dead Ringers (1988): David Croneberg's award-winning account of the circumstances that led twin gynecological surgeons Beverly and Elliot Mantle to madness and eventual destruction.

Death of a Soldier (1986): A mentally unbalanced American serviceman stands trial in Australia during World War II for the murders of three local women.

Death Warrant (1990): A cop with a martial arts background goes behind bars to expose the maniac responsible for a series of gruesome prison murders.

Desire and Hell at Sunset Motel (1992): A paranoid salesman and his seductive wife encounter lust, betrayal, and murder at a seedy California motel.

Disturbed (1990): The unorthodox head of a mental institution begins to fear for his own sanity following the arrival of a seductive young patient.

Do You Remember Love? (1985): A 50-year-old college professor is tragically stricken with Alzheimer's disease at the height of her career.

The Dream Team (1989): A quartet of institutionalized mental patients find themselves abandoned on the streets of Manhattan after their doctor is knocked unconscious by thugs.

Easy Prey (1986): A teenager kidnapped by a psychotic serial killer submits to his demands.

Edge of Sanity (1989): Dr. Jekyll's research leads to drug addiction and his transformation into a scalpel-wielding maniac in this variation on Robert Louis Stevenson's story.

83 Hours 'til Dawn (1990): A fact-based account of a businessman's race against time to locate and rescue his daughter who has been buried alive by a calculating psychopath.

The End of Innocence (1990): A neurotic woman comes to terms with her compulsions after her parents send her to a rehabilitation center.

Everybody Wins (1990): A private eye begins to believe that his client, a prostitute with schizophrenic tendencies, might know more about the murder of her psychiatrist than she admits.

Fatal Attraction (1987): A happily married corporate lawyer's weekend of passion with a seductive but unstable woman threatens to destroy his life.

Fear Stalk (1989): A successful TV executive matches wits with a psychopath who, in an insane attempt to take over her life, has stolen her belongings.

Five Corners (1987): 1963 Brooklyn is the setting for a confrontation between urban youths and a psychotic ex-con with a score to settle.

Flight of the Black Angel (1991): An Air Force captain races against time to save Las Vegas from a psychotic flight student who intends to destroy the city with a stolen nuclear bomber.

Friday the 13th—A New Beginning (1985): A mentally unbalanced young man picks up where Jason left off, killing unsuspecting teenagers in gruesome fashion.

Getting Even (1986): America's survival is at stake when a Texas industrialist and his mad rival battle over possession of a deadly gas.

Halloween 4 (1988): The infamous mass murderer escapes from his sanitarium and heads back to Haddonfield, Ill., to continue the homicidal rampage he started 10 years ago.

Hamlet (1990): His murdered father's spirit induces a Danish prince to feign insanity.

Haunting Fear (1990): A private eye's investigation into a neurotic woman's nightmares leads to a brush with the supernatural.

The Hearse (1990): A schoolteacher tries to recover from a nervous breakdown at a home which is besieged by demons.

Heart of Darkness (1994): A young man searches for an insane ivory trader in the jungles of Africa.

Hider in the House (1989): A recently released mental patient becomes a voyeuristic intruder in a young family's newly renovated home.

Homer & Eddie (1989): A mentally retarded man embarks on a voyage of discovery after he is befriended by a homicidal schizophrenic.

The Housekeeper (1986): An Englishwoman attempts to hide her dyslexia and her mental instability from her latest employers.

House of Usher (1989): A young woman is held captive by a psychotic aristocrat.

Howling IV: The Original Nightmare (1985): A therapeutic trip to the country brings an emotionally unstable novelist face to face with a community of werewolves.

An Indecent Obsession (1985): An Australian military hospital serves as the backdrop for romance between a nurse and a disturbed soldier during World War II.

In My Daughter's Name (1992): An outraged mother takes the law into her own hands after the man who raped and murdered her daughter is acquitted by reason of temporary insanity.

I Saw What You Did (1988): Two teenagers get the wrong number when their telephone prank connects them to a psychotic murderer.

Kansas (1988): While traveling through the Midwest on his way to a friend's wedding, a young man falls under the influence of a psychopath.

Killer (1989): A soulless maniac with a penchant for flesh slices a corpse-laden path through the Southern countryside.

Killer Instinct (1988): A psychiatrist's career is thrown into limbo after an institutionalized patient she is forced to release commits murder.

Lady Beware (1987): A window dresser's suggestive displays fascinate a mentally disturbed man.

The Lady Forgets (1989): An amnesia victim, unable to recall the events from the last two years of her life, becomes endangered when the terrifying truth begins to resurface.

Ladyhawke (1985): A young pickpocket aids two lovers, a 13th century Spanish knight and his lady under the curse of an insanely jealous bishop.

Landslide (1992): An amnesiac geologist's search for his true identity may lead to lethal consequences.

Light Blast (1985): A San Francisco police inspector battles against time to save the city from the destructive force of a mad scientist's deadly laser weapon.

Lisa (1990): A psychotic killer responds to a teenager's prank phone calls by selecting her as his next victim.

The Lookalike (1990): A woman whose daughter perished in a car accident is driven to madness after spotting her dead child's exact look-alike.

Loose Cannons (1990): A policeman suffering from multiple personalities is teamed with a no-nonsense partner to investigate a string of pornography-related murders.

Lost Angels (1989): A rebellious teenager's acts of violence and irresponsibility land him in a less than sympathetic mental institution.

Lunatics: A Love Story (1991): A paranoid agoraphobic and a woman who attracts misfortune like a magnet meet and fall in love.

Maniac Cop (1988): Disguised as a patrolman, a killer stalks the streets of New York City.

Maniac Cop 2 (1991): A monstrous former cop joins forces with a serial killer who preys on strippers in Manhattan's Times Square district.

The Mean Season (1985): A Miami reporter becomes swept up in the media blitz when a psychopathic murderer chooses him to be his sole spokesperson.

Miami Blues (1990): A Miami detective pursues a psychotic thief who is using his stolen badge and gun to carry out a series of daring crimes.

Misery (1990): Based on Stephen King's best seller about a novelist held hostage by his psychotic "number one fan."

Mr. Frost (1990): A series of unusual events leads a British psychiatrist to re-examine an institutionalized killer who claims to be the devil.

Moon Over Parador (1988): A neurotic American actor is called on to impersonate the dead dictator of an island.

The Mosquito Coast (1986): Fed up with contemporary American life, a brilliant but unstable inventor and his family create what they hope will be their Utopia in the jungles of Central America.

Murder: By Reason of Insanity (1985): When her husband's emotional instability manifests itself in violent ways, a terrified woman begins to fear for her life.

Murder by Night (1989): An amnesiac who witnessed a brutal murder fears that he may have committed the crime.

Murder in Paradise (1990): A troubled New York cop's vacation in Hawaii is shattered when a rash of murders leads him to believe that the serial killer who eluded him on the West Coast has followed him to the Pacific.

Murderous Vision (1991): A missing persons detective teams up with a psychic when he learns that his latest quarry might have fallen victim to a psychotic serial killer.

Nightmare at Bitter Creek (1988): A group of psychotic killers turn their rage on a quartet of women enjoying a wilderness vacation with their guides.

Nightmare on Elm Street 3: Dream Warriors (1987): Institutionalized teenagers who share similar nightmares join forces to rid themselves of child-murderer Freddy Krueger's evil influence.

Night Vision (1990): Complications arise when a criminal psychopathologist learns that her partner on a homicide investigation has emotional problems of his own.

Nobody's Child (1986): Based on a true story. A Massachusetts woman triumphs over a lifetime of mental illness.

Nomads (1985): A California physician is possessed by the evil spirits of ancient tribesmen after she treats an apparently mad anthropologist.

Nuts (1987): A prostitute attempts to prove that she is mentally competent to stand trial for allegedly murdering a client in this adaptation of Tom Topor's play.

Obsession: A Taste for Fear (1989): Music by Grace Jones and Kid Creole underscores this avant-garde account of a fashion photographer whose obsession with eroticism attracts a depraved killer.

Offerings (1988): A deranged brute escapes from a mental institution to take revenge on the cruel schoolmates who sent him there 10 years ago.

Open House (1987): A series of calls to a psychologist's radio show provides police with their only link to a serial killer preying on real estate agents.

Operation: Paratrooper (1989): A rookie G.I. is forced into a bloody confrontation with his psychotic former commanding officer.

Out for Justice (1991): A streetwise New York cop juggles his relationship with the mob and his allegiance to the force during a city-wide manhunt for a psychotic thug.

Out of the Darkness (1985): Based on the true story of New York City Det. Ed Zig's year-long hunt for the "Son of Sam" killer, a psycho who targeted young lovers in parked cars.

Out on the Edge (1989): An angry and alienated 17-year-old struggles to cope with his shattered existence after being committed against his will to a behavioral treatment center.

Overboard (1987): A carpenter convinces an amnesiac millionairess that she's really his wife.

Pacific Heights (1990): A young couple's plans to turn their Victorian manor into a profitable apartment house backfires when they take on a sociopathic tenant.

Paint It Black (1989): A psychotic art collector's obsession with a sculptor takes a deadly turn when he murders the artist's lover, a conniving gallery owner.

Party Line (1988): A deranged brother and sister lure unsuspecting callers to their deaths.

The Penthouse (1989): A reunion with a high-school friend turns terrifying when a wealthy young woman is taken hostage by her mentally unstable former classmate.

The Perfect Bride (1991): A woman's suspicions take frightening shape when she discovers that her brother's picture-perfect fiancee is actually a homicidal maniac.

Phantasm II (1988): Seven years after being committed to an insane asylum, a young man picks up the trail of the sinister mortician responsible for his brother's death.

Phantom of the Opera (1990): An aspiring singer becomes an object of desire for the disfigured madman haunting the Paris Opera House.

Police Story: The Freeway Killings (1987): Metropolitan police officers deal with personal and professional dilemmas as they search Los Angeles for a homicidal maniac who stalks motorists on the freeway.

Popcorn (1991): A horror-movie marathon turns into a real-life bloodbath when a crazed killer sneaks into the theater.

Pride and Extreme Prejudice (1990): Eastern and Western agents race to locate an emotionally unstable CIA operative sent into East Germany to obtain sensitive military documents.

Promise (1986): After his mother dies, an irresponsible middle-aged bachelor fulfills a promise made 30 years before to care for his mentally disturbed brother.

Psycho III (1986): As he prepares to reopen the infamous Bates Motel, Norman is troubled by a persistent reporter, a potential romance with a would-be nun, and, of course, Mother.

Psycho IV: The Beginning (1990): Through flashbacks, mass murderer Norman Bates re-counts his life as a child, focusing on the psychological trauma inflicted upon him by his schizophrenic mother.

Rain Man (1988): A greedy young hustler develops a relationship with the brother he never knew, an autistic savant who inherited the bulk of their father's estate.

Remote Control (1987): A videotape is suspected of turning its viewers into psychopaths.

Return of Swamp Thing (1989): The evil Arcane's stepdaughter helps the comic-book monster defeat the madman before he can overrun the world with genetic mutations.

Return to Horror High (1987): A film crew is stalked by a psychotic killer while making a movie at a school infamous for a rash of murders.

Rush Week (1989): A student journalist risks her head when she picks up the trail of the ax-wielding maniac terrorizing her campus.

Saturn 3 (1990): A pair of scientists working in a space station are menaced by a mad genius and his knavish robot.

Schizo (1990): An archeologist's son and his companions encounter sinister forces at work in a haunted Yugoslavian monastery.

Schizoid (1980): A scissor-wielding maniac begins the systematic elimination of nubile young psychiatric patients.

Seven Hours to Judgment (1988): A mentally unbalanced widower devises a unique form of revenge for the judge who allowed his wife's killers to walk free.

She's Been Away (1989): An elderly woman moves in with her great nephew and his pregnant wife after the mental hospital she called home for 60 years is forced to close.

Sight Unseen (1990): A wealthy divorcee's recovery from a nervous breakdown crumbles when a detective begins questioning her about the serial killer who murdered her daughter.

Silent Night, Deadly Night 5: The Toy Maker (1991): A psychotic toy maker creates a closetful of murderous playthings led by his own puppetized son.

The Sitter (1991): A remake of the 1952 film "Don't Bother to Knock," the story of a deranged babysitter and the child in her care.

Snake Eater (1989): A Vietnam veteran heads into the bayous in pursuit of the backwoods crazies who killed his parents and kidnapped his sister.

Someone to Watch Over Me (1987): With a psychotic killer on their trail, a married Manhattan police detective falls in love with the socialite murder witness he's been assigned to protect.

Sonny Boy (1990): Psychotic foster parents fear for the worst when their cannibalistic son escapes from the box they kept him in for the past 17 years.

Sorority House Massacre 2 (1990): Comely college coeds find themselves at the mercy of a maniacal murderer.

Stepfather 2 (1989): A divorcee discovers that the man she is about to marry is a psychotic killer whose designs on her family are headed for violence.

Strange Voices (1987): A family finds it increasingly difficult to cope with the emotional effects of the eldest daughter's schizophrenia.

Sweetie (1989): An Australian woman finds her fears resurfacing following the arrival of her emotionally disturbed, domineering sister.

A Taste for Killing (1992): Two wealthy college buddies enter into a dangerous relationship with a merciless sociopath.

Terror at the Opera (1991): A rising young opera star is haunted by a maniac who wants to prove his love by butchering her friends.

Terror Stalks the Class Reunion (1992): Kidnapping and murder are part of the curriculum for a deranged student whose love for a former teacher knows no bounds.

Trapped (1989): A young businesswoman is forced to face her worst nightmare when she finds herself locked in a high-tech office building with a homicidal maniac.

Trapped in Silence (1986): A psychologist becomes emotionally involved in the case of an institutionalized non-communicative teenager.

Twisted (1985): A deadly battle of wills erupts between a sadistic adolescent and the psychotic woman his parents have hired to babysit.

Unlawful Entry (1992): A demented patrolman develops a fatal obsession for a happily married woman.

Voices Within: The Lives of Truddi Chase (1990): A young woman attempts to unravel the mystery behind the multiple personality disorder threatening to destroy her life.

Warning Sign (1985): Research scientists are turned into homicidal maniacs when a secret germ warfare experiment goes haywire.

Weep No More My Lady (1992): Suspicion falls on a wealthy businessman when his fiancee, an unstable movie star, is found murdered.

What About Bob? (1991): A pompous psychiatrist's near-sacred vacation is disrupted by the unexpected arrival of his new patient, a lovable neurotic with a talent for aggravation.

Wild at Heart (1990): David Lynch's controversial tale of an ex-con, his fiery girlfriend, and the bizarre characters they meet while fleeing from her psychotic mother through the American South.

The Wind (1987): A mystery writer is stalked by a psychotic killer on a secluded Greek island.

Without Consent (1994): A rebellious teenager's parents commit her to a private psychiatric center where patient care is often brutal.

Zelly and Me (1988): A loving nanny and a collection of stuffed animals prove to be small comfort for an emotionally unstable orphan entrusted to a domineering grandmother.

Appendix B

Television Shows
about Mental Illness

This appendix lists episodes of prime-time television series described as involving mental illness and aired since 1980. Descriptions have been taken verbatim from the television guide section of the *Washington Post*. Similar to the film listings in Appendix A, some character must have been described in the television guide summary of the program by some term or description of behavior clearly connoting mental illness—that is, by reference to a character as mentally ill, insane, unstable, mad, schizophrenic, a mental hospital patient, hearing voices, psychopathic, and so forth—in order to be included in this listing. Programs described only as dealing with alcoholism, drug abuse, or mental retardation were not included. Programs that may have involved mental illness themes but were not described as such also are not listed, including programs focused on therapy or therapists unless specific patient labels were mentioned. Television specials and daytime fare (soap operas and talk shows) are not included as well. Finally, this alphabetical listing includes only one entry per program, although many programs had numerous episodes (and television guide entries) that would have been appropriate to include.

Acapulco Heat: Marcos, Tommy, Cat, and Krissie are terrorized by a mentally disturbed man when they become stranded on an otherwise deserted island.

Adventures of Robin Hood: The mad sorcerer, Gulnar, seeks his revenge.

Against the Law (season premiere): McHeath clashes with his former father-in-law when he defends a mental patient accused of murder.

Alfred Hitchcock Presents: Two men waiting in a railroad station learn that a dangerous maniac escaped from a nearby institution.

America's Most Wanted: Stephen Eugene Harrington, a murderer who has escaped from a mental institution.

The A-Team: Following the crash of their plane in the Appalachians, the team members are stalked by a crazed band of mountain men.

The Avengers: Two scientists are kidnapped by mechanical robots programmed by a madman intent on also kidnapping an electronics expert.

Banacek: A hypochondriac requests Banacek's help after her $2.5 million computer loaded with medical information disappears from a burglar-proof building.

Baretta: Baretta learns a man he gave a second chance to has become a psychopathic criminal.

Barnaby Jones: A young woman who spent time in a mental hospital for murder becomes the prime suspect when another person is killed in a similar manner.

Barney Miller: A mad bomber threatens to turn the late shift into the last shift for Barney and his detectives.

Baywatch: A psychopathic murderer who has escaped from prison takes Stephanie and Summer hostage in a lifeguard tower.

Beauty and the Beast: A voyeur who has seen Catherine with Vincent terrorizes her with menacing phone calls.

Beverly Hills 90210: While an obsessed Emily refuses to allow Brandon to end their relationship, Dylan and Brenda pursue a new hobby together.

Birdland: Dr. McKenzie is forced to face a case of family mental illness when his nephew, a priest, is diagnosed as a schizophrenic.

Blue Skies: Zoe gets in trouble with an eccentric old woman known as the psycho lady by the local kids.

Bridges to Cross: Peter and Tracy defend a bag lady who has been victimized by devious relatives.

Broken Badges: A maverick undercover cop establishes a crime-fighting unit composed of officers removed from active duty after experiencing psychological problems.

Cagney and Lacey: Cagney and Lacey pose as prostitutes to trap a psychotic.

Charles in Charge: Charles's personality changes drastically when an accident triggers temporary amnesia.

Charlie's Angels: The Angels enter the fashion world to track down a psychotic killer who strangled several beautiful models.

Cheers: Diane fears she's being followed by a deranged actor.

China Beach: Colleen's nightmares resurface until she seeks therapy and discovers the cause of her flashbacks—post-traumatic stress syndrome.

Civil Wars: Eli considers an acting career; Sydney is taken hostage by a disturbed defendant.

Coach: Despite his team's important victory, Hayden remains depressed over his breakup with Christine.

Columbo: An unstable murder witness along with the absence of a body and murder weapon complicate a case against an American war hero.

The Commish: Tony searches for two missing police officers, undermines a drunk driver, and takes care of a man who thinks he is from another planet.

Confessions of Crime: An emotionally disturbed teen-ager kills the children she is baby-sitting.

Cops: From Tuscon, Ariz.: rescuing a baby from a deranged father.

Crossbow: Stefan fakes insanity to be committed to an asylum where he believes Tell is imprisoned.

Dallas: Relying on fellow patients, J.R. plots to leave the asylum; Bobby turns to his cyclist friends to find April; J.R. faces drug therapy.

David Susskind: Part 1: We can't stop dieting—Victims of Anorexia; Part 2: When fear takes over—Agoraphobia.

Days and Nights of Molly Dodd: Psychiatrist Janet Litchfield reveals why she no longer wants Molly as a patient.

Dear John: Club members help Mary Beth overcome depression after she loses her job.

Designing Women: Suzanne and Julia are shocked to learn that their half-brother, recently released from a mental institution, wants to be a stand-up comic.

Doogie Howser, M.D.: On Christmas Eve, Doogie gets sidetracked by a schizoid patient who thinks he's Santa Claus.

Dragnet: Friday and Gannon deal with a mentally ill man and a dying assault victim when they work out of Central Receiving Hospital.

Eischied: Eischied's efforts to locate a psychotic gunman targeting beautiful young women are hampered by interference from two competing journalists.

Empty Nest: A small kindness backfires for Harry when a neurotic woman refuses to leave him alone.

The Equalizer: A divorcee with a history of psychiatric problems tries to convince McCall that her husband is attempting to drive her insane.

Equal Justice (season premiere): Michael agrees to prosecute a man who slept with a woman without telling her he had AIDS; Briggs' eyewitness has multiple personalities.

Falcon Crest: Angela is harassed in the psychiatric ward; Richard gains custody of the children.

Family Ties: The Keatons discover that Elyse's Aunt Rosemary is suffering from Alzheimer's disease.

Flamingo Road: Lute-Mae Sanders is attacked by the emotionally disturbed son of a prominent Truro family.

48 Hours: A look at schizophrenia—in the mental hospitals and on the streets—and the efforts being made to better understand this disease.

Friday the 13th: The Series: An insane scientist works on a cure for his daughter's degenerative disease by conducting brain experiments on innocent victims.

Frontline: This look at schizophrenia includes profiles of the National Institute of Mental Health Twin Study and New York's Project Reachout.

Gabriel's Fire: An unstable young man takes Gabriel Bird and six others hostage after a failed robbery attempt.

Get Smart: CONTROL and KAOS join forces in the search for a mad scientist threatening to destroy both East and West.

The Girl from U.N.C.L.E.: April Dancer is forced to run for her life in a Mexican building when she becomes the victim of a maniac THRUSH agent.

Hagen: Hagen searches for an escaped mental patient who is accused of poisoning her roommate the same way she did her stepson years earlier.

Hardball: Kaz provides protection for a waitress who is being stalked by an ex-con, while Charlie must trail the knife-wielding psychopath.

Harry O: Harry searches for a deranged killer who is stalking the wife of a retired admiral.

Hart to Hart: An insanely jealous woman murders those she believes stand between her and her obsession—Jonathan.

The Hat Squad: The brothers track an escaped serial killer through the blind psychiatrist who has been treating him, unaware she is his next intended victim.

Hawaii Five-O: A psychotic sniper endangers the lives of motorists as he fires at cars from a hillside overlooking a major highway.

Highway to Heaven: A former Vietnam nurse suffers from post-traumatic stress disorder.

Hill Street Blues: Bates goes undercover to find a psychopath who's killing prostitutes.

The Hitchhiker: A psychotic criminal under police protection demands reconstructive facial surgery to secure a new identity.

Hotel: Christine becomes involved with a man who has multiple personalities.

House Calls: Articles begin to disappear at the hospital and it becomes clear that a kleptomaniac is at work.

Hunter: A psychotic masked killer murders a TV star.

Incredible Hulk: Banner is taken hostage by three women who [have] escaped from an institution.

In the Heat of the Night: A psychiatrist protects the name of a patient who confessed to a murder even though an innocent man is about to be executed for the crime.

Island Son: A trusted resident's procedures endanger a senator's life. Sam encounters an elderly man who is losing touch with reality.

The Jeffersons: A comedy of errors lands George in a mental hospital where he almost goes crazy trying to convince the staff he is sane.

Knight Rider: A pretty amnesia victim could help Michael prevent the assassination of a foreign head of state if he can unlock the clue from her lost memory.

Knot's Landing: Jill, locked in the throes of psychotic obsession, plans revenge against Val while establishing an alibi for herself.

Kojak: A psychotic killer terrorizes Manhattan with a series of seemingly indiscriminate murders.

Kung Fu: The Legend Continues: Kwai Chang helps a woman in a mental institution.

L.A. Law: Rollins defends a deranged ventriloquist who speaks through his dummy.

Law and Order: An obsessive fan who has been bothering a celebrity claims insanity as a defense tactic, but Stone sets out to prove the stalker is mentally competent.

The Life and Times of Eddie Roberts: Delores becomes a psychiatric patient.

Lou Grant: Charlie Hume's nephew shows up looking for a job and turns out to be a mental case shakily balanced by drugs he doesn't want to take.

MacGyver: An escaped madman plots to kill the policewoman who arrested him for murder and the psychotherapist who pronounced him sane.

Magnum, P.I.: A Vietnam veteran suffering from psychological problems murders a beautiful surfer.

A Man Called Sloane: A madman with a powerful weapon threatens to sink a freighter and its cargo of nuclear waste materials.

The Man from U.N.C.L.E.: A psychotic doctor, a beautiful astrologist, and a band of Yucatan savages send Solo and Illya into deadly THRUSH territory.

Mann and Machine: A released psychiatric patient reeks [sic] havoc in the city to even a score with Bobby.

Married with Children: Peggy is depressed when a neighborhood Peeping Tom peeps at everyone but her.

M*A*S*H: While a search goes on for a dog that bit Radar, Hawkeye defies Frank to take care of a case of hysterical paralysis.

Masterpiece Theater: The Jewel in the Crown: Merrick returns to Delhi from Pankot; Perron discovers that the Major has seen Susan's psychiatric records.

Matlock: A psychopath who blames Matlock for his brother's suicide holds the lawyer's associates hostage.

Matt Houston: A vengeful madman stops at nothing in his plan to kill Matt, including the use of C.J. as a pawn.

McCloud: McCloud investigates the murder of a rodeo star and searches for a psychotic preying on women in Central Park.

McMillan and Wife: The McMillans enlist the help of a psychiatrist to identify a psychopathic killer.

Miami Vice: A stripper with a dual personality goes on a killing spree.

Midnight Caller: Devon is stalked by a relentless psychopath and Jack may be the only one able to help.

Mrs. Columbo: A deadly game of cat and mouse unfolds as Mrs. Columbo stalks a deranged ventriloquist who believes his actions are controlled by his fiendish dummy.

Monsters: A psychotic patient at a mental hospital sculpts clay figures into which he hopes to transfer his soul.

Murder She Wrote: An old friend of Jessica's is confined to the psychiatric ward because she may have killed her husband.

Murphy's Law: Kimi is held hostage in Murphy's office by a deranged claimant.

The New Avengers: A demented genius plots to take over the world using an army of birds.

Newhart: Dick hires an unusual illustrator who's in the same sanitarium as Michael.

The New Untouchables: Capone gets a taste of his own medicine when an unstable former mistress stalks the mobster and his family.

Night Court: A paralyzing snowstorm leaves Harry stranded in the courthouse with a group of lunatics.

Nightingales: The arrival of Chris' ex-husband complicates her budding romance with Garrett; a psychotic terrorizes the hospital.

Northern Exposure: Hermit Adam's hypochondriac wife holds Joel hostage.

Perry Mason: Mason and Drake investigate the identity of a girl suffering from amnesia.

Picket Fences: After Mayor Howard Buss experiences a particularly humiliating Alzheimer's episode, Kevin Buss feels he must act to save his father's remaining dignity.

Police Story: Joe Forrester clashes with a more conservative officer in searching for a mentally ill fugitive.

Police Woman: Pepper goes undercover to search for a psychotic strangling middle-aged women.

P.O.V.: "A Season in Hell" recounts Regina Hatfield's three-year struggle with anorexia and bulimia.

Project U.F.O.: A woman takes movies of four circling blue-and-white lights she claims to have seen on two previous occasions—before being placed under psychiatric care.

Quantum Leap (season finale): In a mental institution, Sam undergoes electroshock therapy which results in his having multiple personalities—from past leaps, and Al loses contact.

Quincy: An investigation into a suspicious fire leads Quincy into the company of a disturbed pyromaniac.

Ray Bradbury Theater: A hypochondriac seeks the help of a bone specialist to cure his latest ailment.

Reasonable Doubts: Tess and Dicky differ on her handling of a mentally impaired assault suspect.

Remington Steele: An amnesiac targeted for death surprises Laura and Remington by having multiple identities and several wives.

Return of the Saint: A psychotic threatens to destroy London with strategically placed bombs unless a beautiful sculptress is publicly guillotined in Hyde Park.

Robocop: The Series: Children riot and steal as Robocop faces an unstable man who thinks he is Commander Cash, a cartoon character.

Rockford Files: Rockford, ordered to join a therapy group, tries to help a patient who claims she is receiving threats from the underworld.

St. Elsewhere: The doctors of Boston's St. Eligius Hospital search for a missing mental patient while a young resident fights to prevent a deadly operation.

Seaquest DSV: Bridger intervenes when a dictator being followed by enemies takes hostages to gain access to the ship's technology in hopes of helping his autistic son.

Secret Service: Based on the actual files from the nation's oldest law enforcement agency. Tonight: the manhunt for a psychotic would-be presidential assassin.

Seinfeld: Hypochondriac George gets advice from a "holistic" healer for his claimed heart attack.

Shannon's Deal: Jack's daughter Neala asks him to help a friend whose father has placed her in a home for the emotionally unstable.

Silk Stalkings: Chris and Rita are pulled into the life of Carrie, a young woman who suffers from multiple personality disorder.

Simon and Simon: Unaware of the danger he poses to them, A.J. and Rick are hired to accompany a mental patient to San Francisco.

The Simpsons: Homer is committed to a rest home where his roommate believes he's Michael Jackson.

Sirens: A disturbed child killer suspect exploits Molly.

Sledge Hammer: A madwoman becomes enamored with Hammer and threatens to kill Doreau unless Sledge gives in to her advances.

Soap: Corinne moves out. Burt announces the return of his schizophrenic ventriloquist son Chuck.

Something Is Out There: Jack and Tara investigate a spooky wax museum operated by the twin brother of a deranged killer.

Starsky and Hutch: Starsky and Hutch impersonate a patient and a doctor in order to unravel the mysterious deaths of patients in a mental hospital.

Star Trek: Capt. Kirk finds his brother dead and the entire population of the planet Deneva insane.

Star Trek: The Next Generation: Trapped in a Tyken's Rift with the crew slowly going insane, only Data and Troi are left to save the Enterprise.

Superboy: Pa Kent's past haunts him when a disturbed Korean war veteran blames him for his capture and torture.

Tales from the Crypt: A down-and-out journalist pursues a tip, hoping to apprehend a deranged killer.

Tattingers: Nick helps apartment dwellers deal with a disturbed neighbor.

Taxi: Latka's girlfriend from the old country is bombarded by romantic overtures from both sides of Latka's split personality.

Three's Company: Jack and Janet mistake Terri's co-worker for an escaped patient from the psycho ward.

T.J. Hooker: Stacy is in danger after she falls into the hands of an escaped madman.

Top Cops: A deranged husband sets fire to his home.

Tour of Duty: Anderson risks a court-martial when he fights to keep battle-fatigued soldiers from being returned to combat too soon; Ruiz's emotional collapse worsens.

Tracey Ullman: Sketches: A woman assaults an attacking mugger; a patient expresses her fears to her psychiatrist; lounge singers croon a tragic love song.

Trapper John, M.D.: Trapper and Gonzo try to uncover the motives behind a deranged Vietnam veteran's attack on another hospital patient.

The Trials of Rosie O'Neill: Shocked when a mentally handicapped man is found fit for trial, Rosie defends him against charges of killing a young girl.

True Blue: Geno must do his best Elvis impersonation when an unstable gun-wielding Presley fan insists on seeing the King; a traffic helicopter ditches in the Hudson.

20/20: Patty Duke talks about her fight to recover from manic-depression, her suicide attempts, her family, and the drug lithium.

Twilight Zone: Bob Wilson is flying home after a six-month convalescence from a nervous breakdown.

The Untouchables: The syndicate engages a psychotic war veteran to dispose of Ness.

Vegas: In San Francisco, Dan teams up with two policewomen to find the psychotic killer who is murdering police officers.

Werewolf: Eric feels responsible when an elderly woman is committed to an insane asylum after she reports seeing a werewolf to the police.

White Shadow: Reeves learns a new lesson in tolerance when a mainstreaming program places an autistic boy on his team.

Wild, Wild West: West is kidnapped by a madman who plans to create an underwater kingdom that will control shipping lanes.

Wings: Antonio believes he is being stalked by a sociopath when he fingers a robbery suspect.

WIOU: Hank's ex-wife arrives to write a magazine story about him; a mental patient contacts Eddie and takes his life in front of the camera.

Wiseguy: Sonny's demented nephew poses a threat to Vinnie and the Steelgrave organization.

Wonder Woman: Wonder Woman saves the world from a mad computer.

Appendix C

Novels about Mentally Ill Killers

To give readers a more complete picture of the typical content of current fiction featuring mentally ill killers, this appendix provides descriptions of fifteen selected novels. All of the novels were either published since 1985 or re-released since 1985. All appeared in paperback editions and were available at regular bookstores and newsstands. Promotional prose, plot summaries, and other information relevant to the depiction of mental illness are described for each book. These selections are clearly not an exhaustive listing of this type of novel but merely a sampling; these examples, in fact, are culled from a list of over fifty such novels I have found. Limitations of space prevent me from detailing all of these novels. It is hoped that the fifteen selected are sufficient to illustrate the common themes and features of novels in which mentally ill killers are presented as central characters.

> Mary Higgins Clark, *Loves Music, Loves to Dance* (New York: Simon & Schuster, 1991).

Not only does the killer in this novel, the "dancing shoe murderer," strangle young women he has lured through ads in the personal columns of newspapers, but he dances with them after they are dead and retains the shoes of his victims. He also sometimes keeps their bodies in a freezer until he has the opportunity to bury them on a large estate he owns. The killer is referred to as a madman and a psychopath. He functions effectively—as a psychiatrist—most of the time; he is charming, attractive, and respected. Although no specific diagnosis is offered, there is the clear suggestion that multiple personality disorder is at work here, with the crimes committed by Charlie, an alternate identity of the psychiatrist. Clark also includes mentally ill characters in other novels—a murder suspect (although an innocent one) with multiple personality disorder in *All Around the Town* (1992) and "a cunning psychopath" who kills and then photographs female victims in *A Stranger Is Watching* (1977, re-released in 1991).

Nicholas Conde, *Into the Deep Woods* (New York: St. Martin's Press, 1989).

It is estimated that the serial killer in this novel has killed and tortured twenty or thirty women, using tools that include knives, saws, drills, and screwdrivers. He is referred to on the book's cover as "psychotic," and within the novel as a "psychopath," a "wacko," a "maniac," and a "mad-dog killer." The bottom line assessment, however, is that "this kind of killer is nothing less than the embodiment of evil. . . . Pure evil." Concern is expressed that the killer might escape punishment because of his appearance of normality or because his mental illness might result in his being declared insane and put in an institution from which he might someday be released. That worry is taken care of, however, when a driven private investigator (whose own son is a captured serial killer) deliberately kills the murderer and then shoots himself.

Patricia D. Cornwell, *Body of Evidence* (New York: Avon Books, 1991).

A former mental hospital patient is the villain of this book. He has previously killed his mother and now stalks those who resemble her. Diagnoses suggested by authorities in the story include "paranoid schizophrenia," a "psychopathic mentality," "obsessive-compulsive," and "voyeur." He is also referred to as a "madman," a "psycho," a "deranged individual," a "sicko," and a "fruitcake." He is killed at the end by the heroine, whose reaction to killing him is simply: "I was not sorry I had killed him. I was sorry he had ever been born." Cornwell's other best-selling novels with hero Kay Scarpetta include *Post-Mortem* (1990), in which "medical examiner Kay Scarpetta sets out to unmask a maniac" (according to the book's back cover description), and *All That Remains* (1992), involving the search for a serial killer of young couples.

William Cross, *Cut Up* (New York: Berkley Publishing, 1993).

Carlos is an uneducated hospital worker who practices amputations on female victims. That he is mentally ill is verified not only by the description of his increasingly overwhelming hallucinations but by the colorful terms by which other characters refer to him: a "looney tune with a blown head gasket," a "nut case," a "crazy bastard," and a "sicko," who is "off the deep end." The main characters repeatedly voice their desire/intention to kill him, in part fueled by assumptions that mere capture would lead only to psychiatric treatment and release or escape: "This guy needs to have his ticket canceled. If they put him in the cashew ward, he might escape and start again." The good guys get their wish when Carlos falls onto a glass-topped table, has his own arm severed, and dies.

Robert L. Duncan, *The Serpent's Mark* (New York: St. Martin's Press, 1989).

A quote from the *San Diego Tribune* on the back cover promises readers a "deluxe model psycho tale." It goes on to describe the villain of the novel as a "madman" and as "evil incarnate." This villain begins killing people ("harvesting souls") and selects the police officer Peter Stein to bear witness to his godlike power to restore lives. He kidnaps and kills a little girl and sends Stein her severed finger, crucifies a migrant worker to attempt a resurrection, and, eventually, abducts Stein's wife and child to crucify and resurrect the boy. When Stein catches the killer, he kills him, with "no feeling at all for this son of a bitch."

James Ellroy, *Blood on the Moon* (New York: Avon Books, 1984).

"A brilliant detective and a mysterious psychopath . . . come together in a final dance of death," according to a *New York Times* review quoted on the cover. The mysterious psychopath is Teddy Verplanck, a young man who stalks and kills women who remind him of a girl who betrayed him in high school. The novel tells readers that he has killed more than twenty young women, and, as the novel progresses, his killings become more frequent and more vicious, involving mutilation, dismemberment, and immersion in the blood and viscera of his victims. The killer is referred to as insane and crazy, but, apart from the designation of "psychopath" on the front cover, no specific diagnosis is given. Verplanck is killed at the end in a climactic battle with the novel's detective hero.

Thomas Harris, *Red Dragon* (New York: Dell Publishing, 1981; re-released in 1992 following the success of the film *The Silence of the Lambs*).

Francis Dolarhyde kills whole families in gruesome ways, mutilating the bodies of adult females. He is at first known to the police and the press as "The Tooth Fairy" because of the bite marks he leaves on the bodies. He is fascinated by a painting called *The Great Red Dragon and the Woman Clothed with the Sun*, kills people as part of his "becoming," and eventually is directed by voices from the Red Dragon in the painting. He is referred to by various people (authority figures such as policemen and psychiatrists) as a psychopath, a madman, and simply "crazy." The novel also contains a secondary villain who is mentally ill, Dr. Hannibal Lecter, a serial murderer confined in the Chesapeake Hospital for the Criminally Insane. The reader is informed that Dr. Lecter, a psychiatrist, killed nine people and severely injured three others primarily "because he liked it." Lecter appears again in Harris's *Silence of the Lambs* (1988) along with a psychotic killer, Jame Gumb, referred to as "Buffalo Bill" because he skins his young female victims.

James Neal Harvey, *By Reason of Insanity* (New York: St. Martin's Press, 1990).

The back cover description assures prospective readers of two of the basic elements of serial killer novels: "A Psychopathic Killer. Beautiful Young Victims." Boyishly good-looking yuppie Peter Barrows is an advertising manager who dabbles in photography. He also kills young women and then poses and photographs them. His hatred of women is expressed by savagely biting his victims (in the buttocks after killing them). Readers are informed that Barrows was treated in a psychiatric hospital on four occasions and diagnosed as suffering from a cyclothymic disorder. A jumble of other diagnoses are offered as well. A police psychiatrist suggests, for example: "He's subject to manic-depressive mood swings. That's paranoia, of course. And he's very schizophrenic." When Barrows is killed at the end by a police officer, that officer's only thoughts are: "You rotten bastard. I wish you'd had more time to suffer." The mentally ill villain of Harvey's *Painted Ladies* (1992) suffers a similar fate, when the police officer hero of that novel puts his gun into the killer's mouth and pulls the trigger to ensure that he will not escape with an insanity plea.

William Heffernan, *Ritual* (New York: New American Library, 1988).

Browsers who get no further than examination of the cover of this novel will know that "this chilling, edge-of-the-seat thriller follows the bloody trail of a madman as he creeps in the street shadows, waiting to stalk his next female victim for a sacrifice to a bloodthirsty god. . . ." The killer in this novel is also the veteran police officer in charge of the case, Stanislaus Rolk, who fifteen years ago killed his own wife and son. There is little explanation provided for Rolk's murderous actions, in the past or present, other than the suggestion of a multiple personality. Less formal diagnoses offered include a "maniac," a "psychopath who has a deep hatred of women," a "severely disturbed psychotic," or merely a "sick mother." At the end, Rolk is killed by another detective to spare him the shame of a trial and the "years and years in a mental institution" he would have to endure. The same detective confronts and kills another "maniac" in a follow-up novel, *Blood Rose* (1991).

Herbert Lieberman, *Shadow Dancers* (New York: St. Martin's Press, 1989).

The "ghoulish madman [who] stalks the women of New York" in this novel is yet another fictional sufferer of multiple personality disorder. In both personalities he rapes and kills innocent victims (women) in similar ways, leaving bite marks on victims' bodies and cryptic numerical messages nearby. The combined body count is well over a dozen. The confusing array of labels for the killer(s) includes "nut cases," someone who "isn't in his right mind," "borderline autistic," "demented," and simply "crazy . . . fucking crazy." When faced with capture, the killer throws himself into a river and drowns.

Edward Mathis, *Only When She Cries* (New York: Berkley Books, 1989).

The first glimpse the reader has of this novel's killer, Spenser Price, is as a child entering his parents' room with two bloody kittens and announcing gleefully, "I squished them." Soon Price graduates to raping and murdering young women because he finds it exciting and enjoyable, especially when they cry. Price manages to blend in well with society, even becoming a trusted police officer. To confuse investigators, he imitates the killings of an escaped psychiatric patient named Julian Arrowstone, who is described as a "god-damned psycho who'd killed maybe twenty-five, twenty-six girls." Many different diagnoses are offered for Price and Arrowstone, including "psychos," "incurable psychopath," and "dissociative reaction (split personality)." Price and Arrowstone are both killed, just as the detective hero has pledged: "Your run is over, animal! Wherever you are, I'll find you! Wherever you go, I'll hound you until you are dead, dead, dead!"

Rex Miller, *Chaingang* (New York: Simon & Schuster, 1992).

Daniel Edward Flowers Bunkowski is six foot seven inches tall and weighs over four hundred pounds. His nickname is Chaingang because of the heavy chain he likes to use as a weapon. His history includes being a battered and molested child, institutionalization for nearly half his life, and rescue from imprisonment by the U.S. government to become a trained killer in Vietnam. Now he is a conscienceless murderer who kills for the pleasure it gives him. He is driven to kill, sometimes to torture and mutilate his victims and occasionally to rip out their hearts and eat them. He is diagnosed as schizophrenic, but also referred to simply as a "lunatic killer," a "maniac," and even an "insane piece of shit." At the same time he is described as cunning and resourceful, with an almost instinctual sense of how to pick out victims, to avoid capture, and to appear normal. Chaingang appears in a series of Miller novels, including *Slob* (1987), *Slice* (1990), *Savant* (1994), and *Butcher* (1994).

Ridley Pearson, *Probable Cause* (New York: St. Martin's Press, 1989).

This novel borrows liberally from other psycho-killer fare. The killer, like *Psycho*'s Norman Bates, is a former mental hospital patient who manages a motel. One room of the motel is sealed and rigged to suffocate selected victims by infusion of carbon dioxide into the room. The reader is informed that the murderer is thoughtful, clever, and patient and that he takes pleasure in "trapping" and asphyxiating animals and humans. He is also described as a "psychopath," "criminally insane," and a "madman." When he is finally captured, he shoots himself rather than be sent back to a prison or hospital. A second mentally ill character in the book is the mental hospital patient whose style of killing is being imitated. This patient is a convicted murderer in Atascadero State Mental Hospital with whom the investigator bargains for clues about who may be imitating his killings. Like Hannibal Lecter, this "homicidal psychotic" is shrewd, manipulative, and ruthless, is kept under rigorous confinement, and is inclined to bite people if he can lure them close enough to him. As in *The Silence of the Lambs*, he escapes at the end of the novel. Other novels by Pearson that showcase mentally ill killers include *Hidden Charges* (1987), in which a former mental hospital patient tries to blow up a shopping mall, and *The Angel Maker* (1993), which features a "homicidal maniac" veterinarian.

Jeff Raines, *Unbalanced Acts* (New York: Avon Books, 1990).

A veritable smorgasbord of psychopathology is presented in this novel, in which a terrorist kidnaps twelve patients from the fictional New York State Prison for the Criminally Insane and threatens to turn them loose on the streets of New York City. Three patients are labeled "hebephrenic schizophrenics"; one of them has "murdered fifteen teenagers with an assault rifle" and the other two have followed hallucinatory commands to kill all tourists and Jews. Another patient is described as "seven feet one inches tall and suffering from paranoid schizophrenia. He felt short people were out to get him. . . . One day he came out with a sledgehammer and killed seven people, including one man who was six foot two." Four patients are characterized as "masked schizophrenics"; they also have killed many people, including children, patients in hospitals, and young women. The remaining four are labeled "psychopaths." They include a doctor whose unorthodox medical experiments left body parts scattered around his house, a literal ladykiller whose victims number fifteen or more, a young woman who has accumulated a collection of penises from her victims, and an insurance salesman who murdered families so that it would be easier to persuade neighbors to buy life insurance.

John Sandford, *Rules of Prey* (New York: Berkley Books, 1989).

"Mad but brilliant" is how the killer in this novel is characterized. Referred to throughout the book as the "maddog," he works as an attorney, plans his murders carefully, and follows a set of rules so as not to get caught. He strikes only at women and, as the novel progresses, his crimes become more and more violent, involving torture and mutilation as well as rape and murder. Very little information is given about the killer's background except that his father was often absent or busy, that his mother "never contributed," and that childhood experiences killing animals led to a confusion of sexual excitement with killing excitement. When the killer is finally captured and brags that he will plead insanity and spend only a few years at a state hospital, the detective involved proceeds to kill the unarmed and injured murderer without remorse. So successful has Sandford been in creating suspense with mentally ill killers that his detective has been able to pursue his elimination of disturbed villains in *Shadow Prey* (1990), *Eyes of Prey* (1991), *Silent Prey* (1992), and *Winter Prey* (1993).

Notes

Chapter One   Madness, Madness Everywhere

1. Richard Perez-Pena, "After 20 Years of False Identities, Man Admits 3 Killings," *New York Times*, March 10, 1994; Janny Scott, "Doctors Doubt Multiple Personalities Can Hide Killings from One Another," *New York Times*, March 11, 1994.
2. "Health Coverage for the Mentally Ill," letter to the editor, *Washington Post*, March 29, 1994.
3. Robert Wood Johnson Foundation, "Public Attitudes toward People with Chronic Mental Illness," April 15, 1990.
4. Michael Fleming and Roger Manvell, *Images of Madness: The Portrayal of Insanity in the Feature Film* (Cranbury, N.J.: Associated University Presses, 1985).
5. Alan G. Frank, *Horror Movies* (Hong Kong: Cathay Books, 1974).
6. Ibid., 127.
7. See Appendix A for a listing of the films described in the *Washington Post* television guide.
8. Keith Byrd and Timothy R. Elliott, "Feature Films and Disability: A Descriptive Study," *Rehabilitation Psychology* 30 (1985): 47–51.
9. *Entertainment Weekly*, March 16, 1990.
10. Ibid., February 8, 1991.
11. Otto F. Wahl and Rachel Roth, "Television Images of Mental Illness: Results of a Metropolitan Washington Media Watch," *Journal of Broadcasting* 26 (1982): 599–605.
12. We also excluded mental retardation and substance abuse unless the latter were the primary focus of the program. Thus an addict who is used by the police as an informant but plays no other role in the program would not have been counted.
13. George Gerbner, "Dreams That Hurt: Mental Illness in the Mass Media," in *The Community Imperative*, ed. Richard Baron, Irving Rutman, and Barbara Klaczynska (Philadelphia: Horizon House Institute, 1980; George Gerbner, "Dreams That Hurt: Mental Illness in the Mass Media," *Proceedings of the First International Rosalynn Carter Symposium on Mental Health Policy: Stigma and the Mentally Ill* (Atlanta, Ga.: Carter Center, 1985); Nancy Signorelli, "The Stigma of Mental Illness on Television," *Journal of Broadcasting and Electronic Media* 33 (1989): 325–331.
14. Suzy Kalter, *The Complete Book of M*A*S*H* (New York: Henry N. Abrams, 1984).

15. Mary B. Cassata, Thomas D. Skill, and Samuel O. Boadu, "In Sickness and in Health," *Journal of Communication* 29 (1979): 73–80.
16. Laurel Fruth and Allan Padderud, "Portrayals of Mental Illness in Daytime Television Serials," *Journalism Quarterly* 63 (1985): 384–387+.
17. A more complete listing of television program descriptions from the *Washington Post* television guide that suggest mental illness themes is provided in Appendix B.
18. *Entertainment Weekly*, April 29, 1994.
19. Otto F. Wahl and Arthur L. Kaye, "Mental Illness Topics in Popular Periodicals," *Community Mental Health Journal* 28 (1992): 21–28.
20. Still other examples of current popular fiction can be found in Appendix C.
21. From the album "Disney's Silly Songs." Walt Disney Records.
22. Helen Reddy, "Delta Dawn." From the album "Helen Reddy's Greatest Hits." RCA Music.
23. David Bowie, "All the Madmen." From the album "The Man Who Sold the World." RCA Records.
24. Stephen Sondheim, "You Could Drive a Person Crazy." From "Side by Side by Sondheim." RCA Limited.
25. Napoleon XIV, "They're Coming to Take Me Away." From the album "Demento's 20th Anniversary Collection: The Greatest Novelty Records of All Times." Altenburgh Records.
26. Metal Church, "Of Unsound Mind." From the album "Blessing in Disguise." Elektra Entertainment.
27. Billy Joel, "You May Be Right." From "Billy Joel's Greatest Hits." Columbia Records/CBS, Inc.
28. The 1991 *Phonolog Reporter* (self-described as "the recognized Encyclopedia of the Record Industry . . . a comprehensive listing of currently available recordings") lists 136 popular songs beginning with the word "crazy" and 19 recordings with the single title "Crazy." It also lists 18 songs with "psycho" or "psychotic" in the title, 6 with "maniac," and several with title terms such as "lunatic," "schizo" or "schizophrenic."
29. George Gerbner and Percy Tannenbaum, "Regulation of Mental Illness Content in Motion Pictures and Television," *Gazette* 6 (1960): 365–385.

Chapter Two   Words and Laughter

1. Serge Schmemann, "Schizophrenia and Transition in a New City," *New York Times*, February 25, 1990.
2. "Defense Cuts: Not in My Backyard," *Time*, August 6, 1990, 13.
3. "Schizophrenic Environmental Policy," *Finger Lakes Times*, February 14, 1990.
4. Robin Abcarian, "Cereal Schizophrenia Strikes at Grocery Store," *Herald Journal* (Syracuse, N.Y.). February 19, 1990.
5. "Poll Finds Americans Have Schizophrenic Views of the Rich," *Rochester Democrat and Chronicle*, October 22, 1990.
6. "Reformers Now Seek an Antidote for the Navy's Schizophrenia," *Kansas City Star*, August 28, 1992. The confusion of schizophrenia with split personality was even clearer in the article's text: " 'Multiple personality,' " it begins, "is how schizophrenia is defined, a term that illuminates one of the major problems facing the U.S. Navy today."
7. Rob Parker, "Schizophreknicks: MacLeod Looking to Shake Funk," *New York Daily News*, January 21, 1991.
8. Sixty-two percent of lay respondents to a survey about schizophrenia rated multiple personality as a common or very common symptom of schizophrenia. Otto F.

Wahl, "Public vs. Professional Conceptions of Schizophrenia," *Journal of Community Psychology* 13 (1987): 285–291.

9. Bruce Weber, "Cozying Up to the Psychopath That Lurks Deep Within," *New York Times*, February 10, 1991.

10. American Psychiatric Association, *Diagnostic and Statistical Manual of Mental Disorders*, 4th ed. (Washington, D.C.: American Psychiatric Association, 1994).

11. Ibid., 645.

12. It is possible for serial killers to be psychotic. However, they are usually, then, not psychopathic. These individuals kill because of delusions that make them feel threatened, hallucinations that command them, and so forth. But their crimes are typically poorly planned and carried out in a disorganized fashion, according to Robert Ressler and Tom Schachtman, authors of *Whoever Fights Monsters* (New York: St. Martin's Press, 1992). Their breakdowns and poor functioning, moreover, is very evident; it is likely that many people in their lives have identified them as poorly functioning even before their crimes are known.

13. Appendix C summarizes fifteen novels involving mentally ill killers. Most fit the pattern described, presenting characters with an unreal blend of psychopathic and psychotic features.

14. Robert Ressler and Tom Schactman, *Whoever Fights Monsters* (New York: St. Martin's Press, 1992), 20.

15. It should be acknowledged here that some of the confusion in terminology comes from confusion within the field of psychiatry. The official U.S. guide to diagnostic classification of mental disorders, *DSM-IV*, for example, states that "no definition adequately specifies precise boundaries for the concept of 'mental disorder' " (p. xxi). In addition, although most clinicians would strongly agree that differentiation between mental illness and mental retardation is appropriate and necessary, *DSM-IV* does include mental retardation in its classification of "mental disorders."

16. Tori DeAngelis, "Experts See Little Impact from Insanity Plea Ruling," *APA Monitor*, June 1994, 28.

17. Unfortunately, it is often the case that mental health professionals are as careless with psychiatric labels as media professionals. References to "depressives" and "phobics" and "schizophrenics" remain common in professional discussions and even professional writings.

18. Brigitte Goldstein, "Television's Portrayal of the Mentally Ill," in *Understanding Mass Communication*, 3rd ed., by Melvin L. LaFleur and Everette E. Dennis (Boston: Houghton Mifflin, 1988).

19. See Appendices A and B for other program and film descriptions that demonstrate this trend.

20. Lynn Darling, "City as Psych Ward: Four Crazoids Hit the Streets," *Newsday*,. April 7, 1989.

21. David Edelstein, "Psycho-Slapstick to Sleep By," *New York Post*, April 7, 1989.

22. "Outrage at Harmless Ad Is, Well, Crazy," *Staten Island Advance*, April 5, 1992.

23. John Hinckley, Sr., founder of the American Mental Health Fund, a mental health advocacy and education organization, is one person who has asserted that he would like to see the day when "crazy" is as unacceptable a word in public speech as "nigger."

24. *Staten Island Advance*, April 20, 1992.

25. University of Missouri–Columbia Multicultural Management Program, *Dictionary of Cautionary Words and Phrases* (Columbia: University of Missouri, 1989).

26. David O'Reilly, "Hussein: America's Villain of the Month," *Glens Falls Post Star*, August 19, 1990. Additional labeling noted in this article included "makes the Ayatolla look sane" (Jay Leno), "a Middle East madman" (David Letterman), and "unstable and untrustworthy . . . a madman (Akron *Beacon Journal*). Even song

parodies reportedly rendered psychiatric diagnoses: "Hussein is crazy, ooh, ooh. So call his bluff, ooh, ooh. Hussein is crazy, and things could really get rough, ooh, ooh." Tony Rogers, "Radio Crackles with Saddam Song Parodies," *Glens Falls Post Star*, August 19, 1990.

27. Gerald Lieberman, *3,500 Good Jokes for Speakers* (New York: Doubleday & Company, 1975).
28. Michael J. Shannon, *Still More Jokes* (Chicago: Children's Press, 1986).
29. Darling, "City as Psych Ward."
30. *Staten Island Advance*, April 20, 1992.
31. Joseph P. Shapiro, *No Pity* (New York: Times Books, 1993), 37.

Chapter Three   A Breed Apart

1. Jum C. Nunnally, "The Communication of Mental Health Information: A Comparison of the Opinions of Experts and the Public with Mass Media Presentations," *Behavioral Science* 2 (1957): 229.
2. Ted Sennet, *Masters of Menace: Greenstreet and Lorre* (New York: E. P. Dutton, 1976), 43.
3. Ibid., 165–166.
4. Peter John Dryer, "Fugitive from Murder," *Sight and Sound* (Summer 1964): 127.
5. Philip Kemp, *International Dictionary of Film and Filmmakers*, vol. 3 (Chicago: St. James Press, 1986), 389.
6. "Actors with Dirty Faces," *Time*, January 21, 1991.
7. Otto F. Wahl and Rachel Roth, "Television Images of Mental Illness: Results of a Metropolitan Washington Media Watch," *Journal of Broadcasting* 26 (1982): 599–605.
8. Nancy Signorelli, "The Stigma of Mental Illness on Television," *Journal of Broadcasting and Electronic Media* 33 (1989): 325–331.
9. Laurel Fruth and Allan Padderud, "Portrayals of Mental Illness in Daytime Television Serials," *Journalism Quarterly* 62 (1985): 384–387+.
10. Again it must be acknowledged that mental health professionals and advocates are also prone to this usage. Reference to people with mental illnesses or to individuals with psychiatric disorders is clearly more cumbersome than "the mentally ill." In addition, it is only recently that people in the field have given extensive thought to the implications of this terminology. Thus the shorter designation, "the mentally ill" has been widely used for many years and continues to be used, either out of continued lack of awareness of its unwanted implications or simply because of the difficulty of changing long-standing habits of speech. One of the leading mental health advocacy organizations in the United States, known for its passionate and tireless efforts on behalf of individuals with mental illnesses, is the National Alliance for the Mentally Ill (NAMI), an organizational title they are reluctant to change simply because they are so widely known by that name.
11. Within the larger movement to expand the rights and respect accorded to those with disabilities—the disability rights movement—is a clear call to "put people first," both in the way we think about and in the way we speak about those with disabilities. The first word, they argue, should be "people," as in "*people* with disabilities."
12. "Deadly Smoke," *Time*, November 22, 1982.
13. *Entertainment Weekly*, October 26, 1990, 24.
14. "Schizophrenic Writes Nuclear Weapons Article," *The Olympian* (Wash.), December 10, 1993. The officer reportedly also added, "You can't tell on the telephone." One wonders whether the officer is suggesting that, in person, the patient's distinctive appearance would have given him away more quickly.

15. Stacie Larson, "Schizophrenia Is Treatable," letter to the editor published in *The Olympian* (Wash.), December 25, 1993.

16. Thomas Harris, *Red Dragon* (New York: Dell Publishing, 1981), 54.

17. Rex Miller, *Slice* (New York: Penguin Books, 1990), 74.

18. Ibid., 289.

19. Ibid., 308.

20. Ibid., 290.

21. Shane Stevens, *By Reason of Insanity* (New York: Dell Publishing, 1979), 45.

22. Ann V. Bolinger, "Monster Masked as a Human Being," *New York Post*, April 22, 1994.

23. Thomas Rockwell, *How to Eat Fried Worms* (New York: Dell Publishing, 1973), 20.

24. Lee N. Robins, John E. Helzer, Myrna M. Weissman, Helen Orvaschel, Ernest Gruenberg, Jack D. Burke, and Darrel A. Reiger, "Lifetime Prevalence of Specific Psychiatric Disorders in Three Sites," *Archives of General Psychiatry* 41 (1984): 949–958.

25. Carlos Baker, *Ernest Hemingway: A Life Story* (New York: Scribner, 1969).

26. Buzz Aldrin and Wayne Warga, *Return to Earth* (New York: Random House, 1973).

27. Alexander Walker, *Vivien: The Life of Vivien Leigh* (New York: Weidenfeld & Nicolson, 1987).

28. Dick Schaap, "How Lionel Aldridge Defeated Mental Illness," *Parade*, March 1, 1987.

29. Robert Wallace, *The World of Van Gogh* (New York: Time-Life Books, 1969).

30. Katherine Spitz and Robin Witek, "The Odyssey of Fred Frese," *Beacon Journal* (Akron, Ohio), March 6, 1994.

31. Sylvia Nasr, "The Lost Years of a Nobel Laureate," *New York Times*, November 13, 1994.

32. Susanna Kaysen, *Girl, Interrupted* (New York: Vintage Books, 1993).

33. William Styron, "Why Primo Levi Need Not Have Died," *New York Times*, December 19, 1988.

34. Aldrin and Warga, *Return to Earth*, 284.

35. Jane Hillyard, "Reluctantly Told," in *The Inner World of Mental Illness*, ed. Bert Kaplan (New York: Harper & Row, 1964), 160.

36. Lara Jefferson, "I Am Crazy Wild This Minute. How Can I Learn to Think Straight?" In Kaplan, *Inner World*, 5–6.

37. Amanda Bennett, "Back from Hell," *Wall Street Journal*, October 14, 1992.

38. Susan Sheehan, *Is There No Place on Earth for Me?* (Boston: Houghton Mifflin, 1982), 112.

Chapter Four   Murder and Mayhem

1. Appendix A provides a list of films, released since 1985, described as involving mental illness. Readers will find that, in the majority of these, the mentally ill character is a villain or killer or both.

2. Further examples can be found in Appendix B, which provides verbatim television guide descriptions from the *Washington Post*.

3. John Sandford, *Rules of Prey* (New York: Berkley Books, 1989); Sandford, *Shadow Prey* (New York: Berkley Books, 1990); Sandford, *Eyes of Prey* (New York: Berkley Books, 1991); Sandford, *Silent Prey* (New York: Berkley Books, 1992); Sandford, *Winter Prey* (New York: Berkley Books, 1993).

4. Thomas Harris, *Black Sunday* (New York: Dell Publishing, 1975); Harris, *Red Dragon* (New York: Dell Publishing, 1981); Harris, *The Silence of the Lambs* (New York: St. Martin's Press, 1988).

5. Mary Higgins Clark, *Loves Music, Loves to Dance* (New York: Simon & Schuster, 1991).
6. Patricia D. Cornwell, *Post-Mortem* (New York: Avon Books, 1990); Cornwell, *Body of Evidence* (New York: Avon Books, 1991).
7. Ira Levin, *Sliver* (New York: Bantam Books, 1991).
8. Appendix C contains more examples of novels that feature mentally ill killers, along with descriptions of the plots of each.
9. James Ellroy, *Blood on the Moon* (New York: Avon Books, 1984).
10. Gary Paulson, *Night Rituals* (New York: Bantam Books, 1989).
11. Rosamond Smith, *Soul Mate* (New York: Penguin Books, 1989).
12. William Heffernan, *Ritual* (New York: New American Library, 1988).
13. Gene Lazuta, *Bleeder* (New York: Berkley Publishing Group, 1991).
14. Harris, *The Silence of the Lambs*.
15. Kevin Eastman and Peter Laird, *Teenage Mutant Ninja Turtles First Graphic Novel Number Nine* (Chicago: First Comics, 1986).
16. Shel Silverstein, *Uncle Shelby's ABZ Book* (New York: Simon & Schuster, 1961).
17. Ugly Kid Joe, "Madman." From the album "America's Least Wanted." Stardog Records.
18. Metal Church, "Psycho." From the album "The Dark." Elektra Entertainment.
19. GeTo Boys, "Mind of a Lunatic." From the album "Grip It! On That Other Level." Def American Recordings.
20. George Gerbner, "Women and Minorities on Television: A Study in Casting and Fate," in *Report to the Screen Actors Guild and the American Federation of Radio and Television Artists*, June 1993.
21. Otto F. Wahl and Rachel Roth, "Television Images of Mental Illness: Results of a Metropolitan Washington Media Watch," *Journal of Broadcasting* 26 (1982): 599–605.
22. Nancy Signorelli, "The Stigma of Mental Illness on Television," *Journal of Broadcasting and Electronic Media* 33 (1989): 325–331.
23. George Gerbner, "Dreams That Hurt: Mental Illness in the Mass Media," in *Proceedings of the First Annual Rosalynn Carter Symposium on Mental Health Policy* (Atlanta, Ga.: Carter Center, 1985), 8–13.
24. Laurel Fruth and Allan Padderud, "Portrayals of Mental Illness in Daytime Television Serials," *Journalism Quarterly* 62 (1985): 384–387+.
25. Signorelli, "Stigma of Mental Illness on Television."
26. George Gerbner, "Dreams That Hurt: Mental Illness in the Mass Media," in *The Community Imperative*, ed. Richard Baron, Irving Rutman, and Barbara Klaczynska (Philadelphia: Horizon House Institute, 1980), 19–23.
27. Russell F. Shain and Julie Phillips, "The Stigma of Mental Illness: Labeling and Stereotyping in the News," in *Risky Business: Communicating Issues of Science, Risk, and Public Policy*, ed. L. Wilkins and P. Patterson (Westport, Conn.: Greenwood Press, 1991), 61–74.
28. David M. Day and Stewart Page, "Portrayal of Mental Illness in Canadian Newspapers," *Canadian Journal of Psychiatry* 31 (1986): 813–816.
29. Michael Fleming and Roger Manvell, *Images of Madness: The Portrayal of Insanity in the Feature Film* (Cranbury, N.J.: Associated University Presses, 1985), 89.
30. Ellroy, *Blood on the Moon*, 129.
31. Edward Mathis, *Only When She Cries* (New York: Berkley Books, 1989), 47.
32. Ibid., 190.
33. Ibid.
34. Pamela Kalbfleisch, "The Portrayal of the Killer in Society: A Comparison Study," research paper, Department of Communication, Michigan State University, 1979.
35. Fleming and Manvell, *Images of Madness*, 89.

36. Brigitte Goldstein, "Television's Portrayals of the Mentally Ill," M.A. thesis, University of New Mexico, 1980.

37. Melvin L. DeFleur and Everette E. Dennis, *Understanding Mass Communications* (Boston: Houghton Mifflin, 1981), 583.

38. Gerbner, "Dreams That Hurt," 1980.

39. Fleming and Manvell, *Images of Madness*, 89.

40. Robert Duncan, *The Serpent's Mark* (New York: St. Martin's Press, 1989).

41. Bruce Weber, "Cozying Up to the Psychopath That Lurks Deep Within," *New York Times*, February 10, 1991.

42. Elieba Levine, *Double Jeopardy* (New York: Windsor Publishing, 1990), 51.

43. Cornwell, *Post-Mortem*, 38.

44. Robert B. Parker, *Crimson Joy* (New York: Dell Publishing, 1988), 285.

45. Gerbner, "Dreams That Hurt," 1980.

46. Paulsen, *Night Rituals*, 214.

47. Ibid., 238.

48. Mathis, *Only When She Cries*, 248.

49. Rex Miller, *Slob* (New York: Penguin Books, 1989).

50. Sandford, *Rules of Prey*, 348.

51. Duncan, *The Serpent's Mark*, 1989.

52. One of the major problems in arriving at definitive conclusions involves the differing ways studies have defined and measured dangerousness. Some have used post-hospitalization arrest records, some records of in-hospital assault, and others self-reported acts of aggression by those in the community. Moreover, each of these measures may not reflect the kind of intense, injurious acts the public associates with the term "violence." Studies using post-hospitalization arrest records, for example, sometimes have not excluded the minor charges (loitering, trespassing) that are increasingly used to get people with mental illnesses off the streets. Some hospital "assaults" involve little more than shoving someone in a crowded lunchroom and verbal as well as physical altercations. Self-reported violence might include throwing objects at someone else or bruising a child with a hard spanking. Such acts, while clearly unacceptable, are nevertheless not the random savagery one might infer from the term "violence."

53. Eric Silver, Carmen Cirincione, and Henry J. Steadman, "Demythologizing Inaccurate Perceptions of the Insanity Defense," *Law and Human Behavior* 18 (1994): 63–70.

54. Jeffrey W. Swanson, Charles E. Holzer, Vijay K. Ganju, and Robert Tsutomu Jono, "Violence and Psychiatric Disorder in the Community: Evidence from the Epidemiologic Catchment Area Surveys," *Hospital and Community Psychiatry* 41 (1990): 761–770; Bruce Link, Howard Andrews, and Francis T. Cullen, "The Violent and Illegal Behavior of Mental Patients Reconsidered," *American Sociological Review* 57 (1992): 275–292; Menachem Krakowski, J. Jaeger, and Jan Volavka, "Violence and Psychopathology: A Longitudinal Study," *Comprehensive Psychiatry* 29 (1988): 174–181.

55. This is in contrast to the findings of earlier studies. Studies from the 1960s and 1970s tended to find ex-patients to be *less* likely than other members of the general population to be involved in crimes or violent actions following their hospital discharges. When mental health advocates assert, as they still sometimes do, that research shows ex-patients to be no more dangerous than nonpatients, they are probably, if mistakenly, using this earlier data.

56. Sometimes mental illness may even *lower* the potential for violence. Menachem Krakowski, Jan Volavka, and David Brizer point out ("Psychopathology and Violence: A Review of the Literature," *Comprehensive Psychiatry* 27 [1986]: 131–148): "The successful carrying out of certain assaultive acts . . . requires a certain degree of

intact functioning not compatible with the severe impairment found in disorganized psychotic states."

57. John Monahan, "Mental Disorder and Violent Behavior: Perceptions and Evidence," *American Psychologist* 47 (1992): 511–521.

58. Ibid., 519.

59. John Monahan, "The Prediction of Violent Behavior: Developments in Psychology and Law," in *The Master Lecture Series: Psychology and the Law*, ed. C. J. Scheire and D. L. Hammond (Washington, D.C.: American Psychological Association, 1983).

60. Monahan, "Mental Disorder and Violent Behavior," 519.

61. Linda Teplin, Karen M. Abram, and G. M. McClelland, "Does Psychiatric Disorder Predict Violent Crime among Released Jail Detainees? A Six-Year Longitudinal Study," *American Psychologist* 49 (1994): 335–342.

62. Monahan, "Mental Disorder and Violent Behavior," 519.

63. Saleem A. Shah, "Violence and the Mentally Ill," *Journal of the California Alliance for the Mentally Ill* 2 (Fall 1990): 20–21.

64. Kenneth Tardiff, "Patterns and Major Determinants of Homicide in the United States," *Hospital and Community Psychiatry* 36 (1985): 632–639.

65. Insanity Defense Work Group, "American Psychiatric Association Statement on the Insanity Defense," *American Journal of Psychiatry* 140 (1983): 681–688.

66. Silver, Cirincione, and Steadman, "Demythologizing Inaccurate Perceptions."

67. Sanford Sherizan, "Social Creation of Crime News: All the News That's Fitted to Print," in *Deviance and Mass Media*, ed. Charles Winick (Beverly Hills, Calif.: Sage Publications, 1978), 206.

68. Peter Carlson, "The American Way of Murder," *Washington Post Magazine*, June 19, 1994, 13.

Chapter Five   So What?

1. Robert Wood Johnson Foundation, "Public Attitudes toward People with Chronic Mental Illness," April 15, 1990.

2. Otto F. Wahl, "Six TV Myths about Mental Illness," *TV Guide*, March 13, 1976, 4–8.

3. Jum Nunnally, "The Communication of Mental Health Information: A Comparison of the Opinions of Experts and the Public with Mass Media Presentations," *Behavioral Science* 2 (1957): 222–230.

4. Thomas J. Scheff, "Social Support for Stereotypes of Mental Disorder," *Mental Hygiene* 47 (1963): 461–469.

5. Otto F. Wahl, "Public vs. Professional Conceptions of Schizophrenia," *Journal of Community Psychology* 15 (1987): 285–291.

6. Eric Silver, Carmen Cirincione, and Henry J. Steadman, "Demythologizing Inaccurate Perceptions of the Insanity Defense," *Law and Human Behavior* 18 (1994): 63–70.

7. Otto F. Wahl, "Post-Hinckley Views of the Insanity Defense," *American Journal of Forensic Psychology* 8 (1990): 3–11.

8. That code also includes a provision stating: "Special precautions must be taken to avoid demeaning or ridiculing members of the audience who suffer from physical or mental afflictions or deformities."

9. Lori Schiller and Amanda Bennett, *The Quiet Room* (New York: Warner Books, 1994), 74.

10. Robert P. Snow, *Creating Media Culture* (Beverly Hills, Calif.: Sage Publications, 1983), 9.

11. George Gerbner, Larry Gross, Michael Morgan, and Nancy Signorelli, "The 'Main-

streaming' of America: Violence Profile No. 11," *Journal of Communication* 30 (1980): 10–29.

12. Ibid.

13. National Institute of Mental Health, *Television and Behavior: Ten Years of Scientific Progress and Implications for the Eighties* (Washington, D.C.: U.S. Government Printing Office, 1982).

14. Snow, *Creating Media Culture*, 166.

15. Otto F. Wahl and John Y. Lefkowits, "Impact of a Television Film on Attitudes toward Mental Illness," *American Journal of Community Psychology* 17 (1989): 521–527.

16. Joann Thornton, "Impact of a Newspaper Account of Mental Illness on Reactions and Attitudes toward Mental Illness," doctoral dissertation, George Mason University, December 1993.

17. National Organization on Disability, "Public Attitudes toward People with Disabilities," survey conducted by Louis Harris and Associates, Inc., 1991.

18. Marcia Lovejoy, "Expectations and the Recovery Process," in *The Experience of Patients and Families: First Person Accounts*, ed. National Alliance for the Mentally Ill (Arlington, Va.: National Alliance for the Mentally Ill, 1989), 24.

19. Joseph R. Piasecki, *Community Response to Residential Services for the Psycho-socially Disabled: Preliminary Results of a National Survey* (Philadelphia: Horizon House Institute for Research and Development, 1975).

20. Sander L. Gilman, "Madness and Representation: Hans Prinzhorn's Study of Madness and Art in Its Historical Context." An essay from the Exhibition Catalog for the Prinzhorn Collection, an art exhibit that toured the United States in 1985.

21. E. Fuller Torrey, *Surviving Schizophrenia: A Family Manual*, rev. ed. (New York: Harper & Row, 1988).

22. Otto F. Wahl and Charles R. Harman, "Family Views of Stigma," *Schizophrenia Bulletin* 15 (1989): 131–139.

23. *Webster's New Collegiate Dictionary* (Springfield, Ma.: G & C Meriam Company, 1977).

24. Erving Goffman, *Stigma: Notes on the Management of Spoiled Identity* (Englewood Cliffs, N.J.: Prentice Hall, 1963), 3.

25. Jum C. Nunnally, *Popular Conceptions of Mental Health* (New York: Holt, Rinehart & Winston, 1961), 46, 51.

26. John L. Tringo, "The Hierarchy of Preference toward Disability Groups," *Journal of Special Education* 4 (1970): 295–306.

27. Alan J. Neff and Baqar A. Husani, "Lay Images of Mental Illness: Social Knowledge and Tolerance of the Mentally Ill," *Journal of Community Psychology* 13 (1985): 3–12.

28. Charles D. Whatley, "Social Attitudes toward Discharged Mental Patients," *Social Problems* 6 (1958): 313–320.

29. Derek L. Philips, "Rejection: A Possible Consequence of Seeking Help for Mental Disorders," *American Sociological Review* 28 (1963): 963–972; Philips, "Public Identification and Acceptance of the Mentally Ill," *American Journal of Public Health* 56 (1966): 755–763; Philips, "Identification of Mental Illness: Its Consequences for Rejection," *Community Mental Health Journal* 3 (1967): 262–266.

30. Bruce Purvis, Richard Brandt, Connie Rouse, Vera Wilfred, and Lillian M. Range, "Students' Attitudes toward Hypothetical Chronically and Acutely Mentally and Physically Ill Individuals," *Psychological Reports* 62 (1988): 627–630.

31. Freedom from Fear, *Public Perceptions of People with Mental Illness*, August 1991.

32. B. J. Morganti, "Love Is . . ." *Journal of the California Alliance for the Mentally Ill* 3 (1992): 15–16.

33. Don H. Culwell, "The National Mental Health Consumer Scene," *Journal of the California Alliance for the Mentally Ill* 3 (1992): 40–42.

34. Anonymous, "How I've Managed My Chronic Mental Illness," *Schizophrenia Bulletin* 15 (1989): 635–640.
35. Wahl and Harman, "Family Views of Stigma."
36. D. B. Fisher, "Disclosure, Discrimination, and the ADA," paper presented at a conference on the Rehabilitation of Children, Youth, and Adults with Psychiatric Disabilities, January 1993.
37. Joan F. Houghton, "Maintaining Mental Health in a Turbulent World," *Schizophrenia Bulletin* 8 (1982): 548–552.
38. Freedom from Fear, *Public Perceptions*.
39. Anonymous, "After the Funny Farm," *Schizophrenia Bulletin* 6 (1980): 544–546.
40. Enoch Calloway, "A Psychiatrist's Depression," *Journal of the California Alliance for the Mentally Ill* 4 (1990): 7.
41. Bruce G. Link, Francis T. Cullen, and Elmer Struening, "A Modified Labeling Theory Approach to Mental Disorders: An Empirical Assessment," *American Sociological Review* 54 (1989): 400–423.
42. Lee N. Robins, John E. Helzer, Myrna M. Weissman, Helen Orvaschel, Ernest Gruenberg, Jack D. Burke, Jr., and Darrel A. Reiger, "Lifetime Prevalence of Specific Psychiatric Disorders in Three Sites," *Archives of General Psychiatry* 41 (1984): 949–958.
43. Wahl and Harman, "Family Views of Stigma."
44. Amerigo Farina and Robert D. Felner, "Employment Interviewer Reactions to Former Mental Patients," *Journal of Abnormal Psychology*, 82 (1973): 268–272.
45. Amerigo Farina, Robert Felner, and Louis A. Boudreau, "Reactions of Male Workers to Male and Female Mental Patient Job Applicants," *Journal of Consulting and Clinical Psychology* 41 (1973): 363–372.
46. Kim C. Oppenheimer and Max D. Miller, "Stereotypic Views of Medical Educators toward Students with a History of Psychological Counseling," *Journal of Counseling Psychology* 35 (1988): 311–314.
47. Wahl and Harman, "Family Views of Stigma."
48. Stewart Page, "Effects of the Mental Illness Label in Attempts to Obtain Accommodation," *Canadian Journal of Behavioral Science* 9 (1977): 85–90.
49. Wahl and Harman, "Family Views of Stigma."
50. Gary B. Melton and Ellen G. Garrison, "Fear, Prejudice, and Neglect: Discrimination against Mentally Disabled Persons," *American Psychologist* 42 (1987): 1007–1026.
51. Judith G. Rabkin, "How the General Public and Mental Health Specialists View Mental Illness," paper prepared for the NIMH Depression Awareness, Recognition, and Treatment (D/ART) Program, 1987, 6.
52. Houghton, "Maintaining Mental Health in a Turbulent World," 551.
53. Eli A. Rubenstein, John F. Fracchia, Jeffrey M. Kochnower, and Joyce N. Sprafkin, *Television Viewing Behaviors of Mental Patients* (Stony Brook, N.Y.: Brookdale International Institute, 1977).
54. Personal communication.
55. Bruce G. Link, Francis T. Cullen, Jerold Mirotznik, and Elmer Struening, "The Consequences of Stigma for Persons with Mental Illness: Evidence from the Social Sciences," in *Stigma and Mental Illness*, ed. Paul Fink and Alan Tasman (Washington, D.C.: American Psychiatric Press, 1991), 87–96; U.S. Congress, Office of Technology Assessment, *Psychiatric Disabilities, Employment, and the Americans with Disabilities Act* (Washington, D.C.: U.S. Government Printing Office, 1994).
56. Wahl and Harman, "Family Views of Stigma."
57. Gerbner, Gross, Morgan, and Signorelli, "The 'Mainstreaming' of America."
58. *L.A. Times* film critic Kenneth Turan, quoted in *Entertainment Weekly*, August 5, 1994, 7.
59. The full text of the trailer is as follows: "This story is based on the tragic lives of

Adam and Ewa Berwid. Adam's violent behavior is not intended to be a general reflection of the mentally ill, the vast majority of whom never commit a violent act. Indeed, they are not more prone to violence than the non-mentally disordered."

60. Wahl and Lefkowits, "Impact of a Television Film."

61. I am not suggesting that groups with status and power do not warrant respect or consideration for their feelings. Everyone deserves such consideration, and sensitivity to people's reactions and preferences is almost always appropriate. I am only suggesting that the case for those with mental illnesses is even more compelling because of their long-standing lack of status and support.

Chapter Six   So, Why?

1. Michael Fleming and Roger Manvell, *Images of Madness: The Portrayal of Insanity in the Feature Film* (Cranbury, N.J.: Associated University Presses, 1985), 17.

2. Pamela J. Kalbfleisch, "The Portrayal of the Killer in Society: A Comparison Study," research paper, Department of Communication, Michigan State University, 1979.

3. Robert P. Snow, *Creating Media Culture* (Beverly Hills, Calif.: Sage Publications, 1983).

4. An analogy would be the concern expressed with respect to recent action/adventure films about the portrayal of Arabs as terrorists. A single portrayal of an Arab as a terrorist is not strictly inaccurate. There are Arab terrorists. As Arab antidefamation groups have been quick to point out, however, repeated, consistent portrayal of Arabs as terrorists and little else provides an unacceptable and inaccurate image of Arabs in general as murderous terrorists.

5. Edith Hamilton, *Mythology: Timeless Tales of Gods and Heroes* (Boston: Little, Brown, 1969).

6. Gerald N. Grob, *The Mad Among Us: A History of the Care of America's Mentally Ill* (New York: Free Press, 1994), 58–60.

7. The idea of mental illness as devil possession is not as much a relic of the past as one might think. One sufferer of a mental disorder wrote only recently: "There are those who see mental illness as a demonic possession. My own Sunday school teacher has confessed that he believes this is true in some cases." Dorothy Minor, "Third Side of the Coin," in *The Experiences of Patients and Families: First Person Accounts*, ed. National Alliance for the Mentally Ill (Arlington, Va: National Alliance for the Mentally Ill, 1989). In April 1991, ABC TV's program *20/20* showed the attempt of a Catholic priest to treat a sixteen-year-old girl with mental illness by performing, on camera, an exorcism. Notions of mental illness as demon possession are still alive and well in parts of our society.

8. Oscar K. Buros, ed., *The Third Mental Measurements Yearbook* (Highland Park, N.J.: Gryphon Press, 1949), 200–202.

9. Sander L. Gilman, *Seeing the Insane* (New York: John Wiley, 1982).

10. They were also frequently shown carrying a walking stick, what Gilman refers to as a "staff of madness" because of its use to signify the person being portrayed was mad. The walking stick or staff, according to Gilman, later became a forked one and, later still, with the medieval connection of mental illness with devil possession and witchcraft, became a devil's pitchfork or a witch's broomstick.

11. The chaos expected of early asylums like Bethlehem Hospital even provided us with a lasting addition to our vocabulary, as the popular abbreviation for Bethlehem Hospital—"Bedlam"—became an accepted term for describing a scene of noisy confusion.

12. Janet Colaizzi, *Homicidal Insanity, 1800–1985* (Tuscaloosa, Ala.: University of Alabama Press, 1989).

13. Ibid., 73.

14. Fleming and Manvell, *Images of Madness*.
15. Ibid.
16. American Psychiatric Association, *Diagnostic and Statistical Manual of Mental Disorders*, 4th ed. (Washington, D.C.: American Psychiatric Association, 1994), 424–429.
17. George Gerbner and Percy Tannenbaum, "Regulation of Mental Health Content in Motion Pictures and Television," *Gazette* 6 (1960): 365–385.
18. Ibid., 370.
19. Ibid.
20. David Kantor and Victor Gelineau, "Social Processes in Support of Chronic Deviance," *International Journal of Social Psychiatry* 11 (1965): 280–289.
21. Sander L. Gilman, *Disease and Representation: Images of Illness from Madness to AIDS* (Ithaca, N.Y.: Cornell University Press, 1988), 11.
22. Ibid., 12.
23. Ibid., 12–13.
24. George Gerbner, "Dreams That Hurt: Mental Illness in the Mass Media," in *The Community Imperative*, ed. Richard C. Baron, Irving Rutman, and Barbara Klaczynska (Philadelphia: Horizon House Institute, 1980).
25. Otto F. Wahl and Gary Axelson, "A Note on News Staff Views of Mental Illness and Its Coverage," *Journal of Community Psychology* 13 (1985): 80–82.

Chapter Seven   Future Images

1. Robert Wood Johnson Foundation, "Public Attitudes toward People with Chronic Mental Illness," April 15, 1990.
2. Lee N. Robins, John E. Helzer, Myrna M. Weissman, Helen Orvaschel, Ernest Gruenberg, Jack D. Burke, and Darrel A. Reiger, "Lifetime Prevalence of Specific Psychiatric Disorders in Three Sites," *Archives of General Psychiatry* 41 (1984): 949–958; Irene Elkin, M. Tracie Shea, John T. Watkins, Stanley D. Imber, Stuart M. Sotsky, Joseph F. Collins, David R. Glass, Paul A. Pilkonis, William R. Leber, John P. Docherty, Susan J. Fiester, and Morris B. Parloff "NIMH Treatment of Depression Collaborative Research Program: General Effectiveness of Treatments," *Archives of General Psychiatry* 46 (1989): 971–983.
3. Joann Thornton, "Impact of a Newspaper Account of Mental Illness on Reactions and Attitudes toward Mental Illness," doctoral disseration, George Mason University, December 1993.
4. This estimate of viewer numbers includes theater attendance and video rentals and is provided in the April 29, 1994, issue of *Entertainment Weekly*.
5. "Mental Illness: Information for Writers." Produced and distributed by the National Alliance for the Mentally Ill, Arlington, Virginia.
6. Consumer protest has been a central part of the strategies of most misrepresented minorities in trying to improve their media images. This approach and other strategies used to influence mass media are described in Kathryn Montgomery, *Target: Prime Time* (New York: Oxford University Press, 1989).
7. Carolyn Adler, "Promotion for Movie Protested: Ad for 'Crazy People' Is Called Offensive," *Philadelphia Inquirer*, March 31, 1990.
8. The National Stigma Clearinghouse is currently the only organization devoted exclusively to monitoring and responding to media images of mental illness. Although a relatively small organization, it has achieved substantial recognition and its participants are sometimes referred to (and proudly refer to themselves as) "Stigmabusters."
9. Mark Potts, "Superman's Fatal Flaw" *Washington Post*, September 5, 1992.

10. Bill Hoffman, "Plot to Kill Man of Steel Gets Super Boos," *New York Post*, September 13, 1992; David Arnold, "Death by Stereotype: Plot for Superman Stigmatizes Mentally Ill, Advocates Say," *Boston Globe*, September 12, 1992.

11. Lawrence R. Ricciardi of RJR Nabisco, for example, has been critical of attacks on advertising: "Increasingly," he has asserted in a May 20, 1994, article in *New York Newsday*, "this willingness to criticize virtually any statement or idea because it may be offensive to some constituency—no matter how small—has become part of our everyday lives and a nightmare for marketers and American businesses." Ricciardi has specifically mentioned the National Stigma Clearinghouse in his remarks, along with food service workers who protest ads mocking school cafeteria food, those expressing concern about waiflike clothes models who may encourage anorexia, and those who have objected to the apparently child-oriented cigarette advertising with his company's Joe Camel.

12. There are occasions when media watch activities have been more confrontive and coercive, with demonstrations and even boycotts organized. These have been rare, however, and used mainly when stigmatization appears particularly blatant and the media professionals involved particularly unresponsive to the issues being raised. It is also possible that, for some media professionals, almost any consumer complaint is perceived as coercive.

13. Demitri F. Papolos and Janice Papolos, *Overcoming Depression* (New York: Harper & Row, 1987), 20.

14. In order to encourage efforts to inform and destigmatize, the American Psychiatric Association Legislative and Public Affairs Network offers awards each year for outstanding projects.

15. Amanda Bennett, "Back from Hell," *Wall Street Journal*, October 14, 1992; Elizabeth Neuffer, "For Task Force Aide, Mental Health Issue a Personal One," *Boston Globe*, April 5, 1993; Theresa J. Collier, "The Stigma of Mental Illness," *Newsweek*, April 26, 1993; Katherine Spitz and Robin Witek, "The Odyssey of Fred Frese," *Beacon Journal* (Akron, Ohio), March 6, 1994.

16. Susanna Kaysen, *Girl, Interrupted* (New York: Vintage Books, 1993).

17. Peter D. Kramer, *Listening to Prozac* (New York: Penguin Books, 1993).

18. Thomas E. Backer, "Powers Untapped: Enhancing Mass Media Depiction of Mental Illness," in *Proceedings of the First International Rosalynn Carter Symposium on Mental Health Policy: Stigma and the Mentally Ill* (Atlanta, Ga. Carter Center, 1985).

19. Otto F. Wahl and Gary Axelson, "A Note on News Staff Views of Mental Illness and Its Coverage," *Journal of Community Psychology* 13 (1985): 285–291.

20. Thomas E. Backer, ed., *Proceedings: Portraying Mentally Ill People in Films and Television—Invitational Workshop for Writers, Directors, and Development Executives.* Encino, Calif., March 31–April 1, 1984.

21. Martella Walsh made these observations as a panel participant in a national teleconference, "Stigma: The Misconceptions of Mental Illness," October 8, 1992.

22. Wahl and Axelson, "News Staff Views."

23. Readers may notice that most of the conferences on stigma mentioned were conducted in the 1980s. The apparently smaller number of such efforts in the 1990s is, in large part, a result of the redirection of the efforts of mental health advocates toward issues of national health care.

24. Backer, *Proceedings: Portraying Mentally Ill People.*

25. Lawrence K. Beaupre, "Battling the Stereotypes of Mental Illness," *Gannett Westchester Newspapers*, June 4, 1989.

26. Otto F. Wahl, "Media Images of Mental Illness: A Review of the Literature," *Journal of Community Psychology* 20 (1992): 343–352.

Chapter Eight   Exit Lines

1. President's Committee on Employment of People with Disabilities, "The Media and Its Continuing Stereotyping of People with Mental Disorders," position paper for November 1992 Mental Health Summit.
2. Abigail Padgett, *Child of Silence* (New York: Warner Books, 1993).

Index

Beaupre, Lawrence, 159–160
Beauty and the Beast (animated movie), 10
Benny & Joon (movie), 20
Bergman, Ingrid, 4
Berwid, Adam, 92, 204–205n59
Berwid, Eva, 204–205n59
Bethlehem Hospital ("Bedlam"), 117, 205n11
Beverly Hills 90210 (TV show), 59, 181
Bianchi, Kenneth, 18, 84
Bible, the, reference to mental illness, 115
Billy (Streiber), 10
bipolar disorder, *see* manic-depression
Black Cat, The (movie), 56
Blacks, as objects of projected anxiety, 126
Black Sunday (Harris), made into film, 61
Bleeder (Lazuta), 61
Bleuler, Eugen, 15
blindness, hysterical, 8
Blood Brothers (play), 11
Blood on the Moon (Ellroy), 61, 68, 70–71, 191
Blue Steel (movie), 5, 57
"boarding out" of persons with mental illness, 19th-century, 119
Bob Newhart Show, The (TV show), 30
Body of Evidence (Cornwell), 61, 190
Boorstin, Robert, 152, 155
Born Loser (Sansom), 16
Boston Globe, 146, 152, 155
Bowie, David, 12, 196n23
brain disorders, 18
Brizer, David, 201–202n56
broadcasting, codes governing, 89, 123, 202n8
Buffalo Times, 16
Building New Links of Understanding (Mental Health Association of Hawaii), 137
bulimia, 7
Bundy, Ted, 18, 84
Buster Goes Berserk (record album), 22–23
Butcher (Miller), 70, 193
By Reason of Insanity (Harvey), 192
By Reason of Insanity (Stevens), 46, 69

Cabinet of Dr. Caligari, The (movie), 3, 56
Cagney and Lacey (TV show), 59, 181

Calloway, Enoch, 101
camera, subjective use of, 3
cancer and schizophrenia, comparative stigma study, 98–99
Caputo, Ricardo, 2, 90
Carlson, Peter, 85
Carter, Jimmy, 138
Carter, Rosalynn, 138, 140–141
Carter Center (Emory University) media initiative, 138, 166
cartoons, 16, *17*, *34*, 35, 38, *40*
Cassata, Mary, 8
CBS-TV, *Dallas* episode protested, 150
"Certifiably Nuts," packaged peanuts, 24, *25*, 140
Chaingang (Miller), 70, 193
Charlie's Angels (TV show), 8, 181
Cheers (TV show), 9, 181
child-rearing practices, as proposed cause of mental illness, 122
children: advertising targeted to, 207n11; media for, 61–63
Chill Rain in January, A (Wright), 10
Christie, Agatha, 11
cinema, *see* movies
civil rights of persons with mental illness, 119
Civil Wars (TV show), 59, 181
Clark, Mary Higgins, 61, 189–190
CLIO awards, 140–141
Coalition on Portraying Mentally Ill People, 159
codes, media: Hollywood Production Code, 123; NAMI language guidelines, 138, *139*; National Association of Broadcasters, 89, 202n8
coercion, versus education, 146, 207nn11–12
coffee mug, successful response to, 150
Colaizzi, Janet, 118, 119
Collier, Theresa, 152
comedy, *see* humor, harmful
comics, 61, 62, 74, 145–146. *See also* cartoons
command hallucinations, 19
commitment, involuntary, 119–120
*Complete Book of M*A*S*H, The* (Kalter), 6
Conde, Nicholas, 190
conferences and workshops, for media and mental health professionals, 158–160, 207n23

About the Author

Otto Wahl received a B.A. in psychology from Wesleyan University and a Ph.D. in clinical psychology from the University of Pennsylvania. He is currently an associate professor of psychology at George Mason University in Fairfax, Virginia. He is also on the Board of Advisors of the National Stigma Clearinghouse, a member of the Advisory Council of the Northern Virginia Mental Health Institute, and chairman of the Advisory Council for the Compeer program of the Mental Health Association of Northern Virginia. Dr. Wahl has written extensively on stigma and media depiction of mental illness and has made presentations on this topic at numerous mental health conferences, as well as on radio and television.